THE ROMAN TEXTILE INDUSTRY AND ITS INFLUENCE

THE ROMAN TEXTILE INDUSTRY AND ITS INFLUENCE

A Birthday Tribute to John Peter Wild

Edited by
Penelope Walton Rogers
Lise Bender Jørgensen
Antoinette Rast-Eicher

Oxbow Books

Published in the United Kingdom by
OXBOW BOOKS
10 Hythe Bridge Street, Oxford OX1 2EW

and in the United States by
OXBOW BOOKS
908 Darby Road, Havertown, PA 19083

First printed 2001
Paperback reprint 2014

Paperback Edition: ISBN 978-1-78297-740-7
Digital Edition: ISBN 978-1-78297-864-0

A CIP record for this book is available from the British Library

For a complete list of Oxbow titles, please contact:

UNITED KINGDOM
Oxbow Books
Telephone (01865) 241249, Fax (01865) 794449
Email: oxbow@oxbowbooks.com
www.oxbowbooks.com

UNITED STATES OF AMERICA
Oxbow Books
Telephone (800) 791-9354, Fax (610) 853-9146
Email: queries@casemateacademic.com
www.casemateacademic.com/oxbow

Oxbow Books is part of the Casemate Group

Cover: A Late Roman tapestry from the at-Tar Caves in Iraq (see chapter 7)

CONTENTS

Later Strands

JOHN PETER WILD: AN APPRECIATION

John Peter Wild

John Peter Wild comes from a family associated with the Lancashire cotton industry since early in the industrial revolution. He was educated at Manchester Grammar School and Downing College, Cambridge, where he read Classics, a subject in which he developed a passionate interest at school. When seeking a topic for research after graduating in 1961, Roman clothing and textile manufacture were uncharted waters which combined his family background and classical interests, as well as giving full scope to his archaeological and linguistic expertise. His research was undertaken at Cambridge under the supervision of Professor Jocelyn Toynbee, with a year at the university of Bonn to collect the continental material. He recalls with wry amusement how, on Professor Toynbee's retirement to Oxford, it was suggested to him 'Now you can do a proper topic'. He was not impressed. His thesis was eventually published in two parts: clothing in *Bonner Jahrbücher* 168 (1968), textiles as a separate monograph, *Textile Manufacture in the Northern Roman Provinces* (1970).

In 1965 he was appointed Assistant Lecturer in Classics at Manchester University, transferring as Lecturer to the newly-founded Department of Archaeology in 1968. He was appointed Reader in Archaeology in 1993. During his early years in Manchester, his study of textiles was to some extent eclipsed by his other archaeological interests, especially his work in the Nene Valley, Peterborough, where he had directed excavations since 1966 and is currently Chairman of the Nene Valley Archaeological Trust. Two occurrences in particular, perhaps, helped to restore textiles to the forefront of his research: firstly, an outstanding research student, Gillian Eastwood, who introduced him to the practicalities of the subject (on one memorable occasion she had the complete Wild family spinning with drop spindles after Sunday lunch!) and secondly, his meeting with Lise Bender Jørgensen in the early 1980s and the setting up of the North European Symposium for Archaeological Textiles (NESAT) in collaboration with Lise, and Klaus Tidow. The Symposium's meeting provided a forum for like-minded scholars and craftspeople from throughout Northern Europe and increased recognition of ancient textile studies as an academic discipline in its own right. A third milestone was the setting up, with Dr W. D. Cooke of UMIST, of the Manchester Ancient Textiles Unit, which has attracted students and scholars from many countries engaged on a wide variety of textile-related projects. These students have included Jane Batcheller, Ulla Mannering, Elizabeth Peacock and Antoinette Rast-Eicher, each of whom has contributed to this volume. Few can now doubt the propriety of textiles as a topic for research!

In 1968 John Peter was elected Fellow of the Society of Antiquaries of London and since 1975 has been a corresponding member of the German Archaeological Institute. A bibliography of his work so far appears at the end of this volume, but we imagine that there will be much more to come. This *Festschrift* only marks the turning point at which John Peter lays down his university administrative chores. As he moves into his next phase of life, we all hope that textiles will remain at the forefront of his work.

ABOUT THE AUTHORS

Nettie K. Adams

Nettie Adams has done archaeological work in the Nile Valley over a period of 29 years. Beginning in 1976, she and Elisabeth Crowfoot participated in several seasons of excavations at Qasr Ibrim. The results of their work on the textiles from this site, which range in date from the seventh century BC to the 19th century AD, have been reported at conferences and published in archaeological and textile journals (final reports in preparation).

Carmen Alfaro Giner

Carmen Alfaro is Professor of Ancient History at the University of Valencia. Her research interests include aspects of ancient economy, especially textile production in the Roman period, and women's work as it relates to this. She is author of two books and various articles on the subject.

Johanna Banck-Burgess

Johanna Banck-Burgess studied archaeology at Freiburg and Kiel Universities and holds an MA and PhD in Archaeology. She has specialised in textile archaeology for over fourteen years and currently has a DFG project in Freiburg, South Germany, researching Alamannic textiles.

Jane Batcheller

Graduate of the Clothing and Textiles Department of the University of Alberta, Canada. Worked as a textile analyst at the University of Alberta before starting a research degree in Textile Archaeology at the University of Manchester. Currently completing a PhD on the late Roman textiles from Karanis.

Lise Bender Jørgensen

Lise Bender Jørgensen is Professor of Nordic Archaeology at the Norwegian

University of Technology and Science, Institute of Archaeology, Trondheim, Norway. She was born in Denmark and educated at the University of Copenhagen, Department of Archaeology (mag.art.1976, dr.phil.1993). She has worked in Denmark, Sweden, Norway, travelled widely in Europe and excavated in Egypt.

Dominique Cardon

Dr Dominique Cardon is currently working as Chargée de Recherche in the Centre National de la Recherche Scientifique. She has trained both as a historian (Universities of Paris and Montpellier) and as a weaver and dyer (in Ireland and Peru). She is the author of *Guide des Teintures Naturelles*, a catalogue of the medieval textiles preserved in the South of France and *La Draperie Médiévale – Essor d'une Grande Industrie Européenne.*

Elisabeth Crowfoot

Elisabeth Crowfoot became involved in textiles in 1951, through assisting her mother, G. M. Crowfoot, with her publications. She joined the Ancient Monuments Laboratory as archaeological textile consultant, and has published over a hundred reports, including the 1992 Museum of London volume, *Textiles and Clothing*, with Pritchard and Staniland. She was senior textile consultant at Qasr Ibrim, Egypt, 1976–1988.

Corinne Debaine-Francfort

Corinne Debaine-Francfort wrote her doctoral thesis in oriental languages and civilizations. She is specialist in the archaeology of North and North-West China at the CNRS (UMR 7041, Nanterre) and co-director of the Sino-French archaeological mission in Xinjiang.

Sophie Desrosiers

Sophie Desrosiers obtained her doctoral thesis in ethnology in 1987. Maître de conférences at the Ecole des Hautes Etudes in Paris since 1990, she works and teaches on the relationship between textile techniques and their social context, in the Andean region, around the Mediterranean Sea and in West-Central Asia during late Antiquity and the Middle Ages.

Heidemarie Farke

Heidemarie Farke is an archaeological conservator, specialising in organic materials. After 30 years' work in the Thüringischen Landesamt für Archäologische Denkmalpflege in Weimar, as instructor on the Conservation course, she moved to Schleswig, in 1992, to the Archäologische Landesmuseum at Schloss Gottorf. She is the chair of a working party for restoration and her main concerns are the stabilisation and preservation of historic artefacts.

Thea Gabra-Sanders

Thea Gabra-Sanders was born and educated in the Netherlands and came to Britain on a research scholarship. She is currently a free-lance textile analyst and a research associate at the National Museum of Scotland, where she is working on textiles from Viking Age and Medieval Scottish sites.

Daniël De Jonghe

Dr Daniël De Jonghe had a long career in textile education before joining the Royal Museums for Arts and History in Brussels as scientific associate. On the basis of research in developing countries and the analysis of ancient weave constructions, he has aimed to provide an insight into the evolution of weaving techniques.

Abdurassul Idriss

Abdurassul Idriss is Director of the Institute of Archaeology and Cultural Relics of Xinjiang and co-director of the Sino-French archaeological mission in the region.

Jerzy Maik

Jerzy Maik, PhD, is Associate Professor at the Institute for Archaeology and Ethnology, Polish Academy of Sciences, in Łodz, Poland. He is an archaeologist who also conducts research into the history of textiles in Poland, particularly in the Roman period and the Middle Ages.

Ulla Mannering

Born in Denmark and educated at University of Copenhagen (cand.mag.1998) and Manchester Ancient Textile Unit (M.Phil. 1995). She has worked in Denmark and Sweden and excavated in Egypt. Currently Research Fellow at the University of Copenhagen.

Anna Muthesius

Anna Muthesius is Professor of Textile Studies at the Surrey Institute of Art and Design, University College, and Honorary Member of Lucy Cavendish College, Cambridge University. She researches and published on the topic of Byzantine silk weaving (technology, design, uses, and political, economic and religious significance).

Elizabeth Peacock

Dr Elizabeth E. Peacock is professor in cultural history conservation and a conservator. She is Senior Conservation Scientist on the staff of the Conservation Laboratory, Institute of Archaeology and Cultural History, Trondheim. She holds a

BA in mathematics from Lake Forest College, MAC in Art Conservation from Queen's University and PhD in Textile Science from the University of Manchester.

Frances Pritchard

Frances Pritchard worked as an archaeologist on sites in Britain and Spain. In 1977 she joined the Department of Urban Archaeology, Museum of London, where she developed her expertise in excavated textiles. She is currently a Curator of Textiles at the Whitworth Art Gallery, University of Manchester.

Antoinette Rast-Eicher

Antoinette Rast-Eicher studied archaeology and history in Bern. She works in Switzerland as a free-lance archaeologist specialising in textiles, particularly metal-replaced textiles from Iron Age and Early Medieval graves, but also prehistoric textiles from wet sites and medieval material generally.

Kazuko Sakamoto

Kazuko Sakamoto is currently investigating the textile artefacts unearthed in the at-Tar Caves and silk related to the Silk Road, as a visiting scholar at the Institute for Cultural Studies of Ancient Iraq, Kokushikan University, Tokyo, and a visiting specialist at the Ancient Orient Museum, Tokyo. Also a graduate student at Osaka University, studying fabrics of pre-modern times from the viewpoint of inter-cultural exchange between East and West.

Naomi Tarrant

Curator of Costume and Textiles, National Museum of Scotland, since 1985 and before that of the Royal Scottish Museum. Author of several books, including *The Development of Costume* and *Going to Bed*. Her current research is focused on Scottish samplers and textiles related to the home, as well as dress in eighteenth-century Scotland. Treasurer of the Society of Antiquaries of London, and a former Chairman of the Costume Society.

Klaus Tidow

Klaus Tidow is a textile technologist. Since 1976 he has been Director of the Neumünster Textile Museum and City Archives. His published work includes papers on archaeological textile finds and contributions on the history of textile production and the cloth industry in Neumünster. He has been initiator and organiser of many international textile exhibitions.

Chris Verhecken-Lammens

Chris Verhecken-Lammens is a Scientific Associate at the Royal Museums of Art and History, Brussels. She specialises in Coptic textiles and the evolution of pre-industrial textile technology.

Gillian Vogelsang-Eastwood

Gillian Vogelsang-Eastwood has a doctorate from the University of Manchester. She is a free-lance textile and costume historian, specialising in the Near East and Iran. She is also the Director of the Textile Research Centre, Leiden.

Penelope Walton Rogers

Originally a field archaeologist, now manager of Textile Research in Archaeology, York (UK), a unit which provides a service to museums and archaeologists in the field of textiles, dyes, fibres, craft tools and clothing. Fellow of the Society of Antiquaries; qualified in accountancy; editor of *Dyes in History and Archaeology* 1988–1997; author of two books.

Elizabeth Wincott Heckett

Elizabeth Wincott Heckett is a Research Associate and a part-time lecturer in the Department of Archaeology, University of Cork. She has completed research on a range of Irish textiles, with an emphasis on medieval and Viking Age material, but has also studied Bronze Age, Iron Age and early medieval and post-medieval finds from urban and rural sites.

ACKNOWLEDGEMENTS

This volume has been produced with financial aid from the Abegg-Stiftung, Riggisberg (Switzerland), the Marc Fitch Fund (UK), the Textile Research Centre, Leiden (Netherlands) and private donations. The editors would like to express their gratitude for this help.

The editors would also like to thank the international team of contributors, who responded to queries and corrected proofs with such speed and good humour that the formidable task of editing twenty-one papers became easy. Especial thanks are due to Frances Pritchard, Klaus Tidow and Elizabeth Wincott Heckett for their support during editing and fund-raising.

Finally, we should like to thank Felicity Wild for joining in some gentle skulduggery, to keep the secret from John Peter until the volume in his honour was ready for presentation. The Wilds are in many ways a team and we wish them both many fruitful years in archaeology.

Chapter 1

MONS CLAUDIANUS: INVESTIGATING ROMAN TEXTILES IN THE DESERT

Lise Bender Jørgensen and Ulla Mannering

Introduction

In 1987–1993, an international team of archaeologists and philologists excavated the Imperial Roman quarry of Mons Claudianus in Egypt's Eastern desert.[1] Papyri and *ostraca* were the main focus of the researchers' interest, but already at the end of the first field season it became clear that textiles were to be a major find category. Accordingly, W. E. H. Cockle approached John Peter Wild on behalf of the Mons Claudianus Project to seek his expert opinion. John Peter informed Dr Cockle that this was a very important collection of textiles, a veritable treasure, and that he had no inhibitions about feeling excited about it. The close dating of the Mons Claudianus textiles was the main reason for John Peter's enthusiasm. By 1987, plenty of late Roman and early Byzantine textiles were known from Egypt, but few Early Roman, and almost none derived from well-dated and well-documented contexts.[2] However, in spite of his excitement, John Peter did not take on the challenge of the Mons Claudianus textiles – Egypt had yet to wait for the Wild experience. At that stage, John Peter stayed put in Manchester, content to keep track of colleagues and students travelling abroad.[3] Instead, the task went to Scandinavian textile scholars, but not without plenty of help, encouragement and guidance from him.[4]

Mons Claudianus

Mons Claudianus is situated in the Eastern Desert of Egypt, at the heart of the Red Sea mountains. The altitude is *c.* 700 m; distance to the Red Sea *c.* 50 km, to the Nile *c.* 120 km, and to Cairo some 500 km. The climate is arid and harsh, ranging between frost on winter nights to summer temperatures above 45°C. The Romans started quarrying the grey granodiorite stone of Mons Claudianus in the middle of the first century AD, probably while Nero was Emperor; its zenith was reached in the first half of the second century, during the reigns of Emperors Trajan, Hadrian and Antoninus Pius. After AD 154 the importance of the site dwindled, and some time in the first half of the third century it fell into disuse. The latest evidence of activity is from the Severan period (AD 222–235). In order to work the stone and deliver the characteristic grey pillars for Imperial monuments,[5] a population of – at one point – 920 men were accommodated in a fortified settlement in the main wadi Umm el-Hussein.[6] They consisted of civilian quarrymen, mostly from Alexandria and Syene (Assuan); Imperial workmen (*familia*), many of Semitic or Anatolian origin; soldiers; and some women and children.[7] Supplies for all these people had to be brought from afar, and demanded a well-developed infrastructure and organisation. Life at Mons Claudianus was harsh and demanding, survival and well-being depending on supplies of food and water. For some, at least, it was not without pleasures and luxury,[8] but still everyone dreamt of being sent back to the Nile Valley as soon as possible. A single water-skin could well mean the difference between happiness or despair, and *securitas* was a key word to life at Mons Claudianus.[9]

The rubbish dumps, *sebakhs*, were the main target for the excavations. The dry climate of the desert had secured the preservation of all kinds of stuff, organic as well as inorganic, creating a veritable bonanza for all kinds of specialists. The zoologist and the pottery specialist both had to deal with their share of the finds by weight, and after registration the finds were re-deposited on site. *Ostraca* were of special interest, and with more than 9,000 found, Mons Claudianus qualifies as the largest papyrological haul in this century.[10] Textiles tended to appear in the same contexts as *ostraca*, and in even larger quantities – tens of thousands, filling *cantine* after *cantine*,[11] to be labelled, catalogued, counted and stored in the store-rooms of the Supreme Council of Antiquities in Dendera.[12] This caused the excavators initial despair; later the textile specialists had to think hard to find a way to deal with them. The reality of coping with vast quantities of ancient textiles was something even the good council of John Peter Wild did not prepare us for. At Qasr Ibrim, Elisabeth Crowfoot and Nettie Adams (this volume, pp. 30–37) had a similar experience.

A desert laboratory

The problems of dealing with vast quantities of textiles in the desert are numerous. Getting to examine them is the first. When brought to the Finds Tent and handed over to the specialists, the textiles of Mons Claudianus were usually filled with soil, crumpled and stiff. This made it difficult to analyse them, and cleaning and straightening was necessary. Only when cleaned, colours, decoration and other details truly appear. So the first task of the textile specialists was to establish facilities for cleaning – a kind of textile conservation laboratory in the desert.

The first attempt was a hole in the ground, covered by a large sheet of oilcloth brought from Denmark for the purpose, to be filled with water as a kind of 'sink'. Textiles to be cleaned were sprayed with water to soak, and placed on a fine net to be carefully sunk into the water (Fig. 1.1). The net kept the textiles floating and away from the depositing dirt. The 'sink' worked, but wasn't quite efficient for two reasons: it demanded a strenuous, crouched working position; and soiled water had to be *lifted* out. However, all textiles examined during the 1990 season were washed this way. By 1991 the dug-out sink was replaced by a moveable one: a large Egyptian metal basin that proved much easier to handle, and could be placed on a table at a workable height. Washing was performed outside, the sun providing a good working light (Fig. 1.2).

The limited water supply on site was the next problem: all water was fetched an hour's drive away – every second day 900 litre to serve the needs of the excavation crew of 30. This meant it was not feasible to rinse the textiles as well as European standards demand. The water was first heated by leaving jerry cans in the sun, to allow the textiles to be washed as gently as possible in lukewarm water. Afterwards, the textiles were laid out and straightened. This was a delicate process that required deft hands, wooden nail-pins, and a smooth surface established by covering sheets of Baraka[13] cardboard boxes with stout plastic. During this process, water was liberally sprayed on to the textiles, to keep them flexible and easier to sort out. When neat and straight,

Fig. 1.1 Soaking textiles. Ulla Mannering has sprayed a selection of textiles in preparation for washing them. The textiles are laid out on a plastic-covered Baraka plate, labels with their provenance attached; after spraying, they are covered with a second plastic sheet and left until the next day. Photo: Lise Bender Jørgensen.

Fig. 1.2 Washing and straightening textiles. Ulla Mannering is busy straightening freshly washed textiles on a plastic-covered Baraka plate. To her right, the washing basin, covered with a net that supported the textiles during the cleaning process. Photo: Lise Bender Jørgensen.

they were left to dry in the shade. Space for this, however, proved somewhat difficult to find. Other specialists were accommodated in the Finds Tent too, and some room had to be left for them. The solution to this problem was brought out from Europe the following year: a metal rack, with the Baraka cardboard plates serving as shelves. This made it possible to store the drying textiles in separate layers, away from sun and wind (Fig. 1.3). At a certain stage of drying, textile-watching was quite exciting: suddenly, and vividly, the colours came out.

Fig. 1.3 Drying rack with plastic-covered Baraka plates as shelves. The rack facilitated drying textiles by saving space; left in the shade, it took a full day. Photo: Lise Bender Jørgensen.

Further work, such as drying, analysis, recording and photographing, was carried out indoors. This was due to the glaring sun, fluctuating temperatures, and insistent winds that easily carried textiles away. Small is beautiful when all scientific equipment has to be brought from Europe, within the limits of the airline's 20 kg luggage allowance. The textiles were examined using a simple stereo microscope[14] with an external light source – a plain table-lamp bought in the nearest town. Pre-printed index cards produced in Cairo were used to secure a quick and standardised registration.[15] Drawings or patterns were added if necessary. Photography as documentation increased for each season, with experience and better equipment, and by 1999 slides of *c.* 50% of all recorded textiles are in existence.

Due to the excellent state of preservation the fibre type usually could be determined merely by the look and feel of the fabric; it has not been possible to obtain permission to take samples to Europe for analysis. However, we feel confident to state that the majority of the Mons Claudianus textiles are made of wool. Only a minor part are in plant fibre; these are quite easy to recognise due to their hard and brittle state. Which kind of vegetable fibre cannot be determined without laboratory analyses. Hair cloths like those described by Jane Batcheller in this volume (pp. 38–47) also made up a proportion of the Mons Claudianus textile collection.

The textiles were collected by excavators in plastic bags, gathered from the same stratigraphic layer and supplied with a label recording the provenance. During cleaning and recording, textiles from the same bag were kept together, but not individually numbered before analysis. After examination, each textile was wrapped in acid-free tissue paper before further storage.[16] Numbers were written in the corner of each wrapping to facilitate retrieval; if photographed, the pre-printed number used for identification was left inside with the fabric (Fig. 1.4).

Fig. 1.4 Textiles wrapped in acid-free tissue paper are sorted according to numbers written on the corner, in preparation for storing them in the cantine *standing open behind Lena Hammarlund. Photo: Lise Bender Jørgensen.*

Back-cataloguing in Dendera

Textile investigations only started on site during the fourth season, in 1990. This meant a major backlog awaiting examination and in 1991 the textile team spent half of the season in the store-rooms of the Supreme Council of Antiquities in Dendera. In 1994, 1996 and 1998 there followed three post-excavation study seasons.[17]

Conditions for work in Dendera are somewhat different from those in the desert. Electricity and water are readily available, although the occasional power-cut may cause interruptions. This makes cleaning and analysis much easier, but is still far from laboratory standard. The stored textiles have been recorded and catalogued as antiquities, and examining them requires far more formalities than on the site. Each *cantine* is formally withdrawn from the store for examination, to be re-deposited afterwards. Only a certain number of *cantines* may be taken out at a time, and they are carefully guarded while work is in progress. This necessitates careful planning, as it is difficult to go back to a box to check or compare something, once it has been re-deposited.

Re-storing the textiles presented us with a new problem. Cleaned, straightened and packed in tissue paper, the textiles filled much more than before treatment, and we were not able to fit them into the boxes they came from. Neither was it possible to extend the number of boxes containing textiles. The solution was to dump the contents of at least one metal box after having sorted out any unusual pieces for a selective sample.[18] The discarded textiles were returned to the site from the store in Dendera, to be buried along with pottery and animal bones scrapped by fellow specialists.

Selection of representative textiles

Seven excavation seasons resulted in about 1.25 cubic metres of textiles, filling 12 *cantines* to bursting point with crumpled-up textiles.[19] An estimate suggests that the boxes may contain more than 50,000 textiles (Fig. 1.5). To do them all would take an army of textile specialists and the quantity of textiles made it not feasible to attempt a complete registration. Instead, some hard choices had to be made. First, however, we had to address some important questions. What kind of information did we want from this body of material? Is every detail about every textile fragment essential? What may the textiles contribute to the investigations of Mons Claudianus, and to our knowledge of Roman textiles and clothing?

During three recording seasons around 1,800 textiles were analysed.[20] The first batch, almost 500[21] pieces done during the 1990 season, was a random selection of textiles unearthed concurrently during excavations. They derived from two sources: the large south *sebakh*, and the south-east corner of the Fort. In 1991, another 460 pieces from the south *sebakh* were added to this sample from the backlog in Dendera. Then another strategy was assumed. The purpose was to create two bodies of textiles. The initial, random sample represents the relative proportion of the different types of fabrics deposited at Mons Claudianus. The second, selected sample intends to show the range of variety.

Instead of recording all types of fabrics, textiles were now sorted before wash and analysis. All of the backlog was examined, every plastic bag in every metal box opened and searched for unusual pieces. Criteria for selection were (i) anything unusual – weaves or other techniques, decoration or conspicuous colours, and (ii) all textiles with features related to garments or other recognisable items. The selected sample comprises 228 pieces from the south *sebakh* and 336 pieces from other locations at Mons Claudianus – a total of 564 unusual Roman textiles, gleaned from the contents of seven *cantines*. By 1994, emphasis was placed on adding textiles from locations excavated after 1991 in- and outside the fort to the random sample,[22] which now comprised 70% of all recorded textiles. The number of textiles recorded from the big south *sebakh* and other locations are almost evenly distributed (Table 1.1).

Fig. 1.5 Thousands of textiles in plastic bags are crammed into the cantines. *Lena Hammarlund is investigating a sample. Photo: Lise Bender Jørgensen.*

Although the recorded textiles only make up a few percent of the estimated total number found at Mons Claudianus, the two samples provide us with a general view of the range of textiles present

Location	Random sample	Per cent	Selected sample	Per cent	Total	Per cent
South sebakh	706	38.7 %	228	12.5 %	934	51.2 %
Other locations	556	30.4 %	336	18.4 %	892	48.8 %
In all	1262	69.1 %	564	30.9 %	1826	100.0 %

Table 1.1. Textiles recorded in detail from Mons Claudianus

at the site. Tabby is the most common weave; it constitutes more than 80% of all recorded textiles. In comparison different twills make up 10% of the total number; to these can be added felt, and rarer techniques such as taqueté,[23] Coptic knitting, and tablet weaving. Damask twills, related to those discussed by Dominique Cardon and Daniël De Jonghe in this volume (p. 12 and p. 137) also form part of the Mons Claudianus collection. Among the textiles which can be related to a specific use we may count several items of clothing: a complete baby tunic, four hats, eight belts, a cloth shoe, two knitted socks and at least four small purses. To these can be added three more or less complete tunics – wool relatives of the linen tunics described by Frances Pritchard and Chris Verhecken-Lammens in this volume (pp. 21–29). In addition, fragments of at least another 200 tunics and 45 mantles have been found.[24] Other textiles belong to the group of soft furnishing, such as blankets, cushions, wall-hangings and sleeping-mats.

The textiles from Mons Claudianus display a very varied range of fabrics and indicate what was available to its inhabitants as well as reflecting its wider framework, the Roman World. Simple wool tabbies range from coarse, simple webs to luxurious light materials, and twills display an equally sophisticated variety. Some fabrics are obvious constructed for weatherproof, wind-resistant garbs, others intended to protect against heat and dehydration.[25] Decoration is abundant, as simple stripes or checks, tapestry *clavi* or gammas, or as embroidery, application, and various forms of patterned weaves or piled fabrics. The range of colours bear witness to a well-developed dyer's industry, and indicate what colour combinations were preferred in Roman Egypt.[26] Some of them are quite unusual to a modern western taste. The most common colour is purple, popular for *clavi*. Few, if any, of the purples are likely to be genuine murex (shellfish) purple, but rather 'local purple', mixtures of blue and red, in a wide variety of qualities, some dyed in the wool, others obviously at a later stage. Many Mons Claudianus textiles display similar variations, or imitations, like the so-called shaded bands. Twenty-six stripes (bands) are composed of more than two colours; only a few, however, may be termed true shaded bands, where each colour gradually blends into the next.[27] The remaining are imitations, more or less successful, and presumably accordingly of different value.

Dealing with documentation

Safely back in Europe, the Mons Claudianus Textile Project faced the problem of dealing with a huge amount of documentation such as index cards and slides. To do that comfortably, we needed a systematic and flexible tool to supply us with an overview of the recorded textiles and permit several people to work simultaneously. The answer to this need was a computerised database, constructed by Ulla Mannering in 1995.[28] The database was first set up in Paradox, but later converted into Access for Windows. Details of weaves, spin of warp and weft, fibres, colours, hems and selvedges, stitches and structural sewing may here be quickly and conveniently listed and combined, and linked with archaeological features at the site. Lists of extant slides, drawings or other forms of documentation are also included in the database, facilitating retrieval. The database is still in constant development and will continue to be so during the research process; when our work is completed, however, we aim to make it publicly accessible via the internet.

Future access to the Mons Claudianus textiles requires further study seasons in Egypt. Continued political unrest makes this still more difficult, and demands careful planning, fundraising, and organising. The database, slides, drawings, patterns, and our personal notes, therefore, are our main sources to settle disputed points. Since 1990, the Mons Claudianus Textile Project has grown from one person to a group of six, distributed over three Scandinavian countries.[29] This has emphasized the need for access to those parts of the documentation that could not be included in the original database, particularly slides and drawings. At the time of writing, the slide collection is in the process of being scanned into CD-Rom, copies of which are to be distributed to all project members and, perhaps, at a later stage made accessible via the internet.

A problem may well be turned into a resource. The Mons Claudianus Textile Project has profited from several such problems, practical, geographical, organisational, or economical. Modern information technology has proved a major help, and promises further possibilities. Knowledge of the textiles and clothing from Roman Egypt is still very much under construction, and a major, well-dated collection such as that from Mons Claudianus forms an important part of this process. Fresh questions keep posing themselves during fieldwork, and particularly afterwards. Working conditions in the desert are one aspect of the problem, and, as described here, they play a considerable role in determining what kind of questions it is possible to ask of the material.

Acknowledgements

The Mons Claudianus Textile Project has been founded by many sources over the years. We gratefully acknowledge the British Academy, who made Lise Bender Jørgensen's participation in 1990 possible, and the *VKR's Familiefond* and *Carlsberg-fonden* who funded the 1991 and 1994 seasons. *C. E. G. Gad's Fond* has supported Ulla Mannering's work over several years. 1995–96, the Swedish Research Council for the Humanities and Social Sciences granted the means for Lena Hammarlund to investigate the craftsmanship of the Mons Claudianus weavers. Agnes Geijer's Foundation for Nordic Textile Research provided the resources for Ulla Mannering's study of gammas and other woven decorations, and for Lena Larsson's study of Roman Textile Professions. Lise Bender Jørgensen's work on the Mons Claudianus textiles has been made possible by a Research Fellowship at Göteborg University (1993–96) and since 1996 by a Readership at the Norwegian University of Science and Technology, Trondheim. Since 1999, a generous grant from the Joint Committee of the Nordic Research Councils for the Humanities (NOS-H) has made it possible for Ulla Mannering, Lena Hammarlund and Martin Ciszuk to study the forms of clothing, the construction of twill weaves, and further intricacies of Roman textile technology.

Notes

1 The Mons Claudianus Project is directed by Professor Jean Bingen, Brussels, under the *aegis* of the Institut Francais d'Archélogie Orientale (IFAO), Cairo, and with Dr Hélène Cuvigny, CNRS, as *chef du chantier*. Publications are forthcoming in the monograph series of the IFAO (J. Bingen *et al.* 1992: *Mons Claudianus Ostraca Graeca et Latina* I, DIFAO XXIX, Cairo; *ibidem* 1997: *Mons Claudianus Ostraca Graeca et Latina* II, DFIFAO 32; D. P. S. Peacock & V. A. Maxfield 1997: *Survey and Excavation Mons Claudianus I, Topography and Quarries*. FIFAO 37, Cairo. For a useful overview (in Danish), see A. Bülow-Jacobsen 1996: *Mons Claudianus. Organisation, Administration og Teknik i et Romersk Stenbrud fra Kejsertiden*, Museum Tusculanums Forlag: København. For a complete bibliography, see http://adam.igl.ku.dk/~bulow/MCbib.html

2 Letter from John Peter Wild to Dr W. E. H. Cockle, 17 July 1987.

3 'Gillian [Eastwood] has gone to El Amarna, Elisabeth Crowfoot is at Qasr Ibrim, my embroidery student is in Greece. Do textiles and see the world!' – letter from John Peter Wild to Lise Bender Jørgensen, 10 March 1984.

4 Lise Bender Jørgensen has been quarrelling happily with John Peter over the nature of Roman textile production ever since her Copenhagen MA thesis from 1976. Ulla Mannering took her M. Phil. at Manchester Ancient Textile Unit in 1995, profiting greatly from John Peter's teaching.

5 For an assessment of the meaning of the grey Mons Claudianus stone, see D. P. S. Peacock *et al.* 1994: 'Mons Claudianus and the problem of the 'granito del foro': a geological and geochemical approach', *Antiquity* 68, 209–30; D. P. S. Peacock 1997: 'Charlemagne's black stones: the re-use of Roman columns in early medieval Europe, *Antiquity* 71, 709–15.

6 A. Bülow-Jacobsen 1996: *Mons Claudianus. Organisation, Administration og Teknik i et Romersk Stenbrud fra Kejsertiden*, Museum Tusculanums Forlag: København, p. 12.

7 A. Bülow-Jacobsen 1996: *Mons Claudianus. Organisation, Administration og Teknik i et Romersk Stenbrud fra Kejsertiden*, Museum Tusculanums Forlag: København, p. 20.

8 See e. g. M. van der Veen 1998a: 'A life of luxury in the desert? The food and fodder supply to Mons Claudianus' (with a contribution by Sheila Hamilton-Dyer), *Journal of Roman Archaeology* 11, 101–116. *Ibidem* 1998b: 'Gardens in the Desert', in O. Kaper (ed.): *Life on the Fringe. Living in the Southern Egyptian Deserts during the Roman and early-Byzantine Periods*, CNWS-NVIC, 221–242.

9 Cf. J. Bingen 1998: '*Life on the Fringe*: Some Conclusions', in O. Kaper (ed.): *Life on the Fringe. Living in the Southern Egyptian Deserts during the Roman and early-Byzantine Periods*. CNWS-NVIC, 287–300.

10 A. Bülow-Jacobsen 1992: 'The Excavation and Ostraca of Mons Claudianus', in A. H. S. El-Mosalamy: *Proceedings of the XIXth International Congress of Papyrology, Cairo 2–9 September 1992*, Vol. I, Ain Shams University Center of Papyrological Studies: Cairo 1992, p. 51; D. P. S. Peacock 1992: *Rome in the Desert: A Symbol of Power*. University of Southampton, Southampton, p. 8.

11 *Cantines*: Field suitcases, metal boxes used for storing finds.

12 In 1997, the Supreme Council of Antiquities opened a new store in Qift. All finds from Mons Claudianus were translated from Dendera to Qift and are now kept in the new building here.

13 Baraka mineral water is a staple commodity at any excavation in Egypt, 12-pack boxes bought in quantity to provide delicate Europeans with potable water. But this is not their only merit. Empty bottles may be cut to form useful cups for pens and brushes;

empty cardboard boxes are even more useful, and are quickly snatched up by crew members – to pack finds that are going to the stores, but also as camp furniture, or, as in our case, for tools invented on the spot to serve a particular need.

14 In 1990, and again in 1994 a portable microscope was graciously loaned to us by the First Department of the National Museum of Denmark. The microscope had been acquired for the Department by Dr Margrethe Hald, and it was a great pleasure to apply it to further studies of ancient textiles. By 1991, the Mons Claudianus textile project had acquired an Euromex Model ST portable stereo microscope.

15 The index cards are the same type as designed for the recording of ostraca.

16 In 1994, Hero Granger-Taylor kindly showed us the Masada textiles at the Textile Conservation Centre, then at the Hampton Court Palace. Apart from acquainting us with an important contemporary textile collection, Hero and the TCC staff also demonstrated to us how to fold individual wrappings for textiles out of sheets of tissue paper. This made it possible to solve a major problem: how to pack the MC textiles individually. A first solution, airmail envelopes bought locally, was not satisfactory. Acid-free tissue-paper, however, we had in abundance. In 1990, two large sheaves had been acquired from Museumstjenesten, the Museum Supply Store in Denmark, brought out to Egypt by Professor Adam Bülow-Jacobsen by means of Landrover, and deposited at IFAO's house in Dendera between field seasons.

17 Post-excavation study seasons in Dendera have been headed by Professor Jean Bingen, Brussels, companionably checking disputed readings against the original *ostraca* while members of the textile team worked our way through the *cantines*. Jean has sorted out innumerable problems and – often accompanied by his wife, Marthe – created a pleasant family atmosphere with himself in the role of *père de famille*. During the 1994 season, Lise Bender Jørgensen and Ulla Mannering continued recording. In 1996 and 1998, Lise Bender Jørgensen and Lena Hammarlund have been re-examining the textiles recorded, checking specific pieces, securing additional documentation on colours, and photographing long series of textiles. Life in Dendera is greatly facilitated by the existence of IFAO's house there. *El-Beit Fransa* has been at the disposal for members of the Mons Claudianus project, supplying pleasant accommodation, complete with a beautiful garden, pleasant rooms and the wonderful possibility of hot showers. Fond memories of the French House in Dendera include the exquisite cuisine of our cook Mohammed Said that brightened the 1991 and 1994 seasons. The porters of the house, Khalil, and his sons Abdullah and Hamid, have always made sure that we are taken well care of.

18 MC textiles Nos. 1–468 are kept in Box 1990/4; this box also contains larger pieces of the series 1116–1460. MC Nos. 469–904 in Box 1991/V. MC Nos. 905–115 in Box 1989/20; this box also contains garments, gammas, and other unusual pieces from all series. MC Nos. 1116–1460 are kept in Box 1989/18. MC Nos. 1461–1722 and a collection from Barud (Nos. 1723–51) are kept in Box 1992/20. MC Nos. 1752–63 are re-labelled pieces, mainly kept in Box 1989/20.

19 Metal box (cantine) MC 1987/3; 1988/4; 1989/17, 18, 19, 20, and Varia; 1990/4, 5; 1991/5; 1992/20 and 1993/1.

20 The numbers given in the text do not tally with the numbered textiles referred to in connection with the contents of the cantines. This is because several textile fragments are composite and consist of more than one fabric. Recording was done by Lise Bender Jørgensen, while Ulla Mannering was in charge of sorting and cleaning the textiles.

21 The number of textiles recorded is dictated by the capacity of the recorder and the time spent in Egypt. 500 textiles represent roughly one month's work for one person. This

recently was confirmed by Dr Dominique Cardon, working on the textiles from Maximinion, Krokodilo and Didimoi.

22 At this occasion a group of textiles from Barud, a near-by Roman quarry site excavated by the Mons Claudianus Project 1993, was also examined. They are numbered 1723–51, but not included in the database.

23 The Mons Claudianus taquetés, or weft-faced compound tabbies, have been studied by Martin Ciszuk on basis of documentation made by Lise Bender Jørgensen and Lena Hammarlund. See M. Ciszuk in press: 'The taquetés of Mons Claudianus'....

24 Calculated on the basis of the number of clavi and gammas found. For further details see U. Mannering in press: 'Garments from Mons Claudianus'.

25 Lena Hammarlund is working on this aspect of the Mons Claudianus textiles. For a preliminary version, see L. Hammarlund 1997: 'Textilenes fjerde dimension – håndverkerens kunnskap og redskap', *Spor* 1997/2, pp. 26–29.

26 Colours have been recorded by comparing them to colour charts of the Natural Colours System. No less than 147 shades have been identified; most are faded, and the original range of colours probably was much less. Work on this aspect is in progress.

27 Shaded bands is a term originally used of luxurious fabrics found at various Roman sites in the Crimea, Syria, Israel, Nubia as well as nearby Quseir al-Qadim and tentatively identified with the zonai skiathos mentioned in the Periplus of the Erithraean Sea (G. M. Eastwood 1982: 'Textiles', in D. Whitcomb & J. Johnson: *Quseir al-Qadim 1980. Preliminary Report*. Malibu).

28 In 1995, a planned study season in Dendera had to be cancelled as political unrest in Egypt caused the Dendera area to be closed to foreigners. C. E. G. Gad's Fond had granted Ulla Mannering the travel costs to Egypt, but generously permitted her to spend the money going to Gothenburg instead, to set up the MC database together with Lise Bender Jørgensen who was then a research fellow at Göteborg University.

29 Lise Bender Jørgensen of the Norwegian University of Science and Technology, Dept. of Archaeology is Director of the Mons Claudianus Textile Project. Ulla Mannering, currently at the University of Copenhagen, joined the Project in 1991. Further members are handweavers Lena Hammarlund, Gothenburg, and Martin Ciszuk, Uppsala, both Sweden. Lena Larsson of Göteborg University, has contributed to the project with a study on Roman Textile Professions; recently, Ulla Viklund, a Trondheim postgraduate student, has taken on the task of studying textile design and the use of colours at Mons Claudianus.

Chapter 2

ON THE ROAD TO BERENIKE: A PIECE OF TUNIC IN DAMASK WEAVE FROM DIDYMOI

Dominique Cardon

Introduction

The archaeological site of Didymoi (Fig. 2.1) is a small Roman fortress (*praesidium*) situated in the Eastern Desert of Egypt on the caravan road leading from Koptos (Quft) in the Nile valley to the harbour of Berenike on the Red Sea coast – a place familiar to John Peter Wild. Since 1994, systematic excavations of the *praesidia*, both on this road and on the shorter one from Koptos to Myos Hormos (Quseir), have been carried out under the direction of Hélène Cuvigny, a papyrologist from the University of Paris-Sorbonne.[1] The rubbish heaps that have been preserved on some of these sites (Fig. 2.2) have yielded large numbers of *ostraca*, inscribed pieces of broken pottery, which provide a great deal of information about everyday life in the *praesidia* of the Eastern Desert. They have also produced massive quantities of textile fragments, reflecting the development of techniques in the ancient world during the first three centuries AD and the variety of textile products circulating along these roads. Small

Fig. 2.1 The site of Didymoi in the Eastern Desert of Egypt. Behind the archaeological camp and in front of the small fortress stretches the long rubbish heap where thousands of textile fragments have been discovered.

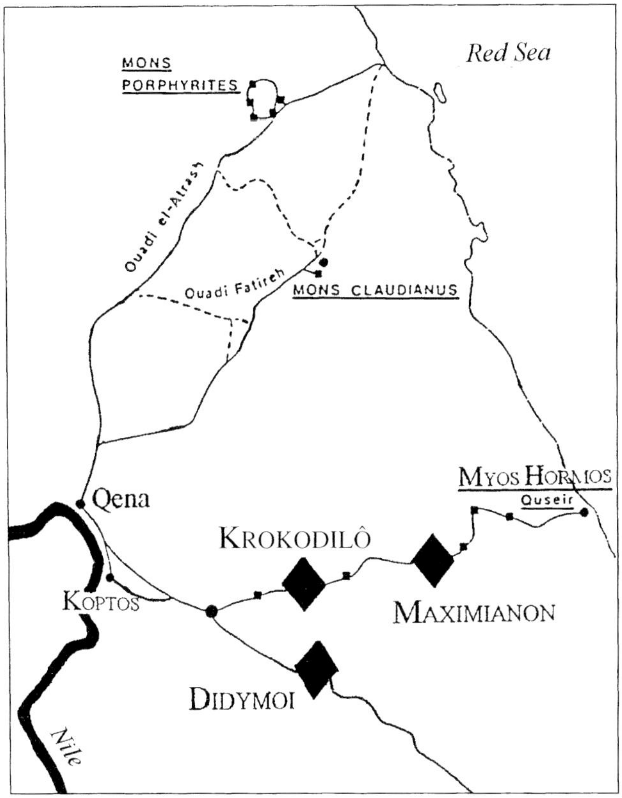

Fig. 2.2 Roman sites of the Eastern Desert of Egypt where archaeological textiles have been found (names underlined or in large capital letters).

groups of textiles from Maximianon, Krokodilô and Didymoi, selected because of their historical importance, have already been published[2] and a chapter on textiles has been included in a forthcoming publication on the Roman sites on the road to Myos Hormos.[3]

The single textile presented here, in honour of J. P. Wild, has been chosen not just because it was discovered on the road to Berenike; there are other good reasons. First, the ground weave of this piece of wool tunic is a damask twill, which makes it one of the earliest examples of the check-patterned textiles identified by J. P. Wild in 1964 as the *scutulata* fabrics mentioned in Latin texts.[4] Moreover, it appears to be the earliest example of a special type of damask twill that has been identified so far in only two silk fabrics, one of which is the silk damask from Holborough, Kent, published by J. P. Wild in 1965[5] and the other a silk damask with a blue warp and a golden yellow weft from Palmyra, Syria.[6] Thanks to the meticulous stratigraphic studies of the rubbish heaps carried out by Jean-Pierre Brun on all the above-mentioned sites, and to discoveries of dated *ostraca*, fairly precise dating of the textile finds is often possible. In the present case, combined archaeological evidence shows that the piece of tunic described here was already much worn and had probably gone through different stages of use when it was eventually thrown out on the rubbish heap some time during Domitian's reign (AD 81–96).

The technical description of the textile will be followed by a discussion of its contribution to the history of textile techniques.

Description of the fragment

Textile 2428.15, discovered in the rubbish heap of Didymoi in 1998, is a long and narrow rectangular fragment of lightweight, ivory-coloured fabric, measuring 605 mm in the warp direction and 104 mm in the weft direction. It is ornamented with a tapestry-woven purple band (*clavus*) 25 mm wide, running at right angles to the selvedge which is one of the long side edges of the fragment (Fig. 2.3). The purple part of the *clavus* runs at a distance of 120 mm from one of the short sides of the rectangle and at 460 mm from the other side, which seems to be the end of the piece (as indicated by a small area of finishing border). The two other edges (one long and one short side of the rectangle) appear to have been neatly torn in a straight line, although at present the fragment is much worn and has many holes. A series of longitudinal creases suggests that it may have been used tightly folded lengthwise, like a kind of strap, or worn like a scarf.

Structural features

The warp is made of undyed, now off-white wool (it still looks shiny white where it has been kept protected by the tightly beaten-in purple weft), hard Z-spun to an angle of 45° or tighter, 29 to 36 threads per cm in the ground weave, 17 ribs, i.e. 34 threads per cm in the *clavus*. The ground weft is made of undyed, now ivory-coloured wool, weaker Z-spun, 54 to 70 threads per cm. The purple weft of the

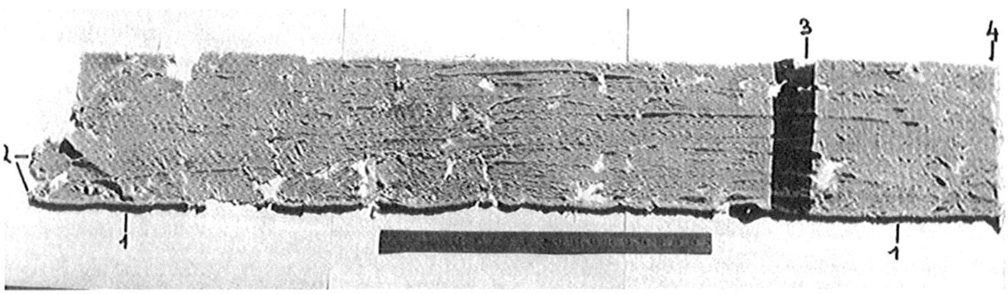

Fig. 2.3 Fragment 2428.15. 1: selvedge; 2: finishing border; 3: purple clavus, *4: corner with faults represented in the diagram of Fig. 2.5.*

clavus is made of wool. Dye and mordant analyses by Witold Nowik, of the Laboratoire de Recherche des Monuments Historiques in Champs-sur-Marne, near Paris, have identified indigotin (woad/indigo), dyers' madder, *Rubia tinctorum* L., and traces of alum and iron. The yarn is Z-spun, extremely thin and regular, with 108 to 124 threads per cm.

The ground weave is 3/1 damask: it is a 3/1 broken twill (or a 4-end satin, décochement 1–2–3–2), alternately warp and weft-faced, forming a chequered pattern of units, 3.5 mm wide by 3.0–3.5 mm high. The basic warp repeat is made up of 12 threads, but within the short width of fabric preserved, four warp sections are composed of only 11 threads and one of only 10 threads. Weft repeats are even more irregular, the most frequent numbers of threads in horizontal sections being 17 and 18, with occasionally as few as 6 and as many as 22 threads, odd numbers being slightly less frequent than even ones. The twill direction[7] changes from one vertical section to the next, but remains unchanged within each vertical section (Fig. 2.4).

Several kinds of warp fault can be observed. The first occurs at the boundary between two vertical sections, where the last thread of a vertical section of 12 crosses over or under the first thread of the adjacent section of 11 threads between two horizontal sections, but keeps working as it should in its normal place (Fig. 2.5, at point marked A). This fault does not run the entire length of the fragment: in the instance shown in Fig. 2.5, the normal order of warp threads reappears in the fourth

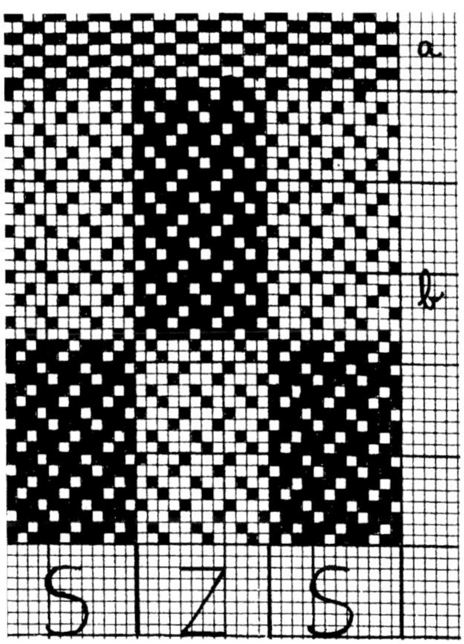

Fig. 2.4 Diagram of the weave structures in fragment 2428.15 from Didymoi: a: 2/2 extended tabby (half-basket weave) of the clavus*; b: 3/1 damask.*

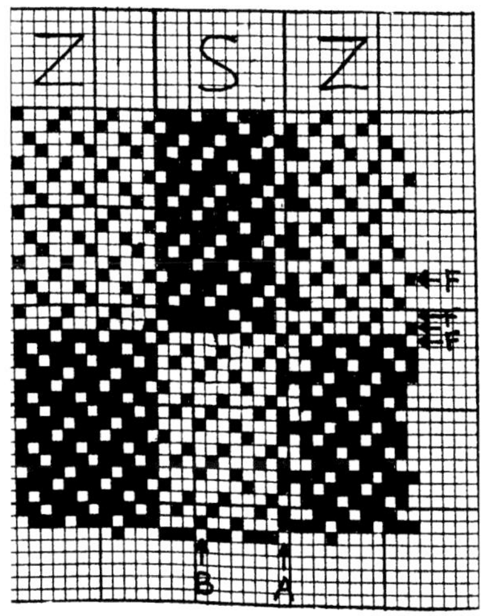

Fig. 2.5 Weave diagram taken from the corner opposite the selvedge and the finishing border, where several faults, here marked A and B, can be observed.

complete horizontal section from the edge of the fragment, nearer to the *clavus*, after the 11th weft thread. Another type of fault can be followed along the whole length of the damask but does not affect the *clavus* weave. This looks like a straightforward entering error, where a warp thread has been attached to the wrong heddle-rod (Fig. 2.5 at point marked B). Another fault, to be found in many places in the damask parts of the fragment, consists of warp and weft floats of various lengths (jumping over 7 to 11 threads of the other system).

The tapestry-woven *clavus* is in regular 2/2 extended tabby, or half-basket weave. On both sides of the purple weft is a 'shadow' of ground-weft yarns following the same course, 19 on the side of the torn edge, 17 on the side of the finishing border (Fig. 2.6).

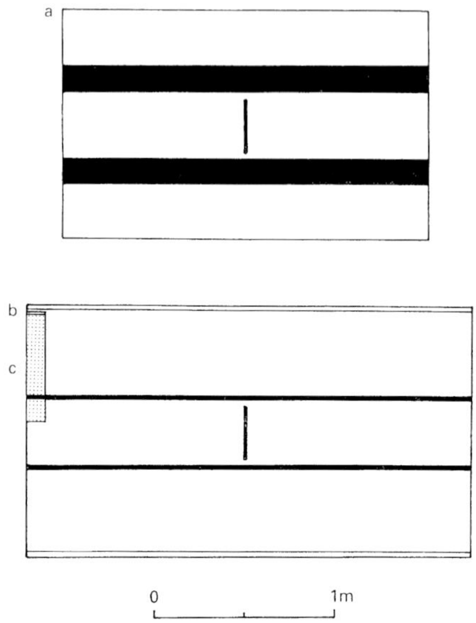

Fig. 2.6 Outline drawings of some surviving sleeveless wool tunics. a: n° 4219 in the Abegg-Stiftung; b: n° 20349 Q150 29/3 from Qustul, Nubia; c (shaded and superimposed on b): fragment 2428.15 from Didymoi.

The selvedge is reinforced by two bundles of six warp threads worked in plain tabby weave. After every eight passes of the main weft, the bundles are wrapped by a supplementary weft unit of four Z-spun yarns, undyed except in the purple part of the *clavus* where the supplementary weft is made of purple threads. The vertical section of the damask next to the selvedge is made up of 10 warp threads, as if the two bundles of the selvedge had been counted as part of a basic unit of 12 warp threads.

The finishing border is preserved as a length of 7 mm at its beginning, at the corner with the preserved selvedge, and as a length of 10 mm further along the last weft. It starts after only two passes of the last horizontal section of the damask, with the two warp-bundles of the selvedge augmented by five threads of the main warp, twisted together in the S-direction into three strands which are then plied Z to form the cord proper. Groups of five to six warp threads, as they issue from the fell of the cloth, are taken up into the three S strands and so into the Z cord.

The contribution of Textile 2418.15 from Didymoi to the history of textiles

As can readily be perceived by textile historians, this rag, discarded by its last users, is a treasure for us, as it encapsulates many pieces of precious information concerning different aspects of textile research.

Fig. 2.7. Close-up of fragment (see Colour Plate I).

The fragment as a piece of a garment

Thanks to the discoveries of complete, or nearly complete, tunics, either contemporary with our fragment, as in the Cave of Letters, in Israel, or a little later, as in Dura-Europos in Syria and Qustul in Nubia,[8] it is now fairly certain that the majority of the fragments of the wool fabrics decorated by tapestry-woven bands in contrasting colours that are found in great numbers in Maximianon, Krokodilô and Didymoi are parts of tunics. They were originally adorned by two vertical *clavi* running from the shoulder to the bottom of the garment on either side of the neck opening. Though it would seem at first impossible, from such a small fragment, to guess whether it once belonged to a one-piece tunic or to a tunic assembled from two identical sheets, each with *clavi*, the preservation of one *clavus*, one selvedge and one finishing border is telling enough. The tiny pieces of the finishing border are enough to show that the fragment represents one of the sides of the tunic. As there is no trace whatsoever of sewing anywhere along the selvedge, it is certain that the fragment belonged to a bottom corner of the front or back of the garment.[9] Lastly, the distance of approximately 490 mm from the inside (neck side) of the *clavus* to the finishing border (side of the tunic as worn) is valuable information, as it allows comparison with the other known pieces of tunics, thus providing a key to what type of tunic the fragment once came from. It corresponds to the neck-to-side measurements of two sleeveless-tunics, one from Qustul, the other preserved in the Abegg-Stiftung (No. 4219), which J. P. Wild proposed to be examples of the *colobium*, the wide sleeveless tunic worn by Romans (Fig. 2.6). Some of these are described in papyri from Roman Egypt, as adorned by two *clavi* that apparently were sometimes dyed with 'pseudo-purple' like the present fragment.[10] Textile 2418.15 from Didymoi may therefore be viewed as a piece of a *colobium* worn in Egypt during the third quarter of the first century AD.

The fragment as an early example of damask weave

In a series of important papers, Daniël De Jonghe, in collaboration with Marcel Tavernier and more recently with Chris Verhecken-Lammens, has studied the extant Roman silk damasks and the complete wool tunic in damask weave preserved in the Abegg-Stiftung[11] (see also this volume, pp. 137–147). These systematic studies have led to a classification of Roman silk damasks into two main technical and stylistic groups and to a proposed schema of evolution from one type to another. A close examination of the faults that can be observed in the silk damasks has allowed D. De Jonghe to demonstrate convincingly that these fabrics could not have been woven on such evolved types of looms as the draw-loom, the horizontal treadle-loom or the Chinese pattern-rod loom. He shows that the silk damasks of the earliest phase, with simple chequered patterns, and the wool tunic preserved in the Abegg-Stiftung could all have been produced on a horizontal loom where the sheds were opened by means of two sets of four heddle-rods (more exactly *baguettes à boucles*), each warp thread being controlled by a single cord loop attached to one of the rods. To open each shed, the relevant rods had to be picked up and lifted. In the case of the chequered damasks ornamented with a *clavus* in half-basket weave (S6 and S38 of Palmyra and the tunic at the Abegg-Stiftung, for example), a shed-rod inserted in front of the heddle-rods and one more heddle-rod would have allowed the weave to be repeated mechanically. Such a loom could be operated by a weaver seated in front of the cloth-beam, with at least one assistant posted at the side of the loom to raise the heddle-rods and insert the auxiliary rods that were also probably used to help open each shed.

These studies provide a firm ground for comparison with the present fragment. Its chequered pattern, the presence of a *clavus* in half-basket weave and the fact that the twill direction remains the same along each vertical section of the damask, provide close parallels to the silk damasks S6 and S38 from Palmyra. The fragment of silk damask from Holborough does not include a *clavus*, but it offers the closest parallel to textile 2428.15, together with S6 from Palmyra, because of their common weave, broken 3/1 twill, with the slant of the twill remaining unchanged in each vertical section.[12] No other instance of this weave has yet been published among the wool damasks that have been discovered in recent years in Quseir al-Qadim, Mons Claudianus, Maximianon, Krokodilô and Didymoi.[13] In the three last sites, the other wool damasks that have been studied so far present alternately warp and weft-faced chequered patterns of regular 2/1 or 3/1 damask twills, where the twill direction remains the same in all warp-face sections, but reverses in the weft-face sections. The weaving faults described above also emphasize the technical similarity between the present fragment and the silk damasks. Fault B in the Didymoi textile only serves to show that in this case too, warp threads were controlled by heddle-rods allowing the mechanical repetition of the weave-pattern; but fault A finds exact, or very close, equivalents in several early silk damasks, where faulty warp floats and warp thread-crossings often occur at the boundary between two vertical sections. In the course of his study of the faults in damask S38 from Palmyra, D. De Jonghe showed how the system of cord loops controlling individual warp threads allows warp threads to cross over each other accidentally without breaking, as happens in the fragment from Didymoi.[14] Several faulty warp and weft floats occurring in various places in the fragment also have the same explanation as already proposed by D. De Jonghe for some silk damasks. They imply the use of auxiliary rods, inserted into the warp behind the heddle-rods, to help open the sheds. In some portions of the warp the auxiliary rods have been inserted into faulty sheds.[15]

It is remarkable that the closest parallels with the wool damask 2428.15 from Didymoi are found among silk damasks reckoned to be later, rather than among the numerous wool damasks of the end of the first and the second centuries AD that have recently been found in the Eastern Desert of Egypt. What it seems to show is that various types of damask weaves were already produced during the second half of the first century AD and that this type of weave was first developed for wool textiles, most probably in Egypt. In favour of an Egyptian origin of fragment 2428.15 is the dye of the purple weft of the *clavus*. It is an imitation of a true shellfish purple, obtained by first dyeing the wool blue in a vat where the source of indigotin was most probably woad, then by dipping it into a madder-bath after mordanting with alum. Iron salts may also have been added to obtain the precise shade of purple required. In the light of a recent series of dye analyses, the systematic – and masterly – use of plant dyes to imitate real purple even in high quality textiles is becoming more and more evident among Egyptian textiles of the Roman period.[16] It is not uncommon either for very high quality textiles of Roman Egypt to be made partly or wholly of Z-spun yarns.[17] In the forthcoming publication of the textiles from the road to Myos Hormos, I have argued that these fine Z-spun yarns may have been spun in the *gynaecea* of the Greek communities settled in Egypt.

Lastly, it must be stressed that the weaving faults observed in fragment 2428.15 from Didymoi add new strength to Daniël De Jonghe's deductions on the type of loom on which the early damask twills may have been produced. However, in the same way as an Egyptian origin is now likely for the earliest wool damasks, an Egyptian origin can also be proposed for the damask loom: it may easily have developed from the horizontal ground loom figured in paintings and models found in Egyptian tombs since the Middle Empire. The weaver – a woman – is effectively sitting in front of the cloth-beam and is helped by one or two other women sitting on either side of the warp, who prepare the sheds for her by manipulating rods. Adding the necessary number of heddle rods and possibly building a stronger frame, one would get a very suitable damask loom... perhaps the Roman horizontal loom described by John Peter Wild?[18]

Notes

1 The excavations are funded by the French Ministère des Affaires Etrangères, with practical help from the Institut Français d'Archéologie Orientale (IFAO) in Cairo.

2 D. Cardon, 'Textiles archéologiques de Maximianon-Al Zarqa et Didymoi: exemples précoces de teinture par réserve sur laine', *Bulletin du CIETA*, LXXV (1998), 14–20; D.Cardon, 'Les damassés de laine de Krokodilô (100–120 apr. J.-C.), *Bulletin du CIETA*, LXXVI (1999), pp. 6–21.

[3] D. Cardon, 'Chiffons dans le désert: textiles des dépotoirs de Maximianon et Krokodilô', in H. Cuvigny (ed), *La Route de Myos Hormos*, Éditions de l'Institut Français d'Archéologie Orientale, Le Caire, forthcoming.

[4] J. P. Wild, 'The textile term '*scutulatus*', *The Classical Quarterly*, N. S., XIV (1964), pp. 263–266.

[5] J. P. Wild, 'A Roman damask silk from Kent', *Archaeologia Cantiana*, 80, 1965, 246–250; J.P.Wild, *Textile Manufacture in the Northern Roman Provinces* (Cambridge, 1970), pp. 51, 101, no. 51, 166 fig. 41.

[6] Silk damask S.6, R. Pfister, *Textiles de Palmyre* (Paris, 1934), 42 and pl. XIIIb; R.Pfister, *Nouveaux Textiles de Palmyre* (Paris, 1937), 36 fig. 17.

[7] Following Daniël De Jonghe's classification of damasks based on 4-end satin: D. De Jonghe, M. Tavernier, 'Les Damassés de la Proche-Antiquité', *Bulletin du CIETA*, XLVII (1978), 42 pl. VIIc–d.

[8] Y. Yadin, *The Finds from the Bar Kokhba period in the Cave of Letters* (Jerusalem, 1963), pp. 204–218, pl. 63–66; R. Pfister and L. Bellinger, *The Excavations at Dura-Europos, Final Report IV, Part II: The Textiles* (New Haven, 1945), pp. 17–19, pl. V–VI; C. Mayer Thurman and B. Williams, *Ancient Textiles from Nubia* (Chicago, 1979), pp. 40–41 and no. 29.

[9] For a discussion of the form of the Roman tunic, see H. Granger-Taylor, 'Weaving Clothes to Shape in the Ancient World: the Tunic and Toga of the Arringatore', *Textile History*, XIII (1) (1982), pp. 3–10.

[10] J. P. Wild, 'Tunic no. 4219: an archaeological and historical perspective', in: *Riggisberger Berichte*, II (1994), pp. 21–27 and figs. 31–34.

[11] D. De Jonghe and M. Tavernier, loc. cit.; D. De Jonghe and M.Tavernier, 'Les Damassés de Palmyre', *Bulletin du CIETA*, LV/LVI (1982), pp. 20–52; D. De Jonghe and C.Verhecken-Lammens, 'Le vêtement damassé 4219 de la fondation Abegg B Riggisberg', *Riggisberger Berichte*, II (1994), pp. 41–71.

[12] J. P. Wild, *Textile Manufacture in the Northern Roman Provinces* (Cambridge, 1970), p. 166, fig. 41; D. De Jonghe and M. Tavernier, 'Les Damassés de Palmyre', XLV fig. 20.

[13] G. Eastwood, 'Textiles', in D. S. Whitcomb and J. H. Johnson, *Quseir al-Qadim 1980 – Preliminary Report* (Malibu, 1987), pp. 286, 287 fig. 3, 304 no. 54; L. Bender Jørgensen, 'Mons Claudianus', *Archaeological Textiles Newsletter*, X (1990), p. 10; L. Bender Jørgensen, 'The Textiles from Mons Claudianus recorded in 1991', *Archaeological Textiles Newsletter*, XII (1991), p.8; L.Bender Jørgensen, 'Textiles from Mons Claudianus: a preliminary report', *Acta Hyperborea*, III (1991), p. 89. For the three last sites, see D. Cardon, notes 2 and 3 above.

[14] Similar faults occur in the Holborough damask, in the yellow silk damask from Trier, the damask silk from Conthey and in fragment S38 from Palmyra: D. De Jonghe and M. Tavernier, 'Les Damassés de la Proche-Antiquité', pp. 23–25 and 41, pl. V–VI; ibid., 'Les Damassés de Palmyre', pp. 39–40, figs.8–9.

[15] Ibid., pp. 23–29, 40–41, figs. 10, 12–13.

[16] The results of a series of dye analyses on the purple yarns present in archaeological textiles of the Roman period from Palmyra, Egypt and France are published in D. Cardon (ed.), *Teintures précieuses de la Méditerranée: pourpre, kermès, pastel / Tintes preciosos del Mediterráneo: púrpura, quermes, pastel* (Carcassonne-Terrassa, 1999–2000).

[17] For example, wool damask no. 2406.1 from Krokodilô, D. Cardon, loc. cit. n. 2, pp.17–19.

[18] J. P. Wild, 'The Roman Horizontal Loom', *American Journal of Archaeology*, XCI (1987), pp. 459–471.

Chapter 3

TWO WIDE-SLEEVED LINEN TUNICS FROM ROMAN EGYPT

Frances Pritchard and Chris Verhecken-Lammens

Introduction

The Whitworth Art Gallery has one of the finest collections of post-Pharaonic textiles in Britain. It is, however, little known despite its use over many decades by students of the University of Manchester, who often come to see it under the guidance of their tutor, John Peter Wild. The situation was very different in the 1890s when the Gallery (then called The Whitworth Institute) first opened to the public and its collection of Coptic textiles from Akhmim (Panopolis) was singled out for press attention: '*there is perhaps nothing in this unique gathering more really interesting than the series of specimens of Graeco-Roman and Egyptian textiles which have recently been found in Upper Egypt*'.[1]

The two linen tunics discussed here were acquired by the Gallery during the 1960s, when textile holdings within Manchester were rationalised.[2] Little is known about their provenance, although it is clear from their staining by body fluids that they were burial garments and there is a strong possibility that they come from Panopolis, which was excavated over many seasons beginning in 1884 by Gaston Maspero, Director of Cairo Museum, and which yielded large quantities of textiles from its extensive burying grounds.[3] The construction and design of the two tunics enable them to be dated to the third and fourth centuries AD and they add significantly to the small corpus of tunics preserved from the period when Egypt was a Roman province and part of the East Roman Empire.

Both tunics were woven to shape in one piece from undyed linen. They have *clavi* and other ornaments tapestry-woven from imitation purple wool embellished with interlace patterns. Once woven, the cloth was turned 90° so that the warp ran horizontally across the tunic when worn. The tunics are also characterised by wide sleeves, almost half the length of the garment. Other details relating to the tapestry technique, for example the grouping of the warp ends and floating threads on the reverse, suggest that the plainer tunic with a three-fold full length *clavus* is earlier in date and, therefore, it will be described first.

Technical information

Tunic A (Fig. 3.1)[4]

Half of one side of the tunic is preserved (the other side and sleeve have been deliberately cut away). Thus the general appearance of the tunic can be reconstructed, with the exception of its sleeve length.

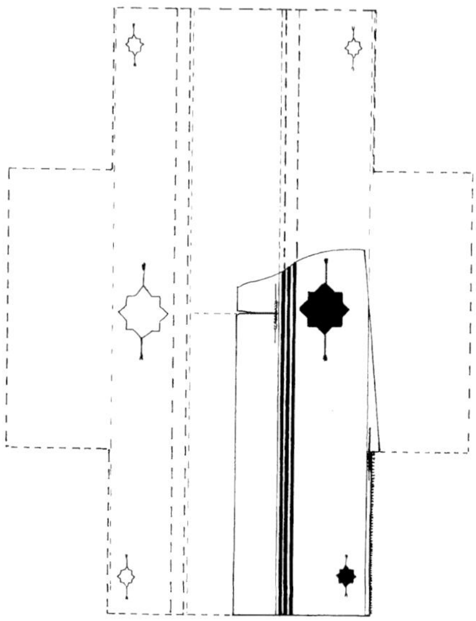

Fig. 3.1. Diagram of Tunic A.

DIMENSIONS

The fabric: length 0.58 m (original length unknown), width 1.40 m (estimated original width 2.40 m)

Tunic: finished length 1.22 m, estimated original width 1.00 m

Sleeves: length unknown (cut off), width 0.77 m (estimated original width 1.12 m)

Decoration: clavus full length, width 50 mm; Shoulder medallion: 190 × 200 mm plus extension at each end of 65 mm and 70 mm; knee medallion: 75 × 75 mm plus extension at each end of 45 mm and 50 mm

MATERIAL AND THREAD COUNT

Ground weave warp: linen, S-spun, 20 threads per cm; weft: linen, S-spun, 10 threads per cm; weave: warp-faced tabby

Tapestry areas warp: as for ground weave, but warp ends are floating, grouped and crossing (see below); weft: (i) tapestry weft: purple wool, S-spun, 42–46 threads per cm; (ii) brocading weft: fine linen, S-spun; weave: extended tabby, 5/1 in the *clavus*, 4/2 in the medallions

FEATURES OF THE WEAVE

The linen fabric is woven in warp-faced tabby. Simple selvedges with densely packed ends form the lower hem and arm seams. The neck opening is formed from an internal simple selvedge strengthened at the sides by a short line of loop-manipulated, twined threads which extend into a discontinuous self-band (a self-band is a band where multiple weft picks are worked as one), 270 mm in length (Fig. 3.2).[5] Two pairs of self-bands between the neckline and the *clavus* act as further reinforcement. A series of self-bands were also woven at the sides. Four pairs extend the full width of the fabric while three discontinuous self-bands run for approximately 170 mm above and below the angle of the arm with the spare weft yarn being deliberately caught into the warp fringe (see below). Apart from the undecorated *clavus*, the only ornaments are octagonal medallions placed at the shoulder and above the bottom edge near the side seam (knee medallion). They have matching interlace brocading worked in a fine linen thread (Fig. 3.2A). The side seam has a short warp fringe of

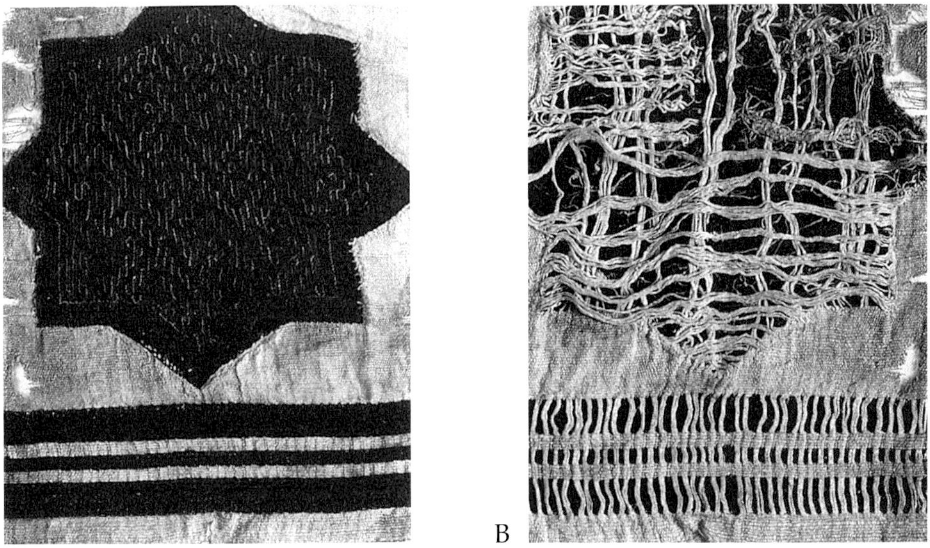

A B

Fig. 3.2. Detail of front and back of Tunic. A showing self-band with twining, clavus *and shoulder medallion: (A) front; (B) back. Note how the threads float and are cut on the back of the medallion. The warp is shown vertically, with the partly twined self-band, next to the neck opening at the top. Photograph: The Whitworth Art Gallery, The University of Manchester.*

cut ends tied continuously with a single thread.[6] The seam allowance of 5 mm to 7 mm is indicated by a line of stitch holes at intervals of approximately 5 mm which extends to within 15 mm of the underarm angle. A few running stitches are preserved worked in double S-spun linen thread and the outermost discontinuous self-band acts as a guide for the position of the seam.

In contrast with the ground weave, the wool ornaments are woven in a weft-faced extended tabby. Different methods can be used to change from a warp-faced to a weft-faced extended tabby.[7] To weave the *clavus* of this tunic, the warp threads were divided in the following manner. One layer is formed of groups of five threads, while the threads of the other layer float behind and only one thread in five binds the weft (Figs. 3.2B and 3.3A). There is no crossing of warp threads. The result is a weft-faced extended tabby in the ratio 5:1, which has caused a slightly puckered openwork effect in the two bands separating the three purple bands of the *clavus*. By contrast, the octagonal medallions on the shoulders and knee are woven in a weft-faced extended tabby in the ratio 4:2. This means the warp threads of one layer have been grouped in fours and in the other layer there are floating threads and crossed threads (Fig. 3.3B). Both these methods (5/1 without crossed threads and 4/2 with crossed threads) were used particularly in early Roman linen textiles, including furnishings as well as tunics, to adapt the density of the warp from a warp-faced weave to a weft-faced weave. The positioning of the medallions has been chosen by the weaver of the ground weave. Before the wool weft is introduced,

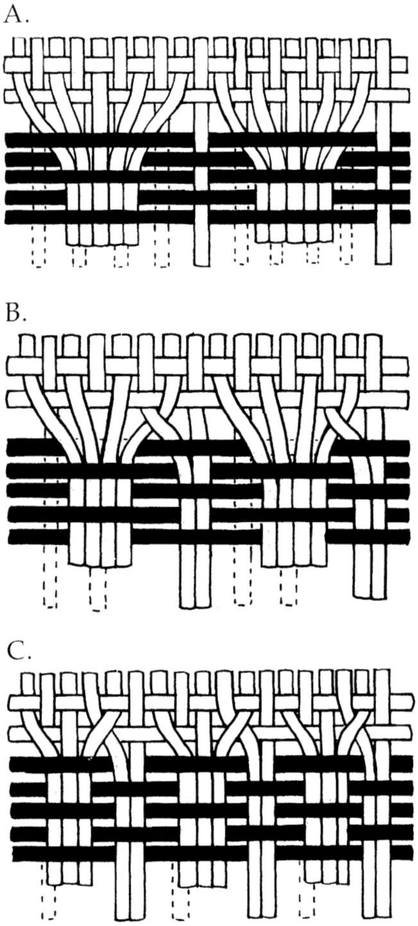

Fig. 3.3. Diagrams showing regrouping of warp threads for areas of weft-faced extended tabby: (A) 5/1, floating and grouped warp threads; (B) 4/2, floating, grouped and crossing warp threads; (C) 3/2, floating, grouped and crossing warp threads.

the ground weft does not interlace with the warp ends but floats over an area determined by the width of the decoration. Once half the ornament has been defined in this manner, the weaving of the ground temporarily stops and the decoration is woven in. First the weft threads of the ground weave are cut in the middle (Fig. 3.2B). Then, across the width of the ornament, a supplementary shed rod is added in order to regroup the warp threads controlled by the shed rod. Once the complete decoration is woven in, the supplementary shed rod is removed and the ground weave alongside the upper section of the ornament is woven. Here again the weft of the ground weave floats on the back of the medallions but the threads are not cut as they are not an impediment to the weaving process (Fig. 3.2B). In the part of the tunic preserved, the cut weft threads are nearer to the vestigial, surviving sleeve and, therefore, it is possible to determine that this sleeve was woven first on the loom.

Tunic B (Figs. 3.4 and 3.5)[8]

This tunic is more complete, with one sleeve intact.

Dimensions

The fabric length: 1.24 m (original length 1.68 m); width 1.78 m (original width 1.84 m)

Tunic: finished length 0.92 m, width 0.93 m

Sleeves: length 0.41 m; width 0.91 m

Decoration: sleeve bands: 0.91 × 0.10 m; shoulder medallions: diameter 220–240 mm; neck bands: 315 × 55 mm plus short *clavi* ending in a small leaf motif, 370 × 50 mm; hem band: 790 × 60 mm plus upright extensions ending in a small leaf motif, 360 × 50 mm; knee medallions: diameter 120–130 mm

Material and thread count

Ground weave: warp: linen, S-spun, 17–22 threads per cm; weft: ground: linen, S-spun yarn, 12 threads per cm; weave: warp-faced tabby

Tapestry areas: warp: as for ground weave, but warp ends are floating, grouped and crossing (see below); weft: (i) tapestry weft: purple wool, S-spun, 50–56 threads per cm; (ii) brocading and small details: fine linen, S-spun; weave: extended tabby 3/2

Features of the weave

The tunic is woven to shape in one piece with the ground weave in warp-faced tabby. Starting with the wide sleeve, a strip of 15mm was woven in tabby followed by a 13mm band of bare ends and two picks of purple wool. Selfbands are woven between these picks of purple and the sleeve decoration. The two sleeve bands, which extend the full width of the sleeve, are woven in warp-faced extended tabby in the ratio 3:2 (Fig. 3.3C) and incorporate the tapestry techniques of slit tapestry and 'lazy lines' (formed by systematically returning weft threads). Most of the patterning is worked in weft brocading.

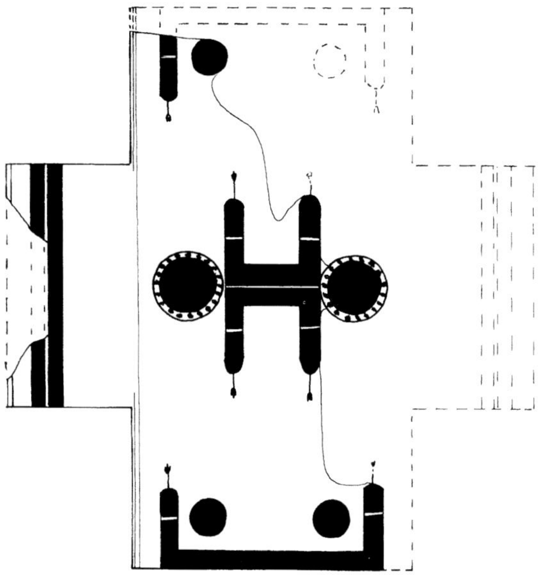

Fig. 3.4. Diagram of Tunic B.

Fig. 3.5. Tunic B. Photograph: The Whitworth Art Gallery, The University of Manchester (see Colour Plate II).

The warp has been extended for 0.46 m on both sides to form the body of the tunic. Here, too, the new sections have a strip of plain tabby followed by a band of bare ends, two purple picks and two self-bands. The purple picks extend a short distance above the armpit into the central warp section, while the self-bands run the full loomwidth. Another sequence of two self-bands woven six picks further into the tunic help to establish the position of the shoulder medallion. In addition to *clavi*, shoulder and knee medallions, the body of this tunic is elaborately embellished with tapestry-woven decoration at the neck and lower edge. The technique of weaving the tapestry decoration differs from that on the first tunic as the ground weft turns back at the edge of the tapestry area instead of floating on the back.

Sewing

The tunic is seamed at the sides and under the arms. Both seams are formed of overlapped edges sewn in running stitch while the tunic was inside out.[9] For the arm seam the seam allowance is 5 mm at the wrist widening to 10 mm near the armpit. The seam continues under the arm and down the sides where the seam allowance remains 10mm wide with the seam lying beside the band of bare ends. The side seam is stitched in a much finer sewing thread, single S-spun linen thread, whereas the arm seam is stitched in four-fold S-spun linen thread. Large running stitches are used throughout, 5mm to 10mm in length and at intervals of 6mm to 10mm. At the underarm angle the seam has been reinforced with four slip stitches using a similar four-fold linen sewing thread.

In addition, overstitches have been used to hold together the long slits between the tapestry decoration and the ground weave at the neck and hem. This has chiefly been carried out in a tightly plied linen thread (S2Z). The tunic has also been repaired on the shoulders between the medallions and the neck band. Double S-spun linen thread was used on one shoulder and a coarser, single S-spun linen thread on the other indicating that the repairs were probably stitched on different occasions.

Decoration

Geometric patterning is used on both tunics and the matching ornaments have been carefully calculated to fill the appropriate spaces using the 'lazy lines' formed by the tapestry technique as a guide for the layout. On tunic A the dark lines between the weft brocading form a pattern of diagonal interconnecting meanders similar to that recorded on various ornaments, roundels, ovals, squares and octagons, in collections in Moscow, Belgium and Switzerland, for example.[10] Overall the patterning on tunic A is very restrained and unusually the shoulder and knee medallions have no contrasting border pattern (Fig. 3.2A).

The patterning on tunic B is based on interlace knots which are cleverly disposed on the shoulder and knee medallions to create contrasting octagonal spaces filled with octofoils. The shoulder medallions have borders of imitation gemstones, pearls alternating with lozenges, in purple on white while the smaller medallions have pearl borders alone. The hem and neck bands have pairs of four-sided knots alternating with lozenges and the *clavi*-like extensions have alternately facing knots similar to those that feature along the sleeve bands. The sleeve, hem and neck bands have dentate edges in white linen. A similar combination of interlace knots and lozenges decorate the ends of a shawl from Antinoë[11] and the reversing of the interlace ribbons on the sleeve bands is paralleled by a pair of bands, which almost certainly come from the cuff of another wide-sleeved tunic, in a Belgian collection.[12]

Discussion

Weaving was a highly skilled craft in the Roman period and analysis of the two tunics shows the considerable attention to detail that went into the weaving of garments in order to ensure that the proportions were correct, the ornaments precisely positioned and the seams accurately aligned. While methods tended to become standardised, subtle differences can be detected, which should eventually enable a number of regional workshop practices to be identified.

The two tunics discussed here possess certain characteristics in common as well as at variance with one another. They are both constructed from purpose-made, cross-shaped loompieces and have wide sleeves typical of the dalmatic, a term first recorded in the mid second century.[13] According to the Edict of Diocletian (AD 301), dalmatics were produced in many centres and in a wide range of grades in the Roman period,[14] and this range in quality is borne out by the few examples that have been preserved.[15] A linen dalmatic from Panopolis, which was acquired by the Victoria and Albert Museum in 1887, is characterised by fine Z-spun purple wool for the tapestry ornaments, elaborately patterned full-length *clavi* and sleeve bands, and an extra band woven in gold as well as purple thread at the side of the skirt.[16] All these features mark it out as a better quality garment than the two Manchester dalmatics. Even more prestigious are two dalmatics made from white silk that are associated with Saint Ambrose (died AD 397), one woven to shape and the other cut out and sewn.[17] But not all dalmatics are of such high status and a closer counterpart to tunic A belongs to a private collection in Israel.[18] This dalmatic has plain, full-length *clavi* and medallions with interlace patterning at the shoulders and above the knees, (the sleeves are missing but the underarm angle indicates their original wide width). In addition, this garment lacks a waist tuck, confirming that the two Manchester tunics are not exceptional in this respect.

The patterning on both tunics makes use of complex geometric interlace, which is characteristic of many purple tapestry-woven ornaments of the third to fifth centuries and was a popular feature of late Roman art.[19] However, such patterning, by itself, is not helpful for dating tunics and the different techniques used for weaving the ornaments are likely to reveal more about chronological trends as well as the place of origin. Tapestry-weaving is used more extensively on tunic B, which also has a greater amount of decoration especially at the neck and hem. Donald King has argued that the increasing concentration of ornaments at the neck and shoulders, including shorter *clavi*, was influenced by military dress and accoutrements and shows cross-cultural influence from Western Asia during the third century.[20] It is considered here that the plainer garment is earlier than the more lavishly decorated example. Nevertheless other sources, for example the mosaics at Piazza Armerina in Sicily dating to the fourth century, show that contemporary tunics were by no means identical in their type of decoration.

The dating of clothing from Roman Egypt remains imprecise due to the poor excavation methods employed on many sites at the turn of the nineteenth century. A fixed reference point is provided by a woven-to-shape linen tunic with narrow sleeves, which is decorated with purple tapestry-woven ornaments patterned with geometric interlace, from the tomb of Elahbel in the Syrian city of Palmyra, which was destroyed in AD 273.[21] The chronology should become better defined as textiles from well dated, recently excavated sites are published. These sites include Mons Claudianus, Didymoi and Berenike, although in contrast with the burying grounds investigated earlier, they are all located further East towards the Red Sea and away from the main centres of population along the banks of the Nile. In the meantime much important new evidence can be discovered about late Roman dress by a careful examination of textiles from Egypt held in many museum collections around the world.

Acknowledgements

Thanks are owed to Ann Tullo for her work on the conservation of the tunics and to Michael Pollard and Derek Trillo for the photography.

Notes

1 The first 'Coptic' textiles acquired by The Whitworth Art Gallery were part of John Charles Robinson's collection. In 1898 these were supplemented by more than 200 textiles, including complete tunics, presented by William Flinders Petrie.

2 The more complete tunic (T.1995.145) was given to The Whitworth Art Gallery by the University of Manchester Institute of Science and Technology (UMIST) in 1964 and the other tunic was probably given by the same institution at the same time. UMIST (formerly called the Technical School or the College of Technology) established a small study and handling collection from its foundation in the 1890s.

3 A. F. Kendrick, *Catalogue of Textiles from Burying-Grounds in Egypt,* Vol.1 (London: HMSO, 1920), p. 9.

4 Accession number WAG T.1996.92.

5 For a description of the same technique used on wool tunics see C. Verhecken-Lammens, 'Two Coptic wool tunics in the collection of the Abegg-Stiftung: a detailed analysis of the weave techniques used', *Riggisberger Berichte* 2 (1994), pp. 73–103.

6 For a diagram of the method used see Marianne Erikson, *Textiles in Egypt 200–1500 a.d. in Swedish Museum Collections* (Göteborg: Röhsska Museet, 1997), p. 79, fig. 1.

7 D. De Jonghe and M. Tavernier, 'Le phénomène du croisage de fils de chaine dans les tapisseries coptes', *Bulletin de Liaison du Centre International d'Etude des Textiles Anciens,*

57–58 (1983), pp. 174–86; H. Granger-Taylor, 'The grouping of warp threads for areas of weft-faced decoration in textiles of the Roman period: a means of distinguishing looms?', *Vlaamse Vereniging Voor Oud en Hedendaags Textiel* (1992), pp. 8–28.

8 Accession number WAG T.1995.145.

9 See Anne Morrell, *The ATN Guide to Structural Sewing: Terms and Techniques* (Manchester, 1989), p. 15.

10 R. Shurinova, *Coptic Textiles: Collection of Coptic Textiles State Pushkin Museum of Fine Arts Moscow* (Moscow: 1969), pl. 46 and catalogue nos. 31, 32 and 51; A. De Moor (ed.), *Coptic Textiles from Flemish private collections* (Zottegem: PAMZOV, 1993), p. 108; Annemarie Stauffer, *Spätantike, früchristliche und islamische Textilien aus Ägypten* (Bern: Bernisches Historisches Museum, 1996), catalogue nos. 9, 19 and 11.

11 Clementina Rizzardi, *I tessuti copti del museo nazionale di Ravenna* (Ravenna: Istituto Poligrafico e Zecca della Stata, 1993), pp. 54–57, catalogue no. 7.

12 A. De Moor, op. cit., p. 11, catalogue no. 20.

13 For a discussion of the term and its secular origin see H. Granger-Taylor, 'The Two Dalmatics of Saint Ambrose ?', *Bulletin de Liaison du Centre International d'Etude des Textiles Anciens*, 57–58 (1983), pp. 127–73 and Marie-Hélène Rutschowscaya, *Coptic Fabrics* (Paris: Adam Biro, 1990), p. 54.

14 V. Gervers, 'Medieval Garments in the Mediterranean World', in N.B. Harte and K.G. Ponting (eds)., *Cloth and Clothing in Medieval Europe: Essays in Memory of Professor E.M. Carus-Wilson* (London: The Pasold Research Fund Ltd., 1983), pp. 279–315.

15 Careful examination of fragments in collections is enabling more examples to be identified see, for example, Susan Walker and Morris Bierbrier, *Ancient Faces: Mummy Portraits from Roman Egypt* (London: British Museum Press, 1997), p. 179, catalogue no. 228.

16 Kendrick, *op. cit.*, pp. 40–41; D. King, 'Roman and Byzantine Dress in Egypt', *Costume* 30 (1996), pp. 1–15; S. Walker & M. Bierbrier, *op. cit.*, pp. 178–79.

17 H. Granger-Taylor, *op. cit.* in note 13.

18 Alisa Baginski and Amalia Tidhar, *Textiles from Egypt 4th – 13th Centuries C.E.* (Tel-Aviv: L. A. Mayer Memorial Institute for Islamic Art, 1980), pp. 36–37.

19 James Trilling, *The Roman Heritage: Textiles from Egypt and the Eastern Mediterranean 300 to 600 a.d.* (Washington: The Textile Museum, 1982) p. 104.

20 D. King, *op. cit.*, p. 4.

21 Rodolphe Pfister, *Textiles de Palmyre, I* (Paris: Les editions d'art et d'histoire, 1934), p. 19, fig. 2, catalogue no. T.20.

Chapter 4

VARIA ROMANA: TEXTILES FROM A ROMAN ARMY DUMP

Nettie K. Adams and Elisabeth Crowfoot

Introduction

Few archaeological publications have been so immediately accepted and recognised as a necessary classic as John Peter Wild's doctoral thesis, *Textile Manufacture in the Northern Roman Provinces.*[1] The combination of a grasp of the technical aspects of the subject, the ability to present it so that even non-weavers could recognise technical processes, and his deep knowledge of the literary and archaeological sources and the historical background, at once brought the subject within the reach of the general reader as well as the prompt consideration of the practical archaeologist.

The extension of his work in later publications, his kind attention to every enquiry, the consideration he gave to students at every stage of study, gave him a special place in the respect and affection of any involved in the world of textile studies, and we are glad of this opportunity of demonstrating our gratitude for many years of co-operation.

Conditions of preservation on the site of Qasr Ibrim on Lake Nasser, on the Egyptian-Sudanese border, have been the reason for the mass of textiles surviving from the Napatan period through the centuries of Christianity and Islamic occupation. However, the excavation season of 1978 brought also dramatic evidence of a Roman military presence at Qasr Ibrim, perhaps for a century or more. Clearance along the southern ramparts revealed a very deep accumulation of Roman period and Roman type refuse.[2] Among masses of good class Egyptian sacking, made from flax with typical spliced thread, and still a good new bright yellow colour, were larger pieces that may have been furnishing for officers billets, curtains and bedspreads with typical decoration, a soldier's knapsack, and one small strip of wool twill, checked blue and white, a relic of duty in the northern regions of which John Peter Wild wrote so well.[3]

Shoulder bag (QI.78T/461)

Fig. 4.1 Shoulder bag from Qasr Ibrim, QI.78T/461

One of the most interesting specimens to come from the dump, because of its completeness, is a well-worn flax shoulder bag (Fig. 4.1). It is triangular in shape, and pieced together from five separate pieces. The largest piece represents one side of the bag. It provides the full width of the woven cloth – selvedge to selvedge – 0.33 m. The other side is made of four irregular pieces, one rectangular, two triangular, and one small corner gusset.

The overall measurements are 0.33 m wide across the bottom and 0.20 m wide at the opening. The two sides taper from the bottom and are seamed together as far as the opening. They are 0.50 and 0.43 m in length to the opening. Above the opening the two sides continue to taper more steeply, narrowing to form the strap, and they probably originally ended in points. Above the opening they are 0.4 and 0.3 m long. Their tapered edges are finished with a heavy hem. The two ends of the strap are raw, and were originally tied in a square knot.

The cloth is undyed, and is the tawny golden colour of old flax. It is badly stained especially near the bottom, where there are several holes and worn places.

Technical Description

Weave: tabby, warp-predominant. *Spin direction*: Warp: S, spliced S; Weft: S, spliced S. *Thread Count*: Warp: 16 per cm; Weft: 5 per cm. *Selvedges*: plain, with no paired warp threads.

Wool fragment (QI.78T/428)

The mass of wool twill weaves of various types from the Roman dump are a constant reminder of Roman army service in other regions. One in particular, 78.T/428, (Outside E. of Unit R.I., level 3) suggests that someone stationed here had seen service in the northern provinces. This is a torn-off strip, 80 × 270 mm, still very solid, a four-shed twill weave, the yarns both Z-spun, 5–7/4 threads per 5 mm (i.e. 10–14 × 8 per cm), with a checked pattern (hound's tooth), in blue (dyed indigo) and natural undyed yarns (Fig. 4.2).

This fragment is strikingly similar to fragments from other Roman-occupied

Fig. 4.2 Checked wool twill from Qasr Ibrim, QI78T/428

sites. Sheffer and Granger-Taylor[4] suggest that the diamond twill weaves from Masada were the property of the Jewish residents, rather than left by the Roman troops; but the connection of twill weaves with the northern Roman provinces is clear in John Peter Wild's doctoral thesis.

Curtain (QI.80T/81)

Among the flax specimens found in the dump were many, many fragments of a large curtain or spread. It has red and white warp stripes; in most cases the red has faded to a light brown, but in a few areas the red colour is well preserved. The stripes are 10–15 mm apart and vary in width from less than 10 mm to about 20 mm. The arrangement of the stripes seems to be strictly random; no pattern could be discerned among the dozens of fragments. The warp face weave is very loose and stringy.

Technical Description

Weave: basket weave; pairs and triples. *Spin direction of yarns*: Warp: Z / S – ply; Weft: Z / S – ply. *Thread count per cm:* Warp: 10 pairs or triples (red yarns finer than white); Weft: 3 pairs or triples. *Edges*: All raw edges.

Curtain (QI.80T/85)

From the same area in the dump, fragments of another curtain or spread were found, this one with blue and white warp stripes. The weave is much finer than 80T/81, and the cloth is much more consolidated. Also unlike 80T/81, the alternating blue and white stripes are roughly the same width as each other. In one area they are approximately 10–15 mm wide, but elsewhere on the same specimen they are 5–8 mm wide.

Technical Description

Weave: very close warp-face tabby and half-basket with paired warp threads. *Spin direction of yarns*: Warp: S; Weft: S. *Thread count of tabby weave*: warp 40 × weft 7–8 per cm. *Thread count of half basket weave*: warp 17 pairs × weft 7–8 per cm. *Edges*: all raw edges.

Textile with gamma figure (QI.80T/283)

Found among a number of dark brown wool fragments was one piece with a gamma figure worked in the tapestry weave. The cloth is very good quality fabric with a close, even weave. The shape of the piece is an isosceles triangle with the short side in the warp direction. One of the longer sides is slightly curved (convex); it and the short side are hemmed with a neat backstitch. The other long side is slightly concave, and is edged by part of a French seam. The dimensions of the specimen are 0.30 m in the warp direction by approximately 0.36 m in the weft.

The gamma figure (Fig. 4.3, C) is dark rose against a brown background. The two arms of the gamma are 100 mm and 85 mm long; the width of both is 45 mm. Its placement within the triangular shape is 100 mm from the shorter side, 85 mm from the concave edge, and 40 mm from the convex edge. It is not notched, and has no 'tail'.

Technical description

Weave: Ground: very close weft-face tabby; Gamma: very close weft-face tabby; Tapestry joins: interlinked. *Spin direction of yarns*: Ground: warp: Z, weft: Z; Gamma: weft: Z. *Thread count*: not available.

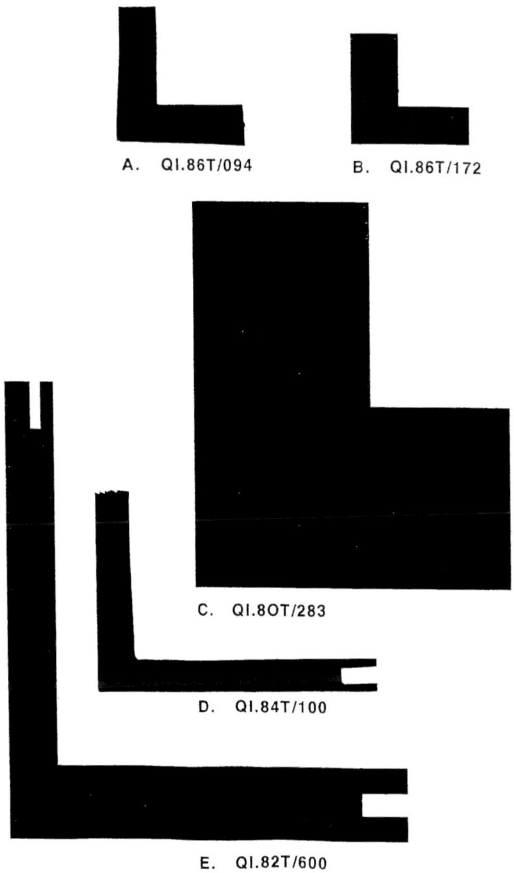

Fig. 4.3 Gamma figures from the Roman army dump at Qasr Ibrim. Scale: 1:2

Other gamma figures from Qasr Ibrim

A number of other textile fragments with gamma figures have been unearthed at Qasr Ibrim, all of which came from contexts other than the Roman dump. One of these dates to the same Roman period, but instead of the wool of the specimen from the dump described above, it has a ground weave of dyed flax with a small purple gamma figure in wool at one corner (QI.86T/172) (Fig. 4.3B).

The gamma remained popular at Qasr Ibrim throughout the centuries following the coming of the Romans. The Nubians began weaving their own fabrics with this motif in the early centuries AD. Some were woven in wool, but the Nubians had a preference for cotton. One example is woven in all cotton, including the small, dark blue gamma figure (QI.86T/094) (Fig. 4.3A). The ground weave of another has a cotton warp and a wool weft (QI.84T/100) (Fig. 4.3D). The colours of the gammas vary from purple to red to blue, and there is also variability in the sizes and shapes of the gamma figures. Some examples can be seen in Figs. 4.3E, 4.4A and 4.4B.

The most spectacular gamma figure from Qasr Ibrim came from a late X-Group (AD *c.* 350–550) context (QI.74T/64). When found it was detached from the ground fabric, and torn into two pieces. It is made entirely of cotton, in three colours: dark blue, lighter blue and undyed, which is now tan, but was originally white. Both arms are approximately 170 mm long and 65 mm wide. The ends of the arms are notched, but there is no 'tail'. Its most extraordinary feature is the very elaborate tapestry-woven figures within the gamma itself. The entire perimeter has been edged in dark blue, with tiny white dots spaced within the blue border. The interior of the figure is divided into rows separated by white lines. The rows alternate between dark and lighter blue chevrons, and lines of tiny motifs which suggest ram's heads with curled horns.

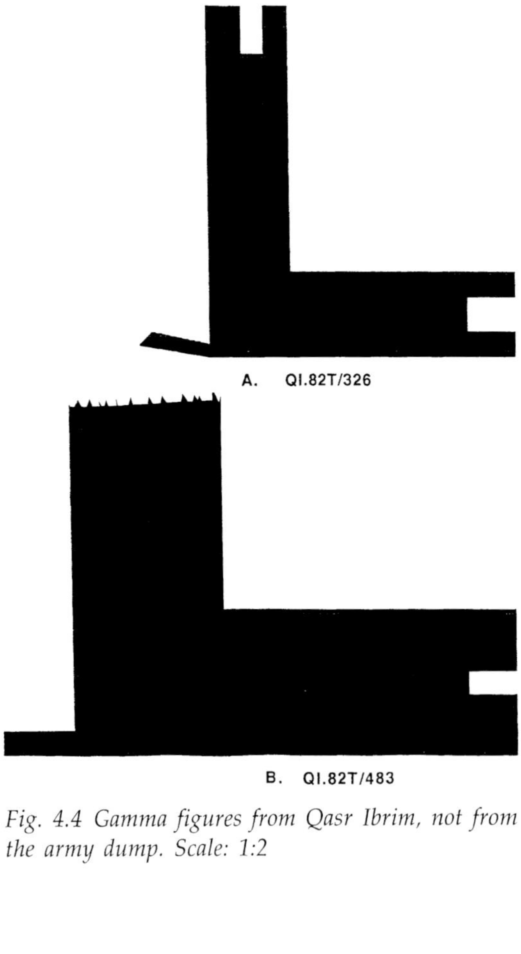

Fig. 4.4 Gamma figures from Qasr Ibrim, not from the army dump. Scale: 1:2

Other archaeological gamma figures

The archaeological site of Gebel Adda, located upstream from Qasr Ibrim in Egyptian Nubia near the Sudanese border, also yielded several specimens with gamma figures. One of the most magnificent came from cemetery V-35, number 97. It is all wool, with purple gammas on a natural ground. The complete size is 3.58m × 2.82m, with a large gamma located in each corner.

The size of the gammas is very much larger than anything from Qasr Ibrim (Fig. 4.5). This piece was used as a burial wrapping. Whether it was specially made for that purpose cannot be known, but it was surely much too large to have been worn as a mantle.[5]

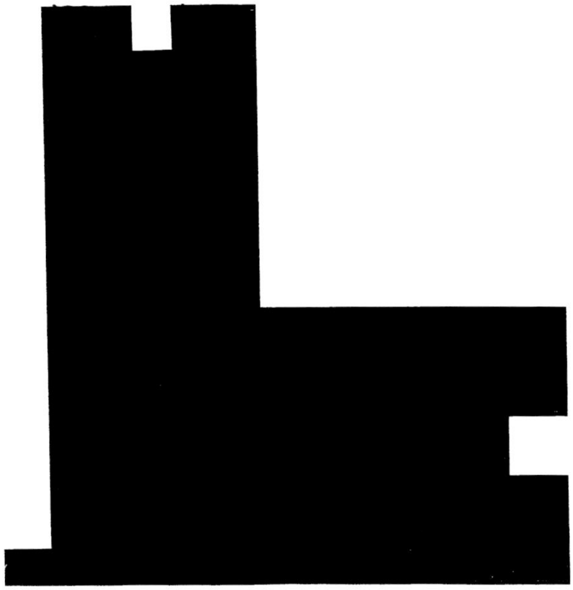

Fig. 4.5 Gamma figure from Gebel Adda. Scale: 1:10

Two other areas in Nubia have yielded gamma figures; all of them were found in a funerary context which belongs to the early centuries AD. The Scandinavian Joint Expedition to Sudanese Nubia excavated a number of cemeteries on the east bank of the Nile, and recovered ten examples of textiles with gamma figures. All are notched, and 'tails' are present in the complete gammas. They occur in orange, red, and blue wool.[6] The Oriental Institute of Chicago also recovered examples of gammas from several cemeteries at Qustal, in the far south of Egyptian Nubia.[7] All of them appear to be notched; on at least one specimen the four gammas have 'tails', but the others are not complete enough to be sure. Their colours are purple, red, brown and blue.

Other archaeological sites have also yielded examples of gamma figures woven in wool. At Palmyra a purple gamma figure on a green ground was found.[8] Beautifully illustrated in colour, the one complete arm is notched, and it does not appear to have a tail, although one cannot be certain. One of the earliest in date was found at Masada.[9] It was found with other fragments of clothing in the casemate wall (locus 1039) dating to the Revolt Period, AD 66–73. From the Cave of Letters[10] six specimens with gamma figures were recovered. All of those illustrated have notched ends and are all similar in size: the arms 90–100 mm long and 30–40 mm wide. They are of various colours, ranging from shades of purple to a red-brown, to red-orange. Dye analyses revealed that madder, indigo, and saffron were used along with several mordants in varying amounts to produce the different shades. All of these textiles can be dated to AD 132–135. An incomplete gamma figure from a somewhat later (late 3rd to early 4th centuries) was found at Karanis.[11] The complete arm is notched at the end, and a small 'tail' extends from the outside right angle. It is described as being originally a dark purple, now badly faded, on a yellow ground.

A recent issue of *Archaeological Textiles Newsletter* contains two mentions of gamma figures. One is from a Roman burial from Les Martres-de-Veyre, France.[12] It is said to date around AD 180. Anothert tantalizing mention is in an article on Roman textiles from the site of Mons Claudianus, located in the Eastern Desert of Egypt. 'In a study on the Gammas and other woven decorative features from Mons Claudianus, Ulla Mannering has established a useful pattern for her future work on the garments from the site'.[13] We await the publication of her report with anticipation.

Finally, a page of drawings of ornamented Coptic tunics[14] contains one drawing with two gamma figures (termed angled bands). They are located near the bottom of the garment, and the arms end in leaf ornaments. Set within the angle of the gamma is a small square. All the illustrations are presumably from actual garments recovered archaeologically, although no identifications are given.

Artistic representations of gamma figures

The earliest representation of gamma figures on clothing comes from the archaeological site Dura-Europus, in Syria.[15] There, the wall of the synagogue has a row of several human figures, two of whom are wearing mantles bearing notched gamma figures. The city of Dura-Europas fell in AD 256, so that the dating of the gamma figures is approximately comparable to those already discussed. From Bawit, in Egypt, a fresco showing the Madonna enthroned with the baby Jesus,[16] has figures wearing robes with gamma figures located at about knee height. The painting is said to be sixth-century, somewhat later than the examples presented above.

A most definitive discussion of representations of gamma figures in art can be found in Yigael Yadin's *The Finds from the Bar-Kokhba Period in the Cave of Letters*.[17] In this same volume there is an extensive section on the dyes in use during this period, the second century AD.[18] He also discusses the possible meaning of the gamma figures and other motifs, but he tends '...to believe that they had no special meaning and that they are merely decorative elements first used by one of the weavers' guilds. There is some similarity between the notched bands and the shuttle, and this tool, as the symbol of the weaver's craft, may have been served as a prototype for the pattern. The gamma is probably none other than a notched band which has been adapted to fit into the corner of a cloth.'[19]

Yadin wrote these words almost two decades before the discovery of un-notched gamma figures at Qasr Ibrim. The textile from the Roman dump, QI.80T/283 was almost certainly brought to Qasr Ibrim with the Roman army occupation, dated by historical records as occurring in 23 BC. The other un-notched gammas (QI.86T/172 and QI.86T/094) are also from this earlier date. These three gamma figures are roughly 150 years older than the gamma figures reported by Yadin from the Cave of Letters. It appears, therefore, that the earliest gamma figures are the simplest in form, and the closest to the letter gamma. We shall probably never know their meaning.

Notes

1 John Peter Wild, *Textile Manufacture in the Northern Roman Provinces* (Cambridge University Press, 1970).

2 William Y. Adams, 'Primis and the Aethiopian frontier', *Journal of the American Research Center in Egypt*, XX (Paris, 1983), pp. 95–104.
William Y. Adams, 'Ptolemaic and Roman occupation at Qasr Ibrim', in Francis Geus and Florence Thil (eds), *Mélanges offerts à Jean Vercoutter* (Paris, 1985), pp. 9–17.

3 Wild *op. cit.*, pp. 47–49.

4 Avigail Sheffer and Hero Granger-Taylor, *Textiles from Masada: a Preliminary Selection* (Masada IV: Israel Exploration Society, The Hebrew University, 1994), item 13.211.

5 We are indebted to Dr. Nicholas Millet, Director Emeritus of the Egyptian Department at the Royal Ontario Museum in Toronto, Canada, for kindly making this information available.

6 Ingrid Bergman *Late Nubian Textiles (Scandinavian Joint Expedition to Sudanese Nubia,* Vol 8, (1975), pp. 47–48, fig. 52, Pls. 60,61,62 and 74.

7 Christa C. Mayer Thurman and Bruce Williams, *Ancient Textiles from Nubia,* (Chicago, 1979), p. 42, nos. 69, 95, 105, 136.

8 R. Pfister, *Textiles de Palmyre,* (Decouverts Par le Service des Antiquites du Haut-Commissariat de la Republique Française Dans la Necropole De Palmyre, Vol. III), (Paris 1940), p. 21 and colour frontispiece.

9 Yigael Yadin 'The Excavation of Masada 1963–64 Preliminary Report', *Israel Exploration Journal,* Vol. 15, Nos. 1–2, 1965, p. 81.

10 Yigael Yadin, *The Finds from the Bar-Kokhba Period in the Cave of Letters,* The Israel Exploration Society, (Jerusalem, 1963), pp. 219–223, Pls. 67, 80, 81, 82, and fig. 75.

11 Lillian Wilson. *Ancient Textiles from Egypt in the University of Michigan Collection* (University of Michigan Press, Ann Arbor, Vol. 31, 1933), p. 33 no. 77 and pl. IV.

12 Carol van Driel-Murray, 'A Set of Roman Clothing from Les Martres-de-Veyre, France' in *Archaeological Textiles Newsletter,* Number 28, Spring 1999, p. 12.

13 Lise Bender Jørgensen, 'The Mons Claudianus Textile Project' in *Archaeological Textiles Newsletter,* No. 28, Spring 1999, p. 19.

14 Klaus Wessel, *Coptic Art in Early Christian Egypt,* (New York: McGraw-Hill, 1965), p. 236.

15 R. Pfister and Louisa Bellinger, *The Textiles* (*The Excavations at Dura-Europus, Final Report IV,* part II) (New Haven, 1945).

16 Gustave di Deneuve, *Form E Colore I Grandi Cicli dell'arte;* 67 'L'Arte Copta' p. 21.

17 Yadin 1963 n. 2, pp. 227–231.

18 Ibid. n. 2. pp. 172–182 and Pl. 58.

19 Ibid. n. 2. 231.

Chapter 5

GOAT-HAIR TEXTILES FROM KARANIS, EGYPT

Jane Batcheller

Introduction

From the collection of more than three thousand textile fragments found during early excavations by members of the University of Michigan at the Roman town of Karanis in the Fayum of Egypt,[1] there is a small group of fragments made entirely of goat hair, seventeen of which are now in the permanent collection of the Bolton Museum, England. This select group of textiles is the subject of this paper.

All of the textiles from Karanis were recovered in the early seasons of excavation (between 1924 and 1926) when the top two levels of the site where investigated and when the buildings of the final period of occupation, from about the middle of the fourth century AD until after the end of the fifth,[2] were unearthed. The hair fragments are from a range of locations spread across the excavated portions of the site. They were found together with other textiles in the in-fill of the abandoned buildings, as well as in refuse middens.[3]

Sheep's wool and flax are the principal fibres of the Karanis textiles, with goat-hair textiles forming only a small portion, approximately three per cent, of the entire corpus. Similar numbers of goat-hair fragments are generally discovered at Roman sites elsewhere in Egypt where textile finds are abundant.[4] The goat-hair textiles of the Karanis collection are easily distinguished from those made of wool, as the goat-hair fibres are much coarser than wool and the yarns made from these coarse fibres are thick and wiry. Consequently, the textiles made from the goat-hair yarns are also thick and usually quite coarse (Table 5.1). In the original cataloguing of the Karanis textiles, the coarseness of the cloth was used as an indication of the presence of goat hair, and in a few instances, textiles composed of wool are listed as hair cloth.[5] In addition, a matted bundle of camel hair is listed as goat hair, and it is likely that similar examples of misidentification exist in the main collection. It is worth noting that within the Bolton collection, goat hair is found only in fragments made entirely of goat hair. The only exception is the use of goat-hair thread for very rough stitching on fragments of wool or flax. The stitching is most often a haphazard joining of mismatched fragments, indicating some sort of re-use of the stitched cloths, unrelated to their original functions.

It is thought that local goats of the Fayum would have provided the fibre source

Museum No. 19.30	Fabric Structure	Yarns/cm wa x we	Fabric Thickness mm	Yarns	Yarn Colour	Spin	Mean† Diameter mm	Mean† Ply Angle°	Ply Turns /cm
.117	tabby	4 x 3.5	2.8	Warp	dark/light blend	S2Z	2.2	30	1.9
				Weft	dark/light blend	S2Z	2.7	23	1.3
.118	tabby	3 x 2.5	3.2	Warp	brown/black	S2Z	2.7	34	1.7
	coarse matting			weft	brown/black	S2Z	4.1	25	0.9
.119	tabby &	4 x 4	–	warp	brown/black	S2Z	–	–	–
	tapestry with	2 x 5	–	weft	brown/black	S2Z	–	–	–
	paired warp								
.120	tabby	2 x 2	5.5	warp	brown/black	S2Z	4.8	32	0.9
	coarse matting			weft	brown/black	S2Z	4.5	32	1.0
.121	tabby	4 x 3	3.0	warp	dark brown	S2Z	2.5	35	1.9
	warp stripes &			warp	white/yellowed	S2Z	2.6	31	1.7
	weft wrapping			weft	dark brown	S2Z	3.0	23	1.2
.122	tabby	5 x 4	3.1	warp	brown/black	S2Z	2.2	25	1.8
	with rows of	2.5 stitch		weft	brown/black	S2Z	2.1	20	1.6
	running stitch	rows/cm		stitch yarn	white/yellowed	S2Z	2.7	31	1.6
.123	oblique twining	7.5	6.1	element	brown/black	Z2S	2.6	34	1.8
	Z-twist			element	white/yellowed	S2Z	2.5	34	1.9
.220	tabby	4 x 3	3.0	warp	dark/light blend	S2Z	3.0	28	1.4
				weft	dark/light blend	S2Z	3.2	28	1.3
.250	tabby &	6 x 6	2.3	warp	brown/black	S2Z	1.4	35	3.4
	interlocking	3 x 14	2.7	grnd weft	brown/black	S2Z	1.6	24	2.3
	tapestry with			tap weft	white/yellowed	S2Z	–	–	–
	paired warp			tap weft	red	S2Z	–	–	–
.251	tabby & tapestry	4 x 4.5	1.9	warp	dk/lt blend	S2Z	2.0	34	2.3
	with paired warp	2 x 16	3.5	grnd weft	dk/lt blend	S2Z	1.9	27	2.2
				tap weft	white/yellowed	S2Z	1.4	19	2.3
				tap weft	red	S2Z	–	–	–
.252	tabby	5 x 6	2.2	warp	brown/black	S2Z	1.7	36	2.7
	crepe-like			weft	brown/black	S2Z	1.7	21	2.0
	texture								
.253	tabby	4 x 4	2.6	warp	dark/light blend	S2Z	1.9	23	1.9
	finishing edge			weft	dark/light blend	S2Z	1.8	31	2.5
.254	tabby	5.5 x 5.5	2.4	warp	brown/black	S2Z	1.7	29	2.5
	finishing edge			weft	brown/black	S2Z	1.9	25	2.1
.255	weft-faced	4.5 x 9	2.2	warp	brown/black	S2Z	1.5	32	3.0
	plain weave			weft	brown/black	S2Z	1.9	26	2.0
.256	tabby	3 x 3	2.8	warp	deep brown/red	S2Z	2.6	34	1.8
				weft	deep brown/red	S2Z	2.9	25	1.3
.257	tabby	2.5 x 2	3.8	warp	dark brown	S2Z	3.9	27	1.0
	coarse matting			weft	dark brown	S2Z	3.7	27	1.1
.258	tabby	4 x 4.5	1.9	warp	dark/light blend	S2Z	1.9	29	2.2
	portion of 251			weft	dark/light blend	S2Z	2.0	24	1.9

† average of 20 measurements

Table 5.1 Fabric and yarn details – goat-hair fragments

for the goat-hair fabrics at Karanis. Documentary evidence indicates that goats were herded together with sheep on the outskirts of the villages in the Arsinoite Nome (the Fayum),[6] and a herdsman, possibly a shepherd responsible for sheep and goats, is recorded on the tax records of second-century Karanis.[7] Goats are still used as a local source of fibre for textile production by the Bedouin of modern day Egypt, and fibre samples from the goats of the Ababda of the eastern Egyptian desert were used to confirm the identity of the goat-hair fibres used in the Karanis textiles.[8]

The fibres

The fibres from the Karanis fragments are of three natural colours: very dark, brownish black; dark brown with a reddish tinge; and white which has yellowed with age. Some of the white fibres were dyed to a deep level red, and are similar in colour to many of the red-dyed wools. Although the dyestuff has not yet been analysed, it is likely to have been madder as madder was a common source of red dye in the late Roman period and so far is the only red dyestuff which has been identified on the Karanis fragments.[9] For a tweedy brown colour, it seems that dark pigmented fibres were mixed with various quantities of white fibre before being spun and plied (see Table 5.2 for percentages of pigmented to white fibre in the mixed-colour yarns). It is also possible that the mixed yarns reflect a natural

Museum No. 19.30	Fibre Source	Yarn Colour	Fibre Diameter (µm)† Mean	Mode	Range	Std.Dev.	Medulla %	Pigment %	Roots/Tips Observed
.117	warp	dark/light blend	73	78	23 – 160	20.8	50	48	tips
.118	warp	brown/black	63	55	14 – 101	17.8	49	100	roots/tips
.120	warp	brown/black	56	56	23 – 105	16.5	79	98	tips
.121	dark warp	dark brown	57	50	32 – 147	18.4	80	86	roots/tips
.121	light warp	white/yellowed	62	63	15 – 108	16.7	96	9	tips
.122	warp	brown/black	76	83	30 – 128	17.5	55	99	tips
.122	stitch yarn	white/yellowed	86	92	48 – 155	19.5	81	2	tips
.123	dark yarn	brown/black	75	75	33 – 123	17.1	66	100	tips
.123	light yarn	white/yellowed	64	63	23 – 99	12.3	63	1	tips
.220	warp	dark/light blend	70	90	34 – 115	18.5	55	61	tips
.250	warp	brown/black	69	59	25 –112	16.5	51	100	tips
.250	weft	white/yellowed	71	63	41 – 131	15.1	74	2	roots/tips
.251	warp	dark/light blend	78	56	46 – 141	18.6	56	73	tips
.252	warp	brown/black	80	63	41 – 163	20.7	64	100	tips
.253	warp	dark/light blend	78	81	39 – 141	19.4	46	94	tips
.254	warp	brown/black	74	60	43 – 141	18.0	47	100	tips
.255	warp	brown/black	78	79	41 – 115	14.8	66	100	tips
.256	warp	deep brown/red	70	64	32 – 147	21.0	62	3	tips
.257	warp	dark brown	63	50	40 – 112	14.6	80	100	roots/tips
.258	warp	dark/light blend	77	80	40 – 119	14.7	50	74	tips

† 100 measurements

Table 5.2 Fibre details.

distribution of dark and white fibres within the coat of a single animal. According to Ryder,[10] colour illustrations of the goats of ancient Egypt suggest that the animals were black, white, tan and piebald, but not grey, the usual colour when white and black fibres are equally present in the coat. In solid-coloured coats, it is also possible for the underwool, or fine fibres, to be paler in colour than the coarse hairs and, when spun, produce yarns of mixed-colour. The dark and light fibres in the mixed yarns of the Karanis fragments are equally distributed in size, regardless of their colour, and some difference in the distribution of the fibre sizes would be expected if the fibres were spun as found in the staples of a single animal. For this reason, it seems probable that some deliberate mixing of dark with light fibres was carried out – perhaps to obtain a single mixed colour from a patchy, piebald animal.

Microscopic analysis only rarely indicated the presence of a truly fine fibre in any of the goat-hair yarns examined. A small number of fine fibres in a coat of mainly coarse hair is reported to be normal for the various species of the so-called 'common' goat,[11] and a double-coated animal, with a significant component of fine hair, was not the type of goat from which these fibres were derived. The absence of fine fibres in a sampling of 100 fibres or more was one feature which distinguished the goat hair of these textiles from the hair of the Egyptian camel (the one-humped, or dromedary, camel). Camel hair is normally comprised of fibres of very different sizes, with a significant component of finer fibres.

The presence of many intact roots and tips was also noted in microscopic examinations of the fibres. These roots and uncut tips indicate that the hair was shed and not sheared from the goats. Collecting the shed fibres rather than shearing the hair from the goats would have ensured that the fibres were as long as possible, an important consideration for the spinning of coarse fibres. In measuring the fibres to establish the distribution of their diameters, it was noted that a gradual narrowing of the fibres occurred toward the tip-ends.The finer diameter segments comprised a significant component of the total fibre mass and are likely to have been important in spinning, being more malleable than the coarser segments, and better able to create the necessary inter-fibre tangling and gripping which would prevent the wiry fibres from sliding apart under tension.

Some of the variation in the graph of the distribution of the fibre diameters shown in Fig. 5.1 reflects the variation in single fibre diameters from root to tip, rather than indicating a range of very differently sized fibres, each of a uniform diameter. Cross-sectional sampling of the fibres from various points in the yarns revealed a large proportion of fibres with round or oval contours and, although mixed with those of flat, elliptical, and kidney-bean shapes, the rounded contour predominated. The largest fibres represented in the distribution of the fibre diameters all possessed large lattice medullae and had flattened or ribbon-like contours resulting from a collapsing of the medullary channel. The major axis of the flattened fibre was recorded as the fibre's diameter, which accounts for some of the extreme values on the high end of the graph.

The fibres in Figs. 5.2 and 5.3 illustrate some of the distinctive visual features of the goat hair which were observed by scanning electron microscopy. The cuticle layer of the coarse goat hair is thin and the scales on the upper fibre of Fig. 5.2 appear very shallow or close to the fibre surface. The leading edges, or margins, of the scales are near or close to one another, and they form a waved pattern across the fibre width. The margins may be described as rippled-crenate: that is, characterised by irregular

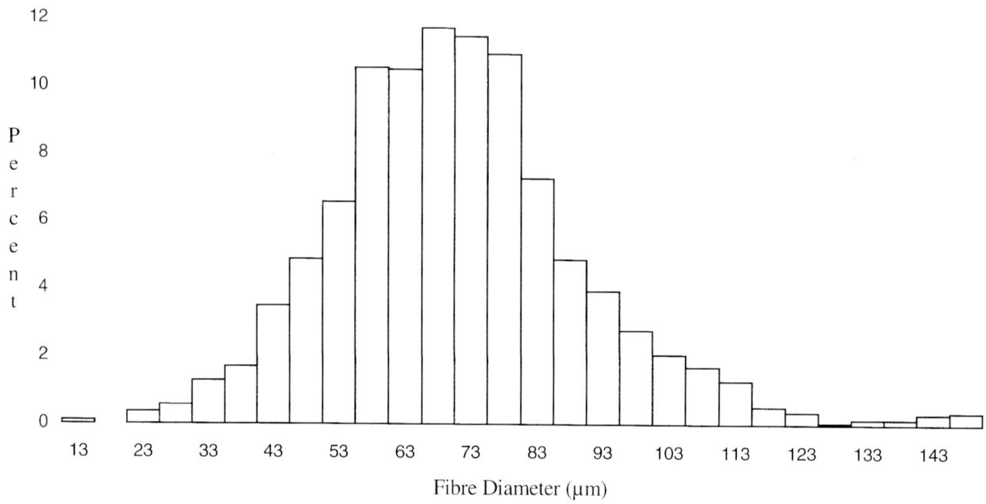

Fig. 5.1. Goat fibre diameter distribution from approximately 2,000 measurements of both white and pigmented fibres. The class divisions of the X-axis are 5 μm and the mean value of every other division is shown on the axis. The final column represents those fibres with diameters greater than 145 μm. The mean diameter is 71 μm and the mode, 75 μm. Values below 40 μm represent the tip ends of fibres (1μm = 1 micron = 0.001 mm).

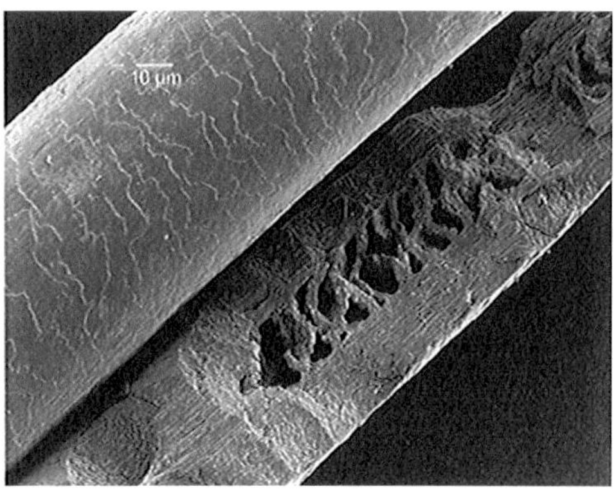

Fig. 5.2. Goat-hair fibres; approximate diameter of upper fibre 68 μm. Cuticle pattern is waved with rippled-crenate margins that are near to close. Fibres from the warp yarn of No. 19.30.118. One fibre with part of the cortex removed and the hollow medullary cavities exposed.

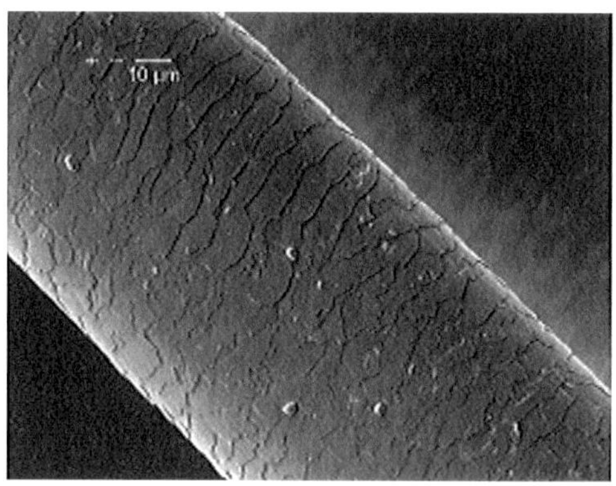

Fig. 5.3. Large, pigmented goat-hair fibre; approximate diameter 100 μm. Cuticle pattern is transitional with smooth margins becoming rippled-crenate across the fibre width. Fibres from the dark yarn of No. 19.30.123.

indentations or notches.[12] The notches that are shallow and taper to sharp points are crenate, while those that are deeper and more rounded are rippled. It is common to find both types in goat hair fibres, except near the root where the scale margins are smooth. Transitional zones[13] with portions of both smooth and rippled-crenate margins are also normal for coarse goat hair and were observed between the root and the tip portion of some of the fibres (Fig. 5.3). Not all fibres examined were as well preserved as those in the figures presented, and subtle variations in the pattern of the scale margins (often best observed by rolled impressions) were not always evident. Even in poorly preserved or heavily soiled specimens, however, some indication of the rippled-crenate pattern could be found. As many coarse animal hairs have rippled-crenate scale margins, this pattern could not be used on its own to identify goat hair. However, it was used to distinguish sheep's wool (especially very coarse wool) from the goat hair and from other coarse animal fibres, since wool fibres have smooth scale margins throughout their fibre lengths (Fig. 5.4).

The lower fibre in Fig. 5.2 has been partially eaten by insect larvae; consequently, the upper half of the cortex layer has been removed and a central medulla of the narrow latticed type[14] has been revealed. In every sampling of the goat hair, a high percentage of medullated fibres was found to be present (Table 5.2), and the medullae were noted equally in the pigmented and white fibres. A variety of medulla types and sizes were found, and a change in the structure from unbroken to fragmental over the length of individual fibres was also common. A series of dark, discoidal shapes, interrupted occasionally by cortex, and sometimes widely separated along the fibre axis, was one of the more frequently observed structures (Fig. 5.5).

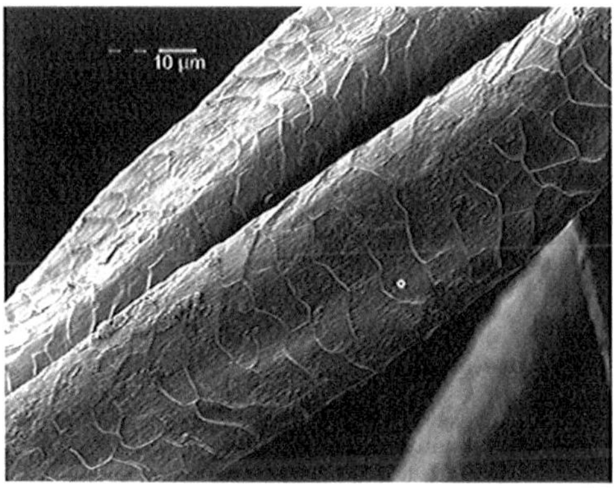

Fig. 5.4. Large, pigmented and medullated sheep's wool fibres; approximate diameter of the major axis 47 µm. Cuticle pattern is irregular mosaic with smooth margins that are near to distant. Fibres from weft yarn of No. 19.30.005.

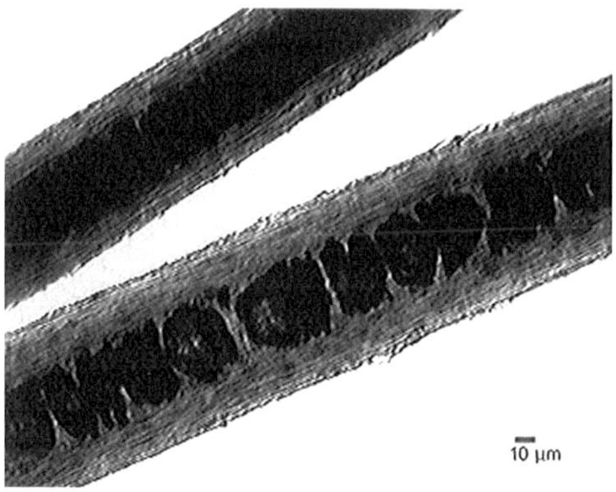

Fig. 5.5. Goat-hair fibres as seen by transmitted light microscopy with unbroken or continuous medulla and dense pigmentation; approximate diameter 73 µm. The dark disk-like shapes are the hollow medullary cavities with intercellular bridges between. Fibres from the warp yarn of No. 19.30.118.

The yarns

All of the yarns in the fragments were found to be 2-ply structures and, with the exception of one, are Z-plied from two S-spun singles (S2Z). In a few of the fragments, the plied yarn structure was difficult to observe without the aid of a microscope, and in heavily worn fragments the structure was also disguised to a certain extent by wear and fibre loss. Nevertheless, the goat hair was not found to have been used in singles yarns, most likely because of the rigid nature of the coarse fibres and their tendency to untwist. This tendency would make a singles yarn difficult to manipulate without some risk of failure. The counter-twist of the ply, on the other hand, would have been reinforced by the untwisting tendency of the original singles.

The fabrics

Twelve of the 17 fragments are various qualities of plain weave (tabby). Nos. 19.30.118, .120 and .257 are very thick, more like heavy matting than fabric, with yarns as large as four to five millimetres in diameter. Another ten fragments are somewhat finer structures. One is a slightly open weave while the remainder are balanced or weft-faced, with little space between the yarns. These plain fragments are not entirely without embellishment. Weft-wrapping (Fig. 5.6a), and contrasting dark and light warp were used, for example, to produce striped effects on fragment No. 19.30.121, while regular rows of running stitch decorated and reinforced the otherwise plain fabric of No. 19.30.122. Several of the textiles included dyed yarns; No. 19.30.256 is entirely of red warp and weft.

Three of the fragments have inserts of tapestry weave. Nos. 19.30.119 and .251 have simple tapestry bands with warp threads crossed and grouped in pairs as illustrated in Fig. 5.6b. A third fragment, No. 19.30.250, has a more ambitious section of discontinuous tapestry weave with a repeating geometric pattern woven in red, yellow and brown weft. An interlinking method of joining the weft colours has been used to weave the tapestry (Fig. 5.6c). This method of colour change is unique to this piece and it may have been necessary to secure the points of colour change by linking the stiff weft yarns in this way. The wool and flax tapestries from Karanis are not interlinked but have various types of dovetailed joins (Fig. 5.6d).

Part of a ribbed selvedge, the only portion of selvedge amongst the hair textiles, is also preserved along one edge of fragment No. 19.30.250, but only in the tapestry section. It consists of four warp yarns used together in one large bundle and a single warp yarn used for a second rib. Each weft yarn returns directly into the tapestry weave and there are no additional passes about the selvedge warps.

Two fragments, Nos. 19.30.253 and .254, share a unique type of finishing border. This edging is not found on any of the wool or flax textiles from Karanis, although many of these fragments are without edges. As might be expected, a single continuous strand of the two-ply warp thread was used to set the warp for each of

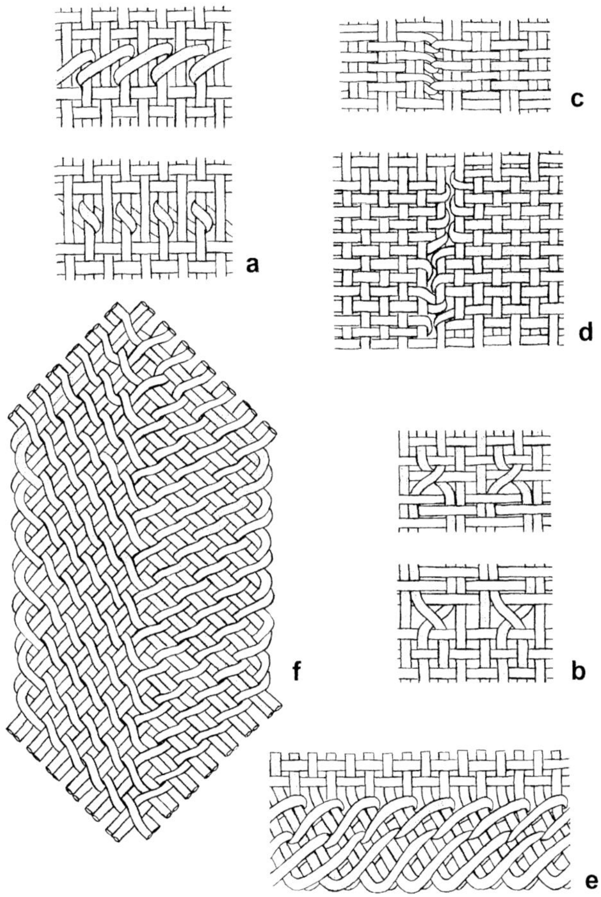

Fig. 5.6. Diagrams of fabric structures: a) wrapping weft yarn in No. 19.30.121. Face and reverse; b) grouping of warp threads to form warp pairs for insertion of tapestry weave in Nos. 19.30.119, .250 and .251; c) Interlocking tapestry weave of No. 19.30.250; d) dovetail tapestry weave, the normal means of colour change in the wool and flax tapestry fragments from Karanis; e) working of the warp loops on the finishing edges of Nos. 19.30.253 and .254; f) Oblique twining of band fragment No. 19.30.123. Paired elements are worked in Z-twining toward the centre of the band.

the fragments, and the loops of continuous warp were used for the final border. To form the edging, each loop in succession was worked horizontally across the fabric as illustrated in Fig. 5.6e. In fragment No. 19.30.254, the working loop enclosed three adjacent loops rather than two. A similar use of the final warp loops for a finishing border was recorded for one of the goat hair textiles from Masada.[15]

In addition to the woven fragments, there is one example of a braided band amongst the textiles, fragment No. 19.30.123. The structure is oblique twining with Z-twined elements.[16] Pairs of dark and light yarns were worked from either side of the band toward the centre point (Fig. 5.6f). The pattern effect is of alternating dark and light arrow heads which come to a point in the centre of the band.

Uses

Aside from the appearance of the fragments which suggests uses for which coarse, hard-wearing cloths are suitable, the documentary evidence suggests that hair fibre textiles were used primarily as sacking and saddlebags.[17] Items of this sort are listed, for example, amongst the personal and household effects in the will of a centurion at Karanis in the early fourth century.[18] The fragments from Karanis provide tangible evidence of what the fibres, yarns and fabrics of these utilitarian items were like.

Acknowledgements

I am grateful to the Bolton Museum and Art Gallery, Bolton, England, and especially to Angela Thomas, the curator, for permission to study the Karanis textiles in the Museum's collection. I am also indebted to the Textiles Department at UMIST for the use of the equipment in the Microscopy Laboratory, and to Trevor Jones who trained me to use the scanning electron microscope and provided very welcome advice regarding the images presented in this paper.

Notes

1 For details of the excavations see A. E. R. Boak and E. E. Peterson, *Karanis: Topographical and Architectural Report of Excavations During the Seasons 1924–28* (Ann Arbor: University of Michigan Press, 1931).

2 For the latest discussion of the dating of finds from Karanis see D. Whitehouse, 'The Date of the Glass from Karanis', *Journal of Glass Studies*, XLI, pp. 168–170.
P. van Minnen, 'Deserted Villages: Two Late Antique Town Sites in Egypt', *Bulletin of the American Society of Papyrologists*, XXXII (1995), pp. 41–56.

3 T. Midgley, unpublished catalogue of the Karanis textiles (Bolton Museum, England, 1930). L. M. Wilson, *Ancient Textiles from Egypt in the University of Michigan Collection* (Ann Arbor: University of Michigan Press, 1933): hereafter Wilson 1933.

4 For example, the recently excavated sites of Berenike and Mons Claudianus. J. P. Wild and F. C. Wild, 'The Textiles', in S. E. Sidebotham and W. Z. Wendrich eds., *Preliminary Report of the 1996 Excavations at Berenike* (Leiden: Research School CNWS, 1998) p. 234. L. Bender Jørgensen 'Textiles from Mons Claudianus', *Acta Hyperborea*, III (1991), p. 86.

5 For example, Textile No. 116 is a wool textile and not a haircloth as described in Wilson 1933, p. 46, Plate IV.

6 J. G. Keenan, 'Pastoralism in Roman Egypt', *Bulletin of the American Society of Papyrologists*, XXVI (1989), p. 177 note 11.

7 P. Mich. 224, l. 6220. H. C. Youtie and O. M. Pearl, *Tax Rolls from Karanis, Michigan Papyri IV* (Ann Arbor: University of Michigan Press, 1939).

[8] Known goat fibre samples from Berenike, Egypt, kindly provided by J. P. Wild.

[9] J. Wouters, 'Dye Analysis of Coptic Textiles', in A. De Moor, ed., *Coptic Textiles from Flemish private collections* (Zottegem: Provinciaal Archeologisch Museum Van Zuid-Oost-Vlaanderensite Velzeke, 1993) p. 53. Some of the Karanis textiles have been analysed for dye by Dr G. W. Taylor, Textile Research Associates, York, and a summary of the results published in G. M. Eastwood, 'Egyptian dyes and colours', *Dyes on Historical and Archaeological Textiles* (now known as *Dyes in History and Archaeology*), III (1984), pp. 9–19.

[10] M. L. Ryder, 'The Use of Goat Hair. An Introductory Historical Review', *Anthropozoologica*, XVII (1993), p. 39.

[11] A. B. Wildman, *The Microscopy of Animal Textile Fibres* (Leeds: Wool Industries Research Association, 1954) p. 119.

[12] *op. cit.*, p. 51. H. M. Appleyard, *Guide to the Identification of Animal Fibres* (Leeds: WIRA, 1978) p. vii.

[13] Wildman *op. cit.*, p. 122, fig. 68b. H. M. Appleyard, *Guide to the Identification of Animal Fibres* (Leeds: WIRA, 1978) p. 10–11, fig. 32b.

[14] Wildman *op. cit.*, p. 50.

[15] A. Sheffer and H. Granger-Taylor, 'Textiles from Masada, a Preliminary Selection', in *Masada IV, The Yigael Yadin Excavations 1963–1965 Final Reports* (Jerusalem: Israel Exploration Society, 1994) p. 179, fig. 44.

[16] I. Emery, *The Primary Structures of Fabrics* (Washington: The Textile Museum, 1966) p. 64.

[17] Edict of Diocletian XI, M. Giacchero, ed., *Edictum Diocletiani et Collegarum de pretiis rerum venalium* (Genova: Istituto di Storia Antica e Scienze Ausiliarie, 1974).

[18] P. Col. 188, l. 17. R. S. Bagnall and N. Lewis, *Columbia Papyri VII: Fourth Century Documents from Karanis* (Ann Arbor: Scholars Press, 1979).

Chapter 6

TWO RESIST-DYED COTTONS RECENTLY FOUND AT KARADONG, XINJIANG (THIRD CENTURY AD)

Sophie Desrosiers, Corinne Debaine-Francfort and Abdurassul Idriss

Introduction

Ever since his participation in the excavations at Berenike, a Red Sea Egyptian port which played an important role in the trade between the Roman East and India, John Peter Wild has scrutinized the hundreds of textiles excavated there each year with the idea of identifying those that were imported by way of the Indian Ocean. He is succeeding now, but the obstacle he has faced since 1995 is the scarcity of available data on Indian textiles of the period. This lack of data is due, on the one hand, to climatic conditions which have not favoured the conservation of fabrics in India, and, on the other, to the poor descriptions of Indian cloth in the written documents of the period.[1] The famous *Periplus Maris Erythraei* lists the types of fabrics loaded on board ships leaving the Indian ports of Barbaricon and Barigaza for the Red Sea, but the textile terms are obscure and it gives no details about these shipments.[2] Among the main characteristics of the material so far excavated from the archaeological strata at Berenike are the dominating presence of cottons woven in 1/1 plain tabby and their division into two groups with threads spun in opposite directions – S/S, typical of Egyptian linen and wool textiles of the period, or Z/Z. In the later group, the discovery of several fragments decorated with a resist-dye technique – which subsequently was mastered in India and is still employed today – motivated John Peter Wild to study the extent of cotton cultivation in Roman times and to make an inventory of archaeological cottons, particularly resist-dyed plain tabbies.[3] The aim of this short contribution is to add two earlier examples to his corpus of fourth- and fifth-century AD resist-dyed cottons from Berenike. The textiles presented here date to the third century AD and were recently excavated by a Sino-French archaeological mission in Xinjiang, or more precisely in Karadong, where other documents testify to the frequent contacts with India.[4]

Karadong

The Sino-French archaeological mission in Xinjiang, headed by Abdurassul Idriss (for the Chinese) and Corinne Debaine-Francfort (for the French), excavated the site of Karadong in the heart of the Taklamakan desert.[5] Karadong is situated along an old course of the Keriya river, which originates in the Kunlun mountains on the Tibetan border, and whose waters vanish into the desert sands (Fig. 6.1). At one time the Keriya valley continued north all the way to the Tarim – as the nearby Khotan valley still does – thus forming a communication link with the Kucha region. An agricultural settlement situated in an irrigated oasis, Karadong is related to the oldest group of historical remains discovered in south Xinjiang: like Niya and Loulan, the site was abandoned during the first half of the fourth century AD.

Following a preliminary survey in 1991, the Sino-French team excavated in 1993 and 1994.[6] Among the finds were pottery that had analogies with pottery from Koushan in north-west India and Pakistan, tablets written in *kharosthi* (these are badly preserved: the inscriptions are almost worn off), and Buddhist wall paintings that are considered to be very Indianized. A comb in sandalwood was discovered by Stein who commented that 'the pattern of this comb is the same as that now common in northern India'.[7] In the conclusion of the first Sino-French publication, its authors note: 'Despite the Chinese suzerainty, the cultural adherence of Karadong, as the Khotan kingdom, to the Indo-Gandharan sphere is a well-established fact, confirmed by the discovery of tablets written in *kharosthi*. The

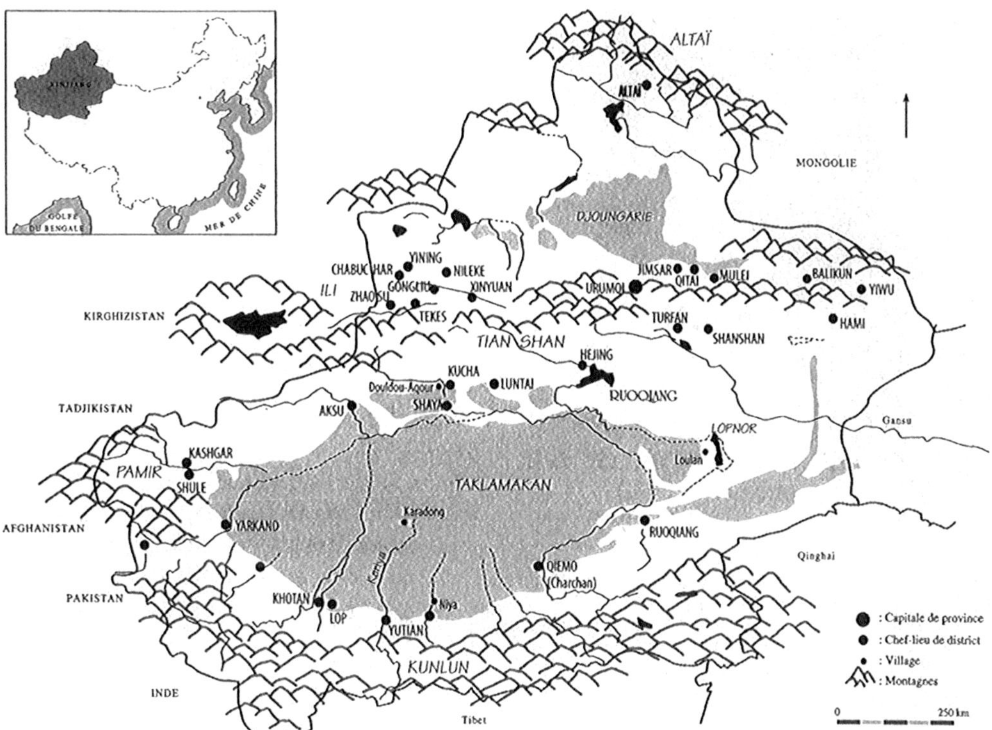

Fig. 6.1 Map of the Tarim basin showing the oasis on the south side of the Taklamakan desert, Xinjiang (copyright Sino-French archaeological mission in Xinjiang).

roads to India through Tibet, the high Indus and Kashmir were functioning, as were those from the West to Bactria through Pamir. The vast Koushan kingdom and its successors favoured these exchanges, which passed through the oasis in the Kunlun foothills.[8]

Fig. 6.2 Three fragments of a resist-dyed cotton tabby found in Karadong. White design on a dark blue ground (copyright Sino-French archaeological mission in Xinjiang).

Fig. 6.3 The reverse of the textile shown in Fig. 6.2 (copyright Sino-French archaeological mission in Xinjiang).

The resist-dyed cottons

The two resist-dyed cottons were discovered in two different houses occupied during the third century AD. The first (inv. 93-KRD25, Fig. 6.2) comprises three small fragments (80 × 33 mm; 42 × 42 mm; 26 × 15 mm); its design is resist-dyed on a dark blue ground but is too incomplete to be identifiable. Nevertheless, as it is at present in Paris for study,[9] it has been possible to determine its technical characteristics. It is a cotton tabby, Z/Z, with 11–12 threads per cm in warp and weft. The first attempt to identify its dye was performed by Claude Coupry and Françoise Froment at the Laboratoire de Spectrochimie Infrarouge et Raman of CNRS in Thiais, and revealed the presence of indigo. Its reverse is dark blue (Fig. 6.3) with a barely visible decoration, which proves that the paste used to resist the dye did not go all the way through the textile. According to John Peter Wild, who examined the photographs in Figs. 6.2 and 6.3, designs are usually more easily visible on the reverse sides of the Berenike specimens. However, this is the only technical difference so far identified between the small group of resist-dyed textiles from Roman Egypt and this first example from Karadong.

The second example (inv. 93-KRD60, Fig. 6.4) comes from house 60, as do some wooden tablets. It is still in Xinjiang (Institute of Archaeology, Urumchi) and only its photograph is available for the moment, but its better preserved design is similar to the fragment with dot rosettes found at Berenike in 1998.[10] Felicity and John Peter Wild compared the latter with another textile fragment which appeared in several publications, identified as having been found in Yutian and dated to the fifth century AD.[11] To be more exact, this fragment comes from Karadong, where it was unearthed in 1959 by Li Yuchun, and its ground is a wool tabby.

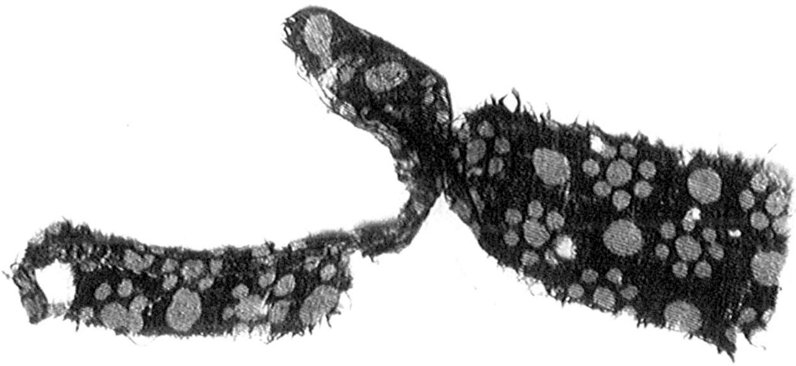

Fig. 6.4 Fragment of another resist-dyed cotton found in Karadong. White design on a dark blue ground (copyright Sino-French archaeological mission in Xinjiang)(see Colour Plate III).

The motifs in art

The Wilds also draw attention to the presence of similar motifs on medieval resist-dyed cottons[12] belonging to a large corpus also discovered in Egypt and whose Indian provenance has been gradually accepted, following Pfister's hypothesis published in1936–1938.[13] The iconographical comparisons with Jain manuscripts from Gujarat, most of which were produced between the twelfth and fifteenth centuries, as well as with contemporary architectural ornaments from the same region, still form the main basis for the attributions to India made by the most recent authors.[14] But these latter are very cautious about using for comparative purposes representations of dress on Central Asian or even Indian paintings because, as Ruth Barnes states: 'the designs are not specific enough for a definite identification'.[15]

In her catalogue of the Newberry Collection housed at the Ashmolean Museum in Oxford, the same author notes in particular the representation of 'rosettes made up of dots and placed on a dark blue ground' (similar to those represented in Fig 6.4) on the dress of a deity painted during the sixth or seventh century AD at Duldur-Aqur, near Kuchan in Xinjiang,[16] although she adds immediately that 'the similarities may be entirely accidental'.[17] The reasons given for such prudence are the absence of direct links between textile representations in paintings and preserved cloth (as in the example from Dunhuang); and the lack of indication as to the method of patterning in the textiles reproduced in these paintings. Our famous rosettes, resist-dyed on a coloured ground are taken again as an example, as they appear above all on silks (and not on cotton textiles), from the Han period found in Central Asia by Sir Aurel Stein, at Loulan and at a site Stein called 'L.M.' (a farm located near the Loulan fort).[18] Even if we support our colleague's caution, the archaeological evidence found in Karadong shows that this connection must not be rejected entirely. The reason is that the Buddhist B sanctuary excavated there (94-KRD62) has wall paintings executed during the third century AD. The imagery includes representations of small buddhas wearing monastic gowns, decorated with rosettes associated with isolated dots, in white on a blackish ground (Fig. 6.5). These are identical to the motifs on our second fragment (Fig. 6.4) and on the wool piece discovered in 1959. On the one hand, the presence of isolated dots associated with rosettes, as on the preserved textiles, introduces a kind of 'realistic' element which shows that it is not like just any other rosette motif: the painter has reproduced real textiles. On

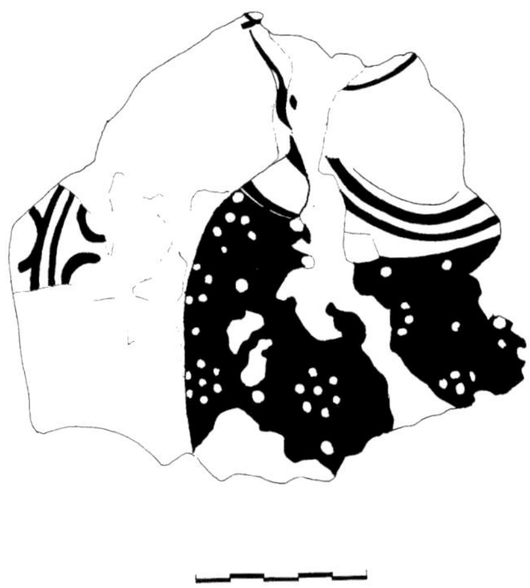

Fig. 6.5 Fragment of wall painting from Karadong. White design on a blackish ground (drawn by J.Suire) (copyright Sino-French archaeological mission in Xinjiang).

the other hand, the strong Indian influence revealed by the study of the paintings, especially in the buddhas' faces, whose features are strongly Indianized, compels us to consider that other parts of the figures, and particularly their garments, may also reflect Indian models.

This type of design is considered typical of India during the medieval period, when it served as a model for Jain manuscripts,[19] to such an extent that Ruth Barnes judged that its presence on a resist-dyed S/S cotton from the Kelsey Museum could be interpreted as an Egyptian production imitating an Indian prototype.[20] One wonders if we are not facing a parallel situation during late Antiquity. There is a strong possibility that the resist-dyed cottons from Berenike and Karadong, so close in technique and design, and found on trade or communication routes between India and western or northern regions, were produced by Indian printers.[21] The question remains open, however, for the resist-dyed silk and wool textiles which have the same, or similar designs. Were they imitations of Indian prototypes? This is possible because resist-dyeing techniques applied to textiles woven with animal fibres were known by then.[22] Or were they printed by Indian artisans, since the indigo-printing technique is essentially the same, on cotton, silk and wool? As Chinese silks were exported from India during the first century AD, we know that this material was available there,[23] as were wool fabrics which are reported in India by Vedic literature as early as the first millennium BC.[24] The identification of textiles of Indian origin among Central Asian finds, as attempted recently by Steven Cohen,[25] together with additional studies, should help answer this question.

Historic wall paintings in India and Central Asia should play a part in this project, for several reasons. First, some of them have accurate depictions of textiles, as shown in the great work of Roger Goepper on the Alchi temple in Ladakh.[26] Second, high-quality photographic reproductions makes them more accessible to a wider audience, as is the case of those from Ajanta painted during the fifth and sixth centuries AD, and magnificently published in 1991 by Amina Okada and Jean-Louis Nou.[27] Moreover, while glancing through the pages of this last volume, we wondered if John Peter Wild would not find therein other parallels to the Berenike cottons, given the number of painted depictions of blue and white chequered fabrics. This is another type of textile frequently encountered among the Berenike Z/Z cottons,[28] on which, since 1995, he and Felicity Wild have placed their microscope in the Egyptian desert.

Notes

1 J. P. Wild, 'Cotton in Roman Egypt: Some Problems of Origin', *al-Rāfidān*, XVIII (1997), pp. 287–298.

2 Wild, *op. cit.*, p. 291. See L. Casson, *The Periplus Maris Erythraei* (Princeton: University Press, 1989).

3 For a more detailed description of the finds at Berenike, see W. Wendrich, 'The Romano-Egyptian Site of Berenike', *Archaeological Textiles News (ATN)*, 18 & 19 (1994), p. 15. F. C. Wild and J. P. Wild, 'Berenike 1995', *ATN*, 20 (1995), pp. 8–9; J.-P. Wild and F. C.

Wild, 'Berenike 1996', *ATN*, 22 (Spring 1996), pp. 20–21; J. P. Wild and F. C. Wild, 'The Textiles', in S. Sidebotham and W. Wendrich (eds), *Berenike 1995* (Leiden, 1996), pp. 245–256; J. P. Wild and F. C. Wild, 'Berenike 1998', *ATN* 28 (1999), pp. 22–23; J. P. Wild, 1997, *op. cit.*

4 The original plan was to publish here a third resist-dyed cottom from Karadong, but problems with the mail have forced us to renounce this plan. A few other silks and wool textiles were discovered at the same site during the 1993–1994 excavations.

5 Debaine-Francfort, Abdurassul Idriss and Wang Binghua, 'Agriculture irrigée et art bouddhique ancien au cœur du Taklamakan (Karadong, Xinjiang, IIe–IVe siècles)', *Arts Asiatiques*, XLIX (1994), pp. 34–52. A comprehensive publication on the Keriya valley archaeological investigations is in preparation by the same authors.

6 Several archaeologists have been to Karadong. First was Sven Hedin who stopped there for two days in February 1896, followed by Sir Aurel Stein who stayed there briefly in 1901 and 1908. They were followed by Huang Wenbi in 1929, Li Yuchun in 1959, and then Wu Zhou and Huang Xiaojiang in 1990 (C. Debaine-Francfort *et al.*, *op. cit.*, notes 13 and 14).

7 A. Stein, *Ancient Khotan* (Oxford: Clarendon Press 1907), I, p. 452: K.002.0.

8 C. Debaine-Francfort *et al.*, *op. cit.*, p. 49.

9 It is at the Valectra laboratory in Saint-Denis, under the 'mecenat' of EDF (Électricité de France Compagny)

10 Wild and Wild, 1999, *op. cit.*, pp. 22–23 and fig. 7a.

11 F. and J. P. Wild cite: *The Silk Road – Textiles from the Han and Tang Dynasties (Sichou zhi lu Han Tang zhiwu)* (Beijing, 1973), cat. 18 and *The Genius of China* (London: Times Newspapers Ltd, 1973), p. 131, cat. 252. It appeared also in Cheng Weiji (ed), *History of Textile Technology of Ancient China* (New York: Science Press, 1992), p. 439 and fig. III-8-4 above.

12 R. Barnes, *Indian Block-Printed Cotton Fragments in the Kelsey museum, The University of Michigan, Kelsey Museum Studies* 8 (Ann Arbor, 1993), cat. 7.

13 R. Pfister, 'Tissus imprimés de l'Inde médiévale', *Revue des Arts Asiatiques* X (1936), pp. 161–164; R. Pfister, *Les toiles imprimées de Fostat et de l'Indoustan,*, (Paris: Les Éditions d'Art et d'Histoire, 1938).

14 See for instance Ruth Barnes, *Indian block-printed Textiles in Egypt. The Newberry Collection in the Ashmolean Museum, Oxford* (Oxford: Clarendon Press, 1997).

15 Barnes, 1997, *op. cit.*, p. 22.

16 Barnes, 1997, *op. cit.*, p. 22, note 4. This fragment is preserved at the Musée Guimet in Paris (inv. EO1122). Barnes cites its publication in J. E. Vollmer, E. J. Keall and E. Nagai-Berthrong (*Silk Roads – China Ships*, Toronto, Royal Ontario Museum, 1983, p. 56); it appeared also in *La Route de la Soie*, exhibition catalogue (Grand Palais, Feb.–March 1976), Paris, Réunion des musées nationaux, 1976, p. 50, no. 220, and M. Hallade, S. Gaulier *et al.*, *Douldour-Aqour et Soubachi* IV, Paris, Éditions Recherche sur les civilisations, 1982 (coll. Asie centrale et Haute-Asie, mémoire no. 9), fig. 36A. There are many other paintings representing textiles with similar motifs, for instance in Ajanta (A. Okada and J.-L. Nou, *Ajanta*, Paris: Imprimerie Nationale, 1991, p. 185) and in Kizil (A. Bhhler, *Ikat Batik Plangi*, Basel: Pharos Verlag, 1972, vol. 3, fig. 259)

17 Barnes, 1997, *op. cit.*, p. 22.

18 A. Stein, *Innermost Asia* (Oxford: Clarendon Press, 1928), vol. 1, p. 194: L.M.I.i.08. (red ground) and L.M.I.i.09 (blue ground), p. 198: L.L.02. (blue ground); illustrations: vol. 3, pl. LXXXVI. A much later example from Khara-khoto appears on this plate (below on the left side). One may remark here that the same precaution is not taken into

consideration when dealing with other iconographical representations as the Jain manuscripts.

[19] Barnes, 1997, *op. cit.*, p. 82, fig. 4.9; see also Pfister 1938, *op. cit.*, pl. XXXIVb.

[20] Barnes, 1993, *op. cit.*, cat. no. 57.

[21] Cotton was grown quite early in Xinjiang but it seems on a limited scale. See Sha Pi-t'i, 'Cotton planting and weaving in Ancient Sinkiang in the Light of Archaeological Data (Conk kaogu fajue ziliao kan Xinjiang gudai de mianhua zhongzhi he fangzhi), *Wenwu*, X (1973), pp. 48–51. Weaving is attested also by a document of the second half of the sixth century AD, found in burial 99 in the Karakhoja cemetery: see E. Trombert, 'Une trajectoire d'ouest en est sur la route de la soie. La diffusion du coton dans l'Asie centrale sinisée (6e–10e siècles)', pp. 205–227, in *La Persia a l'Asia Centrale da Alessandro al X secolo, Atti dei convegui lincei* 127 (Rome: Accademia dei Lincei, 1996), p. 218.

[22] On silks by the Chinese as early as the early Han period according to E. Loubo-Lesnitchenko, 'La technique du "jan-kie" dans la Chine du Moyen-Âge', *Bulletin de Liaison du CIETA*, XXXIV (1971), pp. 75–94 (p. 76), and surprisingly on wool textiles in Egypt as early as the first quarter of the second century AD (D. Cardon, 'Textiles archéologiques de Maximianon-Al Zarqa et Didymoi: exemples précoces de teinture par réserve sur laine', *Bulletin du CIETA*, LXXV (1998), pp. 14–20).

[23] Casson, *op. cit.*, p. 26.

[24] M. Chandra, *Costumes, Textiles, Cosmetics & Coiffure* (Delhi: Oriental Publishers, 1973), p. 5, fn 13, according to S. Cohen, 'The Earliest Indian Textile?', *Textile History* XXX (I), 1999, pp. 5–15 (p. 14).

[25] Cohen, *op. cit.*

[26] R. Goepper, 'Dressing the Temple. Textile Representations in the Frescoes at Alchi ', pp. 100–117, in: J. Tilden (ed), *Asian Art. The Second Hali Annual* (London: Hali Publications, 1995).

[27] Okada and Nou, *op. cit.*.

[28] Wild, 1997, *op. cit.*, p. 287; Okada and Nou, *op. cit.*, pp. 83–86, 105, 108, 131, 139, 144–145, 162, 189.

Chapter 7

A RE-CONSIDERATION OF THE HUMAN-FIGURE EMBLEMS EXCAVATED IN THE AT-TAR CAVES IN IRAQ

Kazuko Sakamoto

Introduction

The question of the human-figure emblems unearthed in the at-Tar Caves was examined in a detailed study in *al-Rāfidān* in 1994.[1] At that time the images on the emblems were considered to be influenced by Graeco-Roman culture and made at the at-Tar Caves. The Caves lie in the south-west desert in Iraq and have been dug parallel to the cliff line which runs along the edge of the salt lake, Bahr al-milh (Razāza Lake). They are 110km to the south-west of Baghdad and 80 km to the west of the ancient city of Babylon. The caves were used in two phases. Their purpose in the first phase, when they were first dug out, is not clear, but in the second phase, which corresponds to the Late Roman period, they were used as a burial place. The emblems considered in this paper are tapestries found on the bodies from the second phase. From the viewpoint of cultural exchange, the location and use of the caves is especially important and the artefacts from the at-Tar Caves need to be considered in relation to the culture of the East, as well as the West. The purpose of this paper is to reconsider the cultural origins of the human-figure emblems.

The tapestries depicting human figures from the at-Tar Caves (Late Roman)

1. *Dionysus represented as a female (Fig. 7.1)*

Specimen C-38-12-1-IV, from Cave F6, 72 × 53 mm

This is a small emblem, in which a female figure is depicted within a double frame, the inner frame a red line and the outer one composed of vertical indented geometric motif and horizontal parapet design. Her hair is decorated with vine leaves and fruit and she wears a diadem with a circular ornament. Her long hair is bound by ribbons. Her face turns slightly to her right and her eyes look in the same direction. The three-dimensional effect seen at the chin and forehead is achieved by inserting the weft diagonally instead of horizontally. This has given a hatched effect in the form of wedge-shaped shading on her cheek and neck. Although the colour of the shading has now faded, darker colour was probably applied in some sections. The human face stands parallel to the warp threads. The emblem is stitched with an extra thread on to a tabby-woven cloth that seems to be a mantle.

Fig. 7.1 Late Roman tapestry-woven emblem from the at-Tar caves, depicting Dionysus as a female. Photo courtesy of ICSAI, Kokushikan University (see Colour Plate IV).

2. Another Dionysus image, half the size of specimen 1 (Fig. 7.2)

Specimen C-38, from Cave F6, 53 × 40 mm

Another image of Dionysus is depicted in this tapestry. Although it is fragmentary, lacking the left half of the face, the design and weaving technique are very similar to the preceding one. The depiction of the head ornament, with vines and diadem, is simplified on this emblem. This tapestry may be regarded as an imitation of the preceding one.

Fig. 7.2 Late Roman tapestry-woven emblem from the at-Tar caves, with another image of Dionysus; half the size of the example shown in Fig. 7.1.

3. A figure wearing a yellow crown (Fig. 7.3)

Specimen C16–132, from Cave C16, 72 × 79 mm

The figure on this emblem wears a crown and is framed in a wavy motif. The crown is barely distinguishable from the background, but its presence is confirmed by visible traces on the reverse and woven slits in the tapestry. The figure wears large earrings. The upper body turns a quarter-turn to the figure's left, but the face is turned in the opposite direction, as if looking back – which is emphasised by the large black pupils. The illusion of shading on the face and neck is produced by weaving threads diagonally and using yarns of graded colours. The figure has been woven at right angles to the warp. This emblem was found sewn to a fragment of tabby-woven cloth with sewing thread which still survives.

Fig. 7.3 Late Roman tapestry-woven emblem from the at-Tar caves, depicting a figure wearing a yellow crown. Photo courtesy of ICSAI, Kokushikan University.

Fig. 7.4 Late Roman tapestry-woven emblem from the at-Tar caves, depicting a woman wearing a decorated cap. Photo courtesy of ICSAI, Kokushikan Univ. (see Colour Plate V).

4. *A female wearing a decorated cap (Fig. 7.4)*

Specimen C16 V-35, from Cave C16, 71 × 76 mm

This emblem has some points in common with specimen 3. First, the number of warp threads is the same, which suggests that they have been woven to the same specifications. Secondly, both of the human images are depicted inside a frame with a wavy motif. Thirdly, the technique used for the three-dimensional effect on the face and neck is the same. Finally, both figures, twisting to see backwards, are woven at right angles to the warp. An elegant feminine atmosphere, however, is created only in this fragment. The female here is wearing a headdress decorated with jewels, and large earrings. Her eyes are woven in light brown and blue-green yarns.

Tapestry emblems from other regions

5. *Tapestry depicting a centaur and a warrior (Fig. 7.5a/b)*

Sinkiang Uighur Autonomous Region Museum, China, AD third–fourth century

This tapestry was discovered in Sampula, Lop County, China, in 1984. It was

a) b)

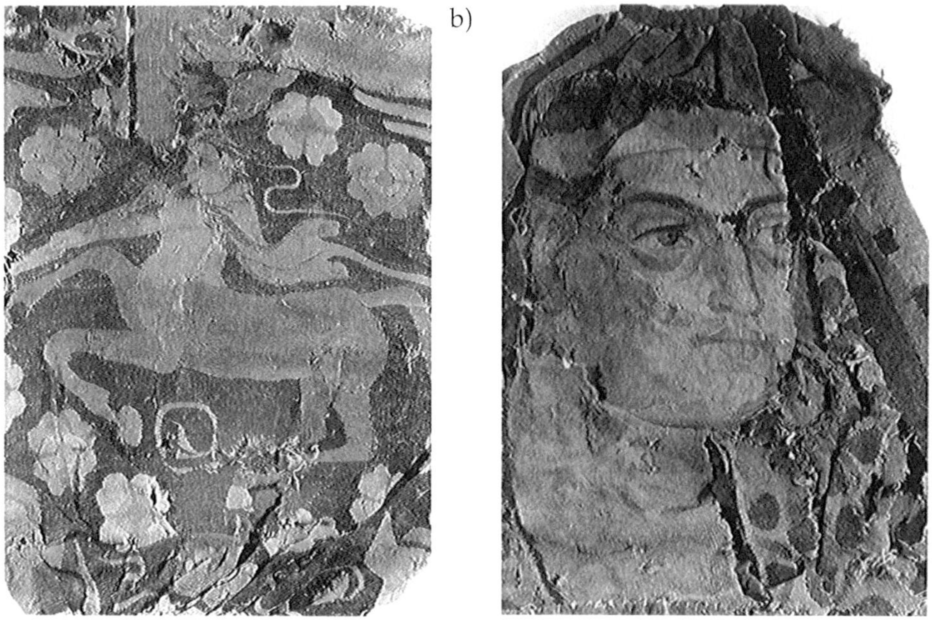

Fig. 7.5 Two parts of a tapestry from Sampula, Lop County, China, dated to the third or fourth century AD, depicting (a) a centaur and (b) a warrior. Sinkiang Uighur Autonomous Region Museum, China.

originally a wall decoration, but has been cut into two parts for use as cuffs of a garment. The upper section of the tapestry is 580 mm long and 455 mm wide. The centaur is depicted in a lozenge made up of four-petal flowers (Fig. 7.5a). He is blowing a horn and running at full speed so that his mantle streams in the wind.[2] The pattern of four petals has shading accomplished by graded colours and is reminiscent of the floral tapestry from Dura-Europos.[3]

The lower section is 610 mm long and 485 mm wide, and depicts a warrior holding a long lance (Fig. 7.5b). His face is turned one-third to his left and his blue eyes look to the left and slightly upwards. The expression of eyes and nose is quite realistic. The hatched, shaded effect has been produced through non-horizontal insertion of the weft, that is, the rose colour weft is diagonally interwoven with the warp in wedge shapes. The graded colours, from rose and pink to white, are used to give a sculpted effect to the eyes, nostril wings and mouth. The image has been woven parallel to the warp. This tapestry has probably come from Bactria.

6. The image of the god of the Nile (Fig. 7.6)

The Pushkin Museum, Moscow, AD third–fourth century, 296 × 294 mm

The image here is of an old man with a white beard, the personification of the Nile.

He holds a cornucopia, which symbolises a plentiful supply, and wears a hair ornament of lotus.[4] While he turns his body slightly to the left, his face is directed the opposite way. The wedge-shaped shading seen on the naked right shoulder and chest gives a hatched effect. Colour grading is ingeniously arranged in highlighted, intermediate and dark wedges. The figure's attitude follows the warp direction.

Fig. 7.6 Tapestry dated to the third/fourth century AD, depicting the god of the Nile. The Pushkin Museum, Moscow.

7. The Figure of Hermes (Fig. 7.7)

New Delhi National Museum, India, AD second–third century, 128 × 133 mm

This was excavated in Loulan.[5] A face with large eyes is represented against a blue background. The face is regarded as that of Hermes because of the caduceus, an attribute of Hermes, at his side. The face is turned towards his right and a three-dimensional effect is visible on his cheeks. This effect is produced by wedge-shaped shading which uses grades of greyish blue, rose, and pink, just as seen on the image of the deity of the Nile described above (no. 6). The Hermes image is, unlike the Nile god, represented in the weft direction, so that the wedge-shaped shading is vertical.

Fig. 7.7 Tapestry from Loulan, China, dated to the second/third century AD, depicting Hermes with his caduceus. New Delhi National Museum, India.

8. Women standing in an attitude of prayer (Fig. 7.8)

The Hermitage, St Petersburg, fifth century BC

This cloth, excavated in Pazyryk, Siberia, is a tapestry depicting two women. The woman in the front has a toothed crown on her head and stands in front of a censer in an attitude of prayer.[6] The parapet motif and indented geometric motif (*cf* no. 1, above) are seen in their veils and garments, and the images are bordered with an indented geometric motif. Censers and an attitude of prayer are

Fig. 7.8 Tapestry from Pazyryk, Siberia, dated to the fifth century BC, depicting women standing in an attitude of prayer. The Hermitage, St Petersburg.

also seen on cylinders and bas-reliefs of Assyria and among the Achaemenids of Persia. The women stand sideways and they are woven at right angles to the warp. The outlining of the figures could be an early attempt at a three-dimensional effect.

The technique of three-dimensional tapestry

The techniques used to represent three-dimensional human images in tapestry have been illustrated here through some typical examples excavated in the East, namely those from the at-Tar Caves and those from other regions. Before turning to the tapestries from the at-Tar Caves, the tapestries from the other regions will be considered. All of the items shown in Figs. 7.5a/b, 7.6 and 7.7 (excluding the early piece, Specimen 8 from Pazyryk), have a hatched effect made from wedge-shaped shading, which is produced by the technique of weaving the weft diagonally across the warp. The style suggests the Hellenic artistic tradition, seen in paintings and mosaics, and the themes of these three are also related to Greek culture. They have further points in common, such as the three-quarters frontal, 'chiaroscuro' (light and dark shading), and the colour scheme. These characteristics can be regarded as the influence of Graeco-Roman culture.

The tapestry with the centaur (Fig. 7.5) and the tapestry depicting Hermes (Fig. 7.7) are both from Sinkiang Uighur Autonomous Region in China. It is reasonable to suppose that these textiles reached this region from Bactria or Gandhara, where an Hellenic culture prevailed as a result of the conquests of Alexander the Great and his generals. They may have come into the Lop region by way of the south side of the Tarim Basin, which is the south road into Central Asia.

Turning now to the emblems excavated in the at-Tar Caves, it is possible to see that the tapestry with the Dionysus image (Fig. 7.1) shares three points in common with the three tapestries just described: first, the wedge-shaped shading produced by a diagonally worked weft; second, its theme related to Greek myths; and third, the figures are depicted facing three-quarters front. The possibility that the second fragment with the image of Dionysus (Fig. 7.2) is an imitation of emblem 1 (Fig. 7.1) has already been discussed. Given that foreign culture is often copied with admiration, the original, no. 1, from which the second, no. 2, has been copied, may have been brought from another land. The parapet and indented geometric motifs seen in Fig. 7.1 are also to be seen in the fifth-century BC Pazyryk tapestry (Fig. 7.8), which is attributed to Western Asia. Since Syria was deeply influenced by Hellenic culture and had a thriving weaving industry, it may be suggested that the emblem in Fig. 7.1 was made in Syria and imported or commissioned from there.

In contrast, the shaded effect produced by wedge-shaped sections cannot be seen in Specimens 3 and 4. Their shading is produced by weft yarns woven diagonally and by the use of different colours such as rose and pink. The attitude of the figures is not frontal but turned slightly sideways. The use of 'chiaroscuro' indicates influence from Graeco-Roman culture. Both the human figures on emblems 3 and 4 are aligned with the weft direction of the tapestry. This is the same as in tapestry no. 8, which suggests that there was an early tradition of weaving horizontal human figures into tapestry in Western Asia. It is therefore reasonable to conclude that emblems 3 and 4 were influenced by Graeco-Roman culture in the depiction of human images and could have been made somewhere near to at-Tar. Pliny says in his *Natural History*: 'weaving different colours into a pattern was chiefly brought into vogue by Babylon, which gave its name to this process'.[7] Since the at-Tar Caves are near Babylon, and 'weaving different colours' is considered to mean tapestry, it may be tentatively suggested that emblems 3 and 4 could have been made in Babylon.

Persian culture and the emblems from the at-Tar Caves

As described above, the figure in emblem 3 is wearing a crown, although it has faded on the front of the tapestry (Fig. 7.3). Flavius Arrianus remarked on the ornaments of Alexander the Great in his *Alexandri Anabasis*, as follows: 'he [Alexander the Great] did not blush to exchange the head-dress (sic) he had long worn as a conqueror for the tiara of the conquered Persians'.[8] Whereas the later figures of Roman Emperors on coins and medals wear a diadem,[9] the kings of the Achaemenids and Sassanids are represented with crowns on their heads.[10] These different depictions reveal that there is the difference between Graeco-Roman and Persian culture in the representation of the ruler's symbol. The human image on the emblem in Fig. 7.3, from the at-Tar Caves is therefore clearly influenced by Persian culture.

Ibn Khaldum says: 'Before Islam, the kings of Persia had placed upon their garments, either the portraits (*suwar*), or likenesses (*ashkal*) of the kings of the country, or certain figures and images designated for this use. The Muslim princes substituted their names for the figures, adding other words considered to be of good augury, in praise of God. Under these two dynasties (the Umayyads, and the Abbasids), it was a most important and honourable concern.'[11]

The emblem shown in Fig. 7.1, with the Dionysus image, has been stitched to another tabby-woven cloth, and so was the example in Fig. 7.3. It may be assumed, therefore, that the tapestry in Fig. 7.4 was also placed upon some garment. Taking these things into consideration, it seems reasonable to suppose that the images on emblems 3 and 4 do not represent some Zoroastrian king of Persia, but some local ruler or his wife who had lived in the region and who had been influenced by Persian culture – although it should be noted that the image is of the Greek god, Dionysus. The bodies with the human-figure emblems in the at-Tar Caves were presumably some local counterparts of kings or their wives, or perhaps some high-ranking officers on whom the emblems were conferred by their lord, as a mark of honour.

What kind of people would have borne the Dionysus image? Regrettably, little is known about the community who used the at-Tar Caves as a graveyard. Further archaeological excavation of the at-Tar Caves and their environs is required to answer this question.

Acknowledgements

Figs. 7.1, 7.3 and 7.4 were provided by the Institute for Cultural Studies of Ancient Iraq, Kokushikan University. I wish to express my thanks to the Institute.

Notes

1 H. Fujii, K. Sakamoto and M. Ichihashi. 'Human-figured emblems by tapestry technique unearthed from at-Tar Cave', *Al-Rāfidān* XV (ICSAI, Kokushikan University, Tokyo, 1994), p. 77–89, pl. 1–10

2 *Roran-okoku to yūkyū no bijo ten katarogu [The Kingdom of Lau-Lan and Eternal Beauty]*, (Tokyo: Asahi-shinbunsya [Asahi newspaper publishing company], 1992), p. 130 & p. 177. 'Shinkyo-Uiguru jichiku hakubutsukan [The Sinkiang Uighur Autonomous Region Museum]' *Chugoku no hakubutsukan, Dai-1-kan [The Museum in China. Vol. 1]* (Tokyo: Kodansha, Wen-wu-shuppansya, 1987), pls. 34–35.

3 A. Stein, *Innermost Asia*, III, Pl. XXX, L.C.iii.010.a (Oxford University Press, 1928).

4 R. Shurinova, *Coptic Textiles* (Moscow. 1967). Catalogue 3. pl. 12. Rutschowscaya. *Coptic Fabrics* (Paris: Adam Biro, 1990), p. 67.

5 T. Yamanobe, *Shiruku-rodo no Orimono [Dyeing and Weaving Technique on the Silk Road]* (Kyoto: Shiko-sha, 1979), pp. 104–105.

6 S. I. Rudenko, *Frozen Tombs of Siberia* (Berkeley & Los Angeles: University of California Press, 1970), pp. 296–297, pl. 177.

7 Pliny. *Natural History*, translated by H. Rackham, Vol. III (Cambridge, Massachusetts: Harvard University Press, 1967), p. 137

8 Arrian, *Anabasis Alexandri IV. Loeb Classical Library*, 236 (translated by E. Iliff and B. D. Robson), (Cambridge, Massachusetts: Harvard University Press, and London, 1967), p. 359. A. Omuta. *Kanazawa-Daigaku bungakubu ronshu, dai-6-kan [Collected Essays by the Faculty of Literature, Kanazawa University]*, trans. & comment, Department of History, 1986. p. 49. 'Flavii Arriani quae exstant omina edidit', A. G. Roos Vol. 1, *Alexandri Anabasis*, editio stereotypa correctior addenda et corrigenda adiecit G. Wirth. Lipsiae in *Aedibus* B. G. Teubneri MCMLXVII.

9 *Jinrui no bijyutsu [The Universe of shapes]*, 'Roma-bijyutsu [Roman Art]' (Tokyo: Shinchosha, 1974), pp. 347–351; *Jinrui no bijyutsu*, 'Kodai-makki no bijyutsu [Late

Antique Art]' (Tokyo: Shinchosha, 1974), pp. 389–393.

10 *Jinrui no bijyutsu*, 'Kodai-iran no bijyutsu [Ancient Iranian 'Art Perse']', I and II (Tokyo: Shinchosha, 1974), pp. 240–251.

11 R. B. Serjeant, 'Material for a history of Islamic textiles up to the Mongol conquest', *Ars Islamica*, IX (University of Michigan, 1942), pp. 60–61. Ibn Khaldun was born in the fourteenth century, and his opinion seems to be based on some earlier historical documents.

Chapter 8

WAS THERE GREEK OR ROMAN INFLUENCE ON SASANIAN WOMEN'S CLOTHING?

G. M. Vogelsang-Eastwood

Introduction

In recent years there have been a number of articles about women's clothing during the Sasanian period (*c.* AD 224–651).[1] One particular assumption made in these articles is that most Sasanian women wore a dress of some kind as their main item of clothing. This has led to the suggestion that the garments worn by Sasanian women were based on classical Greek originals, notably the *chiton* or the *peplos* (see below).[2] In this article I would like to suggest that the mainstay of Sasanian women's wardrobe was a combination of skirt and blouse, and that this represents an Iranian, rather than a Greek, or more accurately, Graeco-Roman inspired, tradition.

Greek and Roman clothing for women

Before looking at the garments worn by women in the western parts of the Sasanian Empire, it is necessary to say something about Greek and Roman clothing traditions for women.[3] One of the basic garments of a Greek woman consisted of a dress, of which there are two main types. Firstly, there is the *peplos* which was made from a long, rectangular piece of cloth (in wool or linen). The upper third of the material was folded over to form an 'overblouse'.[4] The folded edges of the material were then pinned together along the upper arms with *fibulae* (Fig. 8.1). In addition, belts were sometimes used to create and secure the draped, layered effect. The second form of dress commonly worn by Greek women is the *chiton*, which was made out of two rectangular lengths of material sewn along the sides up to the arms.[5] The rectangles were pinned together at intervals along the top, with a space left for the head and neck.

Fig. 8.1 Greek style peplos *and* himation.

A mantle (*himation*) was usually worn over the *peplos* or *chiton*. The *himation* was made out of a large rectangular piece of cloth (usually wool). When out-of-doors, the *himation* was used to wrap the woman's body in such a manner that virtually every part of the wearer was covered. A typical Roman style outfit for a woman consisted of a sleeveless, tunic-like garment called a *subucula* (made from linen), over which were worn one or more similar garments (the *tunica*) which were made out of wool or linen depending upon the time of year.[6] The uppermost garment consisted of a full-length, sleeved dress (*stola*; wool, linen or silk), which was suspended from the shoulders (Fig. 8.2). Usually the *stola* had sleeves which may be sewn on or pinned at regular intervals in a manner similar to the Greek *peplos*. Again, when in public women were expected to be covered in a modest manner, so a rectangular, woollen mantle (*palla*) was draped over the *stola* in order to veil the wearer's head and body.

Fig. 8.2 Roman style tunica *and* palla.

Over the centuries the garments described above changed and developed. In particular the eastern parts of the Roman Empire garments became more elaborately decorated. Nevertheless the basic items described above remained the standard garments worn by women in the eastern Greek and Roman world over the centuries, and it is these items which are normally compared with the Sasanian forms.

Sasanian period clothing for women[7]

One of the major problems when looking for information about women's clothing from Sasanian Iran is the lack of any actual examples. Although garments for men and children have been recorded from excavations in Egypt, and the former Soviet Union, no verifiable garments for women would appear to have survived.[8] Another problem concerning the study of women's clothing from the Sasanian period is the small number of suitable representations available. Nevertheless, there are more representations of women than from earlier periods in Iranian history, and it is clear that they wore a far wider range of garments, especially in the western part of the empire, than is normally recognised.

The most useful sources of information about women's clothing are contemporary silver plates and vessels which are now in collections throughout the world – although the dating of these objects is open to considerable speculation and debate. In addition, it is clear that silver vessels in the Sasanian style were being made well into the Ommayad and later periods. The aim of this study, therefore, is to provide a summary of Sasanian women's clothing, in the form of a typology of the relevant garments, rather than a chronology. It should also be stressed that the women depicted on the silver objects would appear to be goddesses, court women (queens and their attendants), as well as musicians and dancers, so that the range of information concerning their garments is limited to these particular groups. Nevertheless, it does give an indication of the basic garment types which were available, and it would seem reasonable to suggest that 'ordinary' Sasanian women in the western part of the Iranian Plateau wore a similar range of clothing, albeit of different types and quality of cloth.

Fig. 8.3 Sasanian woman wearing a typical blouse and skirt.

It has been suggested by other authors, including R. Ghirshman and P.O. Harper, that Sasanian women wore a long dress with a veil draped around the lower body and passing over the left shoulder.[9] Harper, for instance, suggested that the dress derived from the Greek *chiton* or *peplos*, while the veil was a descendant of the Greek *himation*.[10] However, a close examination of the various representations have shown that most women are not wearing a long dress, but a short blouse with long skirt.

The combination of these garments can be clearly seen on a silver plate now in the Hermitage Museum, St. Petersburg.[11] Although this plate is of a later date (it has been variously dated to the fifth/sixth centuries, and to the sixth/seventh centuries AD), the form of the garments can be traced back to earlier periods. The main figure on the plate is a woman or goddess, who is shown riding on a griffin, while playing a flute (Fig. 8.3). She is wearing a waist-length blouse with long sleeves ending in wide bracelets. The lower edge of the garment has a scalloped hemline. The garment has been decorated with double lines separated by circles. The skirt is long and full, and has a different style of patterning from the blouse, although still using lines and circles.

Blouses[12]

In addition to the plate now in the Hermitage Museum, there are several other silver vessels on which blouses are clearly depicted. On a silver vase now in the National Museum, Tehran, for instance, there is a woman who is wearing a short blouse with long sleeves, a narrow belt and a long skirt (Fig. 8.4).[13] The blouse has a long front opening with rounded edge, which the silversmith has highlighted using three pendants. One of the questions which needs to be asked about this detail is whether the artist was trying to depict a necklace of some kind or the neck opening of the blouse. It is clear, however, that the woman is wearing a heavy, chain-like necklace with large ornament around her throat. As the majority of depictions show Sasanian women wearing one necklace or neck ornament, it would seem reasonable to suggest that the artist was depicting the front decoration of the blouse, rather than trying to show that the woman was wearing a combination of short and long necklaces. It should also be noted that the woman is wearing a long, tightly twisted veil which is draped over her elbows, and then passes around the back of the wearer.

Another woman depicted on a vase in the Heeramaneck Collection, New York, is shown wearing a more unusual version of the blouse and skirt combination (Fig. 8.5).[14] In this case she is wearing a long-sleeved blouse which comes to waist level, but the lower edge of the garment has been indented at the front, producing an upside down V-shape. The front upper edge of the skirt has been draped, so exposing her navel. The silversmith has also indicated a belt with clasp around the top of the skirt. Again she has a long veil draped over her elbows and passing around the back, but this time the veil is not twisted upon itself.

Finally, a woman wearing a sleeveless blouse can be seen on a silver ewer now in the Sackler Gallery, Washington DC.[15] The dancer is depicted wearing a sleeveless blouse decorated around the shoulder, neck opening and cuffs (Fig. 8.6). The garment is tightly nipped in at the waist with a belt. Her skirt is ankle length.

Skirts

One of the few depictions which indicate the nature of the skirts worn during this period can be seen on a silver plate now in the Freer Gallery, Washington. It is dated to the fifth-seventh centuries (Fig. 8.7a–b).[16] It was suggested A.C. Gunter

Fig. 8.4 Sasanian woman wearing a short blouse, belt and skirt.

Fig. 8.5 Dancer (?) wearing an indented blouse, skirt and wide veil.

Fig. 8.6 Dancer wearing a sleeveless blouse with long skirt and belt.

and P. Jett that the decoration on the plate shows a mixture of 'western and eastern elements of iconography'.[17] According to Gunter and Jett the central figure depicts Ariadne, 'who is nude except for drapery across her lower legs' (Fig. 8.7a).[18] However, it would seem more likely that she is wearing a long veil draped around her waist and over her left elbow, and a long, full skirt. Also it would seem that she is sitting on part of her veil. The skirt has been decorated with crescents and dots. To the left of the figure are two female figures moving to the left (Fig. 8.7b). According to Gunter and Jett the women are wearing 'long-sleeved garments and a form of loose trousers and hold scarves over their head or shoulder'.[19] I would like to suggest that the two women are wearing long-sleeved blouses with wrap-around skirts. Due to the movement of the figures the skirts have come open, thus showing bare legs. If this interpretation is correct then the costume worn by the women remains Sasanian rather than western inspired.

In the Heeramaneck Collection, New York, there is a silver bowl with representations of animals, birds and dancers.[20] One of the dancers is wearing a long sleeved blouse, two skirts, and a long narrow veil (Fig. 8.8). The underskirt is represented by horizonal lines, while the wide overskirt is depicted with vertical lines. Over the skirt, the dancer would appear to be wearing a belt made up of shell-shaped panels. Both the skirts and the belt are used to accentuate the hips of the dancer. The low-slung nature of the skirt is used to accentuate the bare mid-riff of the dancer.

In the majority of cases skirts are shown being worn from the lower waist, just above the hipline. In addition, skirts are normally depicted as full, with the lower edges of the garments being represented with generous folds and pleats.

Long dresses

Although the mainstays of Iranian women's wardrobe would appear to be the blouse/skirt

a

b

Fig. 8.7 a. Seated figure of Ariadne wearing a veil and long skirt. b. Two women wearing short blouses and split-sided skirts.

Fig. 8.8 Dancer wearing a blouse and two skirts.

combination, it is clear that some women also wore a range of long dresses. it should be stressed that these garments are not of the *peplos* type with their characteristic fastenings along the shoulders and arms. One of the earliest depictions of a Sasanian woman wearing such a dress comes from the mosaics of Bishapour, which date to the reign of Sapur I (AD 241–272; Fig. 8.9).[21] A woman holding flowers and garlands is shown wearing a long, red dress with full-length sleeves. Over her dress is a light blue wrap which is draped over the left shoulder and over the right hip. There is no indication of a belt. It was suggested by Ghirshman in his description of this find, that her veil was a descendant of the Greek *himation* (which was later adopted by Roman matrons).[22]

Another example of a woman wearing what appears to be a full-length dress can be found on a vase now in the Galerie d'Art Idemitsu, Tokyo (Fig. 8.10).[23] It has been dated to the sixth-seventh centuries AD. The woman in question is wearing a long-sleeved dress which has a belt just above the hips. The belt appears to have a decorative clasp. The dress is unusual in that there is a front slit from just below the breasts to the waist, so that the navel is exposed. There would appear to be a short slit at the neckline, although this may be a necklace. Both the upper and lower parts of the garment are decorated with inverted Vs and dots in equal density. A long veil is draped over both elbows and is passed behind the wearer.

There is another example on a bowl found in Mazanderan (northern Iran), which has been dated to the eighth century AD.[24] The bowl is now in the Archaeology Museum, Tehran. The women in question are musicians and appear to be wearing sleeved, long dresses with accentuated front openings (Fig. 8.11). The ends of the sleeves are hidden by heavy cuffs, which are probably added rather than being part of the garment.[25] In addition, it would appear that the women are wearing heavy bracelets. One of the women is also wearing a belt, but the waist of the second

Fig. 8.9 Figure of a woman from a mosaic at Bishapour wearing a long, red dress, with blue veil.

Fig. 8.10 Figure of a woman wearing a long dress with decorative belt and a twisted veil.

Fig. 8.11 Musician wearing a long dress, narrow belt and veil.

Fig. 8.12 Group of woman wearing respectively: (A) nothing, (B, D, E) a blouse and skirt combination and (C) a tunic-like garment.

woman is hidden. The presence of a belt and the tight-fitting nature of these garments indicate that long dresses are depicted rather than blouses and skirts.

All of the above dresses have long sleeves. However, there is a representation of a female dancer which would indicate that a wide dress, or perhaps more correctly a tunic, without sleeves, was also part of the Sasanian woman's wardrobe. Such a garment can be seen on a fresco from the palace at Bishapour (Fig. 8.12).[26] There are five dancers in the relevant panel. The first of which (A) is naked, apart from her jewellery, the second (B), fourth (D) and fifth (E) dancers appear to be wearing blouses and skirts, while the third figure (C) is wearing the tunic-like garment.[27] The garment has no sleeves and is decorated around the neck opening, side edges and along the lower hem. No further indication is given of its construction. The woman is wearing no veil. No satisfactory parallels for this figure have so far been found.

Veils

As has been seen, the use of different sorts of veils has a long history in this part of the world. It should come as no surprise, therefore, to find them as a major element of women's indoor clothing during the Sasanian period. Their size and shape appear to vary considerably and they appear to have been used in many different ways. Sometimes they are draped over one arm, on other occasions over both arms; they may be draped behind the woman or on other occasions in front. The placing of the veil seems to depend on the status and activities of the woman, so that a musician has her veil well under control, while a dancer is using it as part of her performance.

Sometimes female dancers are shown naked, except for their jewellery, headdress and veil, the veil forming an integral part of the dance. In these circumstances the veils tend to be long and narrow. Such a veil can be seen on an oval plate, which is now in the Baltimore Museum[28] and has been dated to the sixth-seventh centuries AD. In contrast, a goddess(?) on a plate now in the Cleveland Museum of Art is depicted with a long, wide veil (Fig. 8.13).[29] The plate in question has been dated to the fifth/sixth centuries. The woman is wearing the basic garments, namely, a long-sleeved blouse, and skirt. In front of the lower half of her body is draped a wide, diaphanous veil. A similar item can be seen on the fifth/sixth-century vase in the Museo d'Arte Orientale, Rome, already described above.[30]

There is a fifth-century AD plate in the Walters Art Gallery, Baltimore, on which a queen is shown seated with a king (Fig. 8.14).[31] The queen is depicted wearing a long-sleeved garment covered by a large veil, or possibly an indoor cloak, which is fastened on the left shoulder. As the undergarment is covered by the veil it is not possible to say whether she is wearing a long dress or, as would seem more likely given the proposed date of the plate, a blouse and full skirt.

Fig. 8.13 Goddess(?) wearing a blouse and skirt combination with a wide veil.

Fig. 8.14 A queen wearing a large veil fastened at her left shoulder.

Coats

Occasionally goddesses and queens are shown wearing long coats with 'false sleeves'.[32] These garments are worn draped over the shoulder. One of the most famous examples can be seen at Taq-i Bustan (near Kermanshah in west Iran), where a goddess is shown at the investiture of Khosrow II. Her coat is draped over both shoulders and is decorated down the front opening as well as around the sleeve cuffs (Fig. 8.15). The coat comes to about knee length. Further examples of this type of coat

Fig. 8.15 The goddess from Taq-i Bustan wearing a long-sleeved coat over her dress (photograph by the author).

can be seen on a silver plate now in the Abegg Stiftung, Riggisburg,[33] which has been dated to the late Sasanian or early Islamic period.[34] There are two women depicted on the plate, both of whom are wearing coats over their shoulders (Fig. 8.16).

Palmyra

Until now, the emphasis has been on showing what was Iranian about the garments worn by women in the western parts of the Sasanian Empire. There is, however, a degree of overlap in women's clothing along the borders of the Roman and Sasanian Empires. This overlap in (and indeed the differences between) Greek, Roman and Sasanian clothing traditions can be seen when looking at the garments worn by women in wealthy caravan cities such as Palmyra and Dura Europos, which lay on the major trade routes linking Central Asia, Iran, India and Arabia to the eastern Mediterranean. From examination of funerary sculptures from

Fig. 8.16 Two women (possibly goddesses) wearing long-sleeved coats.

the city of Palmyra, in what is now Syria, it would appear that the main garments worn by the wealthier Palmyrene woman were a long, full gown and a broad veil which was draped over the head and down the back and shoulders.[35] There is also a more formal outfit which may be derived from a combination of Graeco-Roman and eastern style garments:[36] in a second-century AD mortuary portrait (slightly earlier than the Sasanian pieces described above), a woman wears a characteristic outfit for the region. She has on an eastern-style tunic, with long sleeves gathered in folds and ornamented with decorated cuffs and armbands, with two, similarly decorated broad strips down the front of the garment (Fig. 8.17). Over the tunic she is wearing a *peplos*-style garment which has been brought under the right arm and then pinned on the left shoulder. The extra material of the garment has been bloused over a belt and allowed to drop to the floor. The woman has drawn her mantle over her head and shoulders, and is shown holding part of it in either hand. By comparing Figs. 8.3 and 8.17 it becomes clear that the appearance of these garments and the way in which they are worn are not the same as those worn by Iranian women.

Fig. 8.17 A Palmyrene-style outfit for a woman.

In conclusion, it may be suggested that women living in western Iran during the Sasanian period had their own clothing tradition. It was based upon the combination of blouse, skirt and veil, or occasionally, a dress and veil. Further, unlike the garments worn by the women in caravan cities such as Palmyra, these garments represent an Iranian tradition, rather than being strongly influenced by, or even descendants of, Greek or Graeco-Roman clothing concepts.

Notes

1 For instance, P. O. Harper, 'Sources of certain female representations in Sasanian art', *La Persia nel Medioevo*, accademia Nazionale dei Lincei Quaderno, CLX (Rome), p. 513; E. H. Peck, 'Clothing iv. In the Sasanian Period', in E. Yarshater (ed.), *Encyclopaedia Iranica*, vol. V (1992), p. 735, 741.

2 For a discussion of Graeco-Roman and Iranian influences on dress from Palmyra and Dura Europos, see B. Goldman, 'Graeco-Roman dress in Syro-Mesopotamia', in J. L.

Sebesta and L. Bonfante, *The World of Roman Costume* (Wisconsin: University of Wisconsin Press, 1994), pp. 163–81.

3 The emphasis in this article has been placed on the western parts of the Sasanian Empire, as more information, in the form of various types of representations, is available about the range of garments worn by women in this region. The clothing worn in the eastern regions will be the subject of future research.

4 Sebesta and Bonfante, *op. cit.*, p. 245.

5 Sebesta and Bonfante, *op. cit.*, p. 243.

6 See J. L. Sebesta, 'Symbolism in the costume of the Roman woman', in Sebesta and Bonfante, *op. cit.*, pp. 54–64.

7 Due to constrictions on space, hairstyles and jewellery are not being discussed in this paper.

8 See for example, A. Geijer, 'Un manteau de cavalier iranien reconstituteé', *CIETA Bulletin de Liaison*, XXVII (1968), pp. 22–4.; A. Jeroussalimskaija, 'Le cafetan aux simourghs du tombeau de Mochtechevaja Balka (Caucase Septentrional)', *Studia Iranica*, VII (1978), pp. 183–211.

9 For example, R. Ghirshman, *Iran: Parther und Sasaniden* (Munich: C. H. Beck, 1962), p. 66; Peck *op. cit.*, p. 739.

10 P.O. Harper, *op. cit.*, p. 513.

11 Acc. no. S-26. See Brussels, *Hofkunst van de Sassanieden* (Brussels: Koninklijke Musea voor Kunst en Geschiedenis, 1993), p. 223, no. 73.

12 There has been a debate as to whether to call these garments, blouses or bodices. According to Yarwood a blouse is regarded a separate, loose bodice of different colour and material from the skirt, while a bodice is the upper part of a woman' dress above the waist (D. Yarwood, *The Encyclopaedia of World Costume* (London: Batsford, 1978), p. 38, 40.

13 M. Duchesne-Guillemin, *Les Instruments de Musique dans l'Art Sassanide* (Ghent: Peters, 1993), no. 36bis.

14 O. Graber, *Sasanian Silver. Late Antique and Early Medieval Arts of Luxury from Iran* (University of Michigan Museum of Art, Ann Arbor, 1967), p. 108, no. 21; Duchesne-Guillemin, *op. cit.*, p. 99, no. 36, fig. 36.

15 Smithsonian Institution, Arthur M. Sackler Gallery, S1987.117. A. C. Gunter and P. Jett, *Ancient Iranian Metalwork in the Arthur M. Sackler Gallery and the Freer Gallery of Art* (Smithsonian Institution, Washington D. C., Philipp von Zabern, Mainz, 1992), 194, no. 35.

16 Freer Art Gallery, acc. no. 64.10: Gunter and Jett, *op. cit.*, pp. 121–7.

17 Gunter and Jett, *op. cit.*, p. 124.

18 Gunter and Jett, *op. cit.*, p. 121.

19 Ibid. As far as I am aware there is no evidence to suggest that Sasanian women from western parts of Iran, or indeed Roman or Greek women in the Eastern Mediterranean world, normally wore trousers.

20 Graber, *op. cit.*, p. 104, no. 17.

21 R. Ghirshman, *op. cit.*, 1956, frontispiece, pls. VII/1, V/1.

22 Ghirshman *op. cit.*, p. 66.

23 S. Fukai, *Study of Iranian Art and Archaeology: Glassware and Metalwork* (Tokyo: Institute of Oriental Studies, 1968); Duchesne-Guillemin, *op. cit.*, no. 40, fig. 40.

24 P. O. Harper, *The Royal Hunter. Art of the Sasanian Empire* (New York: Asia Society, 1978), pp. 77–8, no. 26.

25 Such cuffs can be seen on statues from Palmyra, as well as forming part of Qajar (nineteenth century) dress for dancers and court women.

[26] F. Sarres and R. Ghirshman, *Bîchâpour – Les Mosaïques Sassanides* (Musée du Louvre: Paris, 1956), p. 58, fig. 3.

[27] The second figure almost looks as if she is wearing only a blouse and veil, but this could be the sketchy way in which the figures have been realised in the published drawing.

[28] The Walters Art Gallery, Baltimore; Ghirshman, *op. cit.*, pp. 217, 366, fig. 258.

[29] Cleveland 62.294; Graber, *op. cit.*, p. 109, no. 22.

[30] Museo d'Arte Orientale, Rome, acc. no. 8542. Duchesne-Guillemin, *op. cit.*, no. 40, fig. 4.

[31] Baltimore 57:709. Graber *op. cit.*, pp. 100–1, no. 13.

[32] An example of a queen wearing a coat can be seen on a silver plate now in the Sackler Gallery, S1987.117; Gunter and Jett, *op. cit.*, p. 131, no. 18. The queen appears to be wearing a long dress under the coat.

[33] Abegg-Stiftung, inv. no. 8.4.63; P. O. Harper, 'Sasanian and Early Islamic silver and bronze vessels', *Riggisberger Berichte*, VI, 1998, pp. 226–7, fig. 122.

[34] Ibid.

[35] Goldman *op. cit.*, p. 164.

[36] Ibid., fig. 10:4

Chapter 9

RECENT DISCOVERIES OF GOLD TEXTILES FROM AUGUSTAN AGE GADIR (CÁDIZ)

Carmen Alfaro Giner

Introduction

The city of Cádiz is an ancient Phoenician settlement, strategically sited in the bay of the same name, and it possesses an archaeological wealth which can only be compared with that of the most ancient and important Mediterranean cities. The origin of this emporium is the subject of some controversy among academics;[1] it was built on a small elongated island near the coast, which forms the boundary of a perfectly protected harbour. The city acquired a high economic profile as the centre of a fast-growing commerce which existed between the Middle East and all the region known to ancient authors as the mythical 'Land of Tartessus'.[2] This area would coincide approximately with the territory between the mouths of two rivers Annas and Betis (rivers known to the Arabs as Guadiana and Guadalquivir). The wealth of the region, or at least of some of its inhabitants, was still a reality at the beginning of the Roman Empire. The two tombs which we will describe below will illustrate this wealth in the city of Gadir (ancient Cádiz).

During the summer of 1998, F. Blanco and J. F. Sibón were completing the obligatory rescue excavations prior to the construction of a block of flats at 8–12 Arzobispo Escalzo St., an area on the outskirts of the ancient Punic and Roman necropolis, when they found five rectangular and perfectly aligned funerary monuments.[3] These were built from squared blocks of well-worked limestone of approximately equal size and proportion. The last of these monuments, almost at the edge of the area of investigation, was 2.5 m high × 1.3 m wide × 2.37 m long and yielded objects of significant interest. The stone construction concealed one principal burial (Tomb 25) and four secondary ones. The first, that of an adolescent girl, was situated underneath the monument inside a grave excavated in the sandstone ground. It was cube-shaped and delimited on the inside by four large slabs of stone. The other four were found inside the actual mass of stone blocks forming the monument, in cavities in each of the four corners (Tombs 25a, 25b, 25c and 25d). All the burials were cremations.[4] In the principal tomb, Tomb 25, and in Tomb 25a, gold textiles were found – in very small quantities, but of great historical value because the tombs were clearly dated to the Augustan period (between the end of first century BC and the beginning of 1 AD).

In both cases, the material is difficult to study due to the circumstances of their finding. In the fragments from the principal tomb, the gold was bonded physically to the remains of a badly burned and deformed silver object. According to the verbal accounts of the discoverers, this could have been a small box, perhaps with some type of handle or lifting device; the small fragments of textile were adhering to it. In the case of the secondary tomb (Tomb 25a), the remains of the gold textiles were stuck into one of the lateral walls of the cavity in which the furnishings and the funerary remains of the deceased – apparently another adolescent girl – had been placed. They formed a sort of compact ball of barely 30 mm diameter, with no remains of fibre other than the poorly preserved gold threads.

Our intervention, in order to find the original form of the textiles, was limited to a careful opening up of the compacted mass until it was spread out as far as possible. However, the fragility of the metal brought this to a halt and for the time being this has prevented us from obtaining a complete picture of the design.

Description of the textiles

Composition of the metal

These small fragments of gold first appeared in 1999 and a preliminary report was compiled almost straight away.[5] Now, however, the results of XRF analysis of the gold are available.[6] This quantitative analysis shows that the gold used is virtually pure (97.41%) with a small quantity of silver (1.88%) and another much smaller amount of copper (0.71%), indicating 23.4 carat gold. Analysis of some gold threads from a tomb in Munigua, Mulva, Seville, carried out in the same institute has revealed a slight difference in the alloy, in that case the proportion of silver being a little higher (3.22% silver, 96.34% gold and 0.45% of copper, indicating 23 carat gold).

The gold threads

Both samples (Tombs 25 and 25a) are made from spirally spun gold strip (gold filé).[7] The strip (πέταλον or *bratteola*) is 0.2 mm wide, and 3.6 microns thick, twisted around a fibre core; in both cases the twist is Z. According to literature on gold textiles, the core thread was normally made from silk, linen, or even from very finely spun wool. The final result is a thread of 0.1 mm diameter (100 microns). There are approximately 180 threads per cm, the threads being tightly pressed together and alternately visible on the front and back of the textile, which almost doubles the number which can be crammed together.

The fire from the cremation has destroyed the organic matter, leaving the gold spiral almost hollow, with only the burnt remains of the original elements. For this reason it has been impossible to identify any fibre structure with the scanning-electron microscope (SEM), nor, so far, to determine the chemical make-up.[8] In gold threads of a later date it has been suggested that, for the *bratteola* to adhere better to the inner core, a fine coat of reddish iron oxide may have been used,[9] although in this case, we have been unable to detect any similar substance.

As gold melts between 1048° and 1058° C (when alloyed 90% gold with 10% silver: pure gold melts at 1064° C)[10] we may surmise that the funerary cremation of Gadir must have reached a very high temperature. In general, the threads are more deformed than those of the gold textiles from Munigua.[11] The surface of the gold strip frequently shows round hollows, most probably where the fusion of metal has begun to take place. In this regard, parallels may be drawn with, for example, the remains of tapestries from burials 3 and 4 at Arc-sur-Argens, Var, France, which are a little later than the pieces from Gadir.[12] Sometimes the undulations and distortions give rise to special situations. In a fragment of textile no larger than one square centimetre, one half preserves the appearance of tapestry, whereas the other half looks completely flat (although there are still visible lines which delineate the old threads). This most probably occurred when this small fragment of material was heated up, because half of it was in contact with a hard flat surface which moulded it in this way.

The textile remains from Tomb 25

All that is left of the two groups of textiles from Tombs 25 and 25a, are the elements of gold tapestry which were woven simultaneously with the ground material (which may have been linen, silk or wool), the gold representing the decorative element.[13] The technique is the same as that found in Greek and Roman textiles, always rather badly preserved, and also in Coptic ones, where the weave is more complete and the relationship of the gold thread to the ground weave can be observed.[14] The gold thread, used as a weft, is used for the design, on a relatively thick warp which provides the textile with volume and gives it the typical ribbed tapestry effect. The problem lies in that, when the perishable background material disappears due to action such as fire, it is very difficult to reconstruct the decorative shapes of the gold – especially if, as here, the textiles are not in their original flat position.

Nevertheless, some conclusions may be drawn. The textiles from Tomb 25, physically mixed with the burnt remains of a small silver box (Fig. 9.1), present a much simpler structure than those from Tomb 25a, described below. They suggest a long ribbon in which the weft runs longitudinally, in a design similar to that proposed in Fig. 9.2. There were perhaps two bands, each 15 mm wide, of continuous gold tapestry (that

Fig. 9.1 The burnt remains of a silver object together with the gold thread from Tomb 25.

is to say, with 280 threads 0.1 mm thick in each), between which was some sort of scale pattern.[15] The small size of the object and the fact that it was most probably kept in the aforementioned little silver box leads one to think that this may be an ornamental head-band, a *corolla* or στέφανος, which literature has so often spoken of as part of the furnishings of the young adolescent.

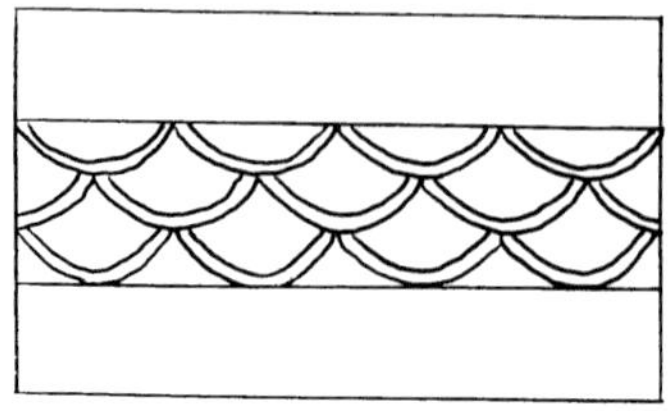

Fig. 9.2 The reconstructed design of the gold head-band from Tomb 25.

The textile remains from Tomb 25a

In this example (Fig. 9.4) the complexity of the design is much greater. As the reconstruction shows, there are two narrow bands of tapestry at the sides and an ample variety of foliage between (Fig. 9.3). The greatest difficulty lies in the fact that these foliage elements have become amalgamated and difficult to separate: some seem to have small stalks (also of gold) which intertwine with others. In Fig. 9.5, an attempt has been made to reconstruct the start of one of the elements of the four-leaved clover which appears in Fig. 9.6. The problem for the weaver was that the weft had to be worked separately in the two upper leaves, but be common to both in their lower part and in the start of the two lower leaves, and then to divide again at their base (Fig. 9.7) – all in scarcely one centimetre square! The same difficulty

Fig. 9.3 A provisional drawing of the design of the gold head-band from Tomb 25a.

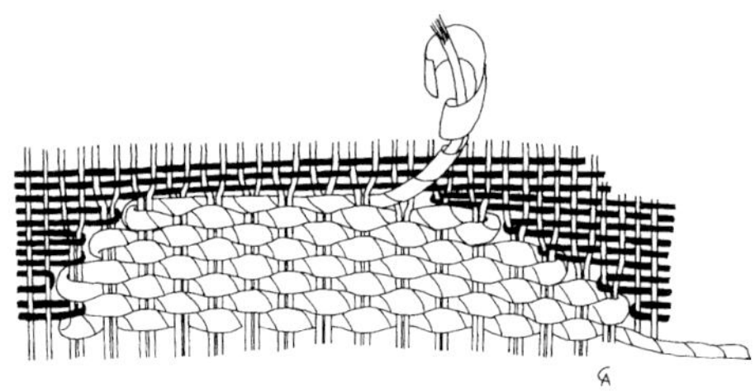

Fig. 9.5 A reconstruction of the tapestry-weaving technique of the four-leaf clover shown in Fig. 9.6.

Fig. 9.4 Partly unfolded textile from Tomb 25a.

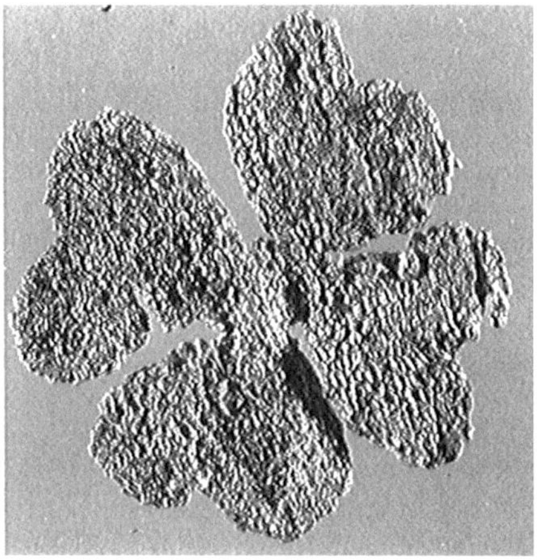

Fig. 9.6 A four-leaf clover made from gold thread, from Tomb 25a.

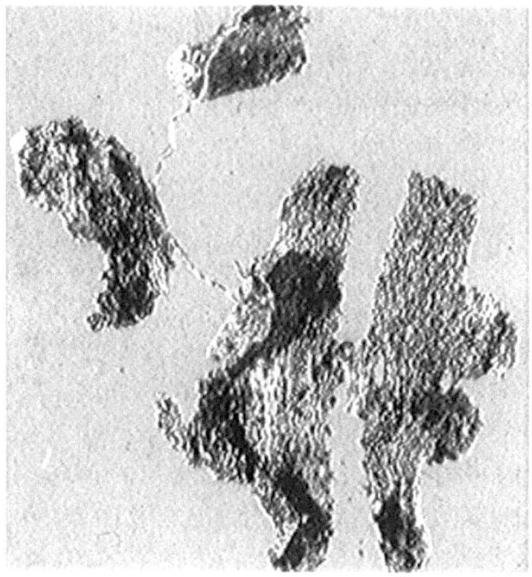

Fig. 9.8 Detail of a flower(?) made from gold thread, from Tomb 25a.

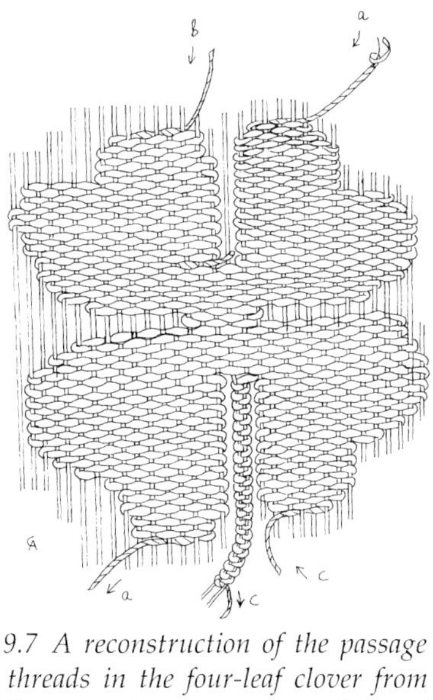

Fig. 9.7 A reconstruction of the passage of the gold threads in the four-leaf clover from Tomb 25a. There are three separate weft threads, a, b and c.

occurs in the case of the double symmetrical leaves or petals of Fig. 9.8. As in the case of the textile from Tomb 25, we think that this small object may have formed part of one of the headbands which were so common in the Graeco-Roman funerary world.

The origin of the Gadir textiles

Geological surveys of the ancient land of Tartessos demonstrate that gold was still present long after the pre-Roman and Roman inhabitants exploited it. The goldwork of the area is of fine quality and craftsmanship, so that the possibility of local manufacture of gold thread cannot be ruled out, especially as the identity of the fibre of the core thread is not known (silk would suggest an import).

A variety of factors, however, point to the import of these products. The two burials in question belonged to people of high social standing, with a taste for antiques or beautiful family heirlooms. The ashes of Tomb 25 were deposited in a Phoenician alabaster urn, clearly dating from the eighth century BC. This family had no difficulty acquiring exotic objects such as ointment jars and sculpted crystal bottles, which have been hollowed out using an exceptional technique of craftsmanship (personal communication from the excavators). These are today on show at the Museum of Cádiz. They may well originate from a city such as Alexandria in Egypt. This would support the theory that the gold headbands were also imported, and one is reminded of the funerary portraits of Egypt at this time. Finally, the fact that the threads are in a Z-twist is a technical detail which suggests a link with the East.

The present day

Sixty years ago in North Africa it was still possible to study at first hand the process of manufacturing gold threads.[16] Today in Europe, narrow strips are still twisted into 'gold threads', and the external characteristics are similar to those we know from antiquity. They are used for the production of highly ornate silk cloths of eighteenth-century style. Workshops of this kind exist in Lyons, France, and on a smaller scale (only one manufacturer) in Valencia, Spain, where silk production has always been a great tradition.[17] According to our source in Valencia, nowadays a 5 mm diameter wire is used, either copper or silver (depending on the desired quality), which is then gilded. This wire is put through a *trefilator*, a machine which slowly draws out the wire, making it thinner until is has 'the thickness of a hair' (approximately 1 mm diameter), at the same time flattening it. The metal strip thus obtained has a width of 1.5 mm. It is spun, using a spinning wheel, around a fine thread of silk or cotton, always turning the metal strip the opposite way from the thread-core.

In Lyons it is possible to visit the factories, according to S. Desrosiers, although our contact in Valencia did not permit us to visit his workshop. To such an extent do craftspeople still jealously guard their professional secrets. And not only that, he did not believe for a second that 2000 years ago it was possible to do work such as his, using almost pure gold, of a greater fineness, and without the machinery which he had available to him.

Notes

1 M. E. Aubet Semmler, *Tiro y las colonias fenicias de Occidente*, (Barcelona: Bellaterra, 1987), pp. 228–238. J. Millán León, *Gades y las navegaciones oceánicas en la Antigüedad (1000 a.C – 500 d.C.)* (Ecija, 1998), pp. 17–31.

2 Herodotus I, 163; Strabo, III, 2, 11–14; Justinus XLIV, 1,14; Avienus, *Ora maritima*, 260–298.

3 We are grateful to both for the facilities which they have generously made available to us for the study of the gold textiles, and the generosity with which they have permitted us to see their preliminary notes and also to publish such extraordinary material. My gratitude extends to the director of the Museum of Cádiz, Dr Cándida Garbarino and Prof. Mercedes Serrato, who let us know of the existence of thiese materials in the Museum. All the finds from 8–12 Escalzo will be published in a monograph, which will allow us to publish any further new data concerning the textiles.

4 Inhumation and cremation alternated in the necropolis, although the second predominated.

5 C. Alfaro Giner, 'Archéologie des textiles anciens dans la péninsule ibérique: à propos de quelques nouveautés', in D. Cardon et M. Feugère eds, *Archéologie des textiles des origines au Ves de notre ère, Lattes* 28–29 Oct. 1999, in press.

6 These analyses have been undertaken by Marisa Hernández, in the Instituto Tecnológico Metalmecánico (AIMME) in Valencia, for whose collaboration we are grateful.

7 J. P. Wild, *Textiles of the Northern Roman Provinces* (Cambridge: C.U.P., 1970), p. 39, 132.
R. Boyer, 'L´inhumation habillée dans le sarcophage n° XX de la nef de l´église haute', in *Vie et mort à Marseille à la fin de l´Antiquité*, (Marseille, 1987)(pp. 45–93), p. 132.
A. Batcheller, 'A Roman Textile Bracelet from Dorchester, Dorset', *Archaeological Textiles Newsletter*, XX (1995)(pp. 5–8), p. 5–6).

8 The better condition of the threads found in Munigua (Mulva, Seville) has made possible, in certain more exposed parts, the analysis of the mineral elements which exist inside them, without being able to determine, at the moment, the organic composition of the fibres of the core.

9 A. Stauffer and F. Weisse, 'Ein frühmittelalterliches Goldgewebe aus Lauchheim', *Fundberichte aus Baden-Württemberg*, 22/1 (1998)(pp. 729–736), p. 730.

10 J. Alsina Benavente, *El oro*, (Barcelona: TI, 1988), p. 213.

11 C. Alfaro Giner, 'Gold textiles from a Roman Burial at *Munigua* (Mulva, Sevilla)', in *Archaeological Textiles in Northern Europe, Report of the VIIth NESAT Symposium* (Edinburgh, in press).

12 G. R. Boyer, S. Arnaud, A. Reymondon and J. Desse, 'Un groupe d´Urnes Cinéraires (Ier et II e siècle) découvert près des Arcs-sur-Argens (Var)', *Gallia* XLIV (1986) (pp. 91–109), p. 93–101.

13 The term *aurum intexere* (Pliny, *Natural History*, VIII, 196), is usually translated as embroidering with gold. We think a more logical interpretation would be: 'woven into the actual material', which we can observe in most gold textiles to have survived from the classical world.

14 M. Flury-Lemberg, *Textil Conservation* (Berne: Abegg-Stiftung, 1988), fig. 448–456.
R. Pfister, *Textiles de Palmyre découverts par le Service des Antiquités du Haut-Commissariat de la République française dans la Nécropole de Palmyre* (Paris 1934), pp. 18, 45, 54.
R. Pfister, *Nouveaux textiles de Palmyre, decouverts par le Service des Antiquités du Haut-Commissariat de la République Française dans la Nécropole de Palmyre (Tour d´Élahbel)* (Paris, 1937), p. 11.
R. Pfister, *Textiles de Palmyre découverts par le Service des Antiquités du Haut-Commissariat de la République française dans la Nécropole de Palmyre* III (Paris, 1937), p. 16.
P. Du Bourguet, *Musée National du Louvre. Catalogue des Étoffes Coptes*, I (Paris: Editions. des Musées Nationaux), p. 76, fig. B26.
D. Benazeth, 'Un rare exemple de tissu copte à fil d´or', *Tissage, Corderie, Vannerie, IX Rencontres Internationales D´Archéologie et d´Histoire, Antibes* (Juan-les-Pins, Octobre 1988), p. 224.

15 S. Desrosiers showed us a very similar design, as yet unpublished, from the textiles of Naintré (Vienne).

16 Vicaire-Le Tourneau, 'La fabrications du fil d´or à Fès', *Hespéris* XXIV (1937), pp. 67–88.

17 Still today the breeding of silkworms in a cardboard box is customary amongst children of all social levels in Valencia, and the city has many white mulberry trees, the leaves of which these insects feed on exclusively.

Chapter 10

ROMAN TEXTILES IN SWITZERLAND

Antoinette Rast-Eicher

Introduction

Textiles of the Roman period are rare finds in Switzerland. This is due to the difficult conditions of preservation in settlements, and the practice of cremating bodies, which dominated the Swiss Plateau North of the Alps and which leaves little textile evidence. Only a few fragments have been recorded, either as chance finds or as discoveries in museum store-rooms. More recently, however, some interesting finds have begun to appear from Valais, a part of Switzerland where both kinds of burial tradition – inhumation and cremation – were practised. Here, excavations are producing new evidence concerning Roman costume in the Alps. Nevertheless, compared with the later, much more abundant, finds from the Migration Period (when textile-types were derived from those of the Roman period), textiles of the Roman period in Switzerland still remain scarce.

Textiles from settlements

Most of the Roman textiles from settlements have already been published, by Wild.[1] The old finds from Windisch (Roman *Vindonissa*), Aarau, include small groups from the fort and from the fort's rubbish dump. They are woven in tabby and twill and one is a fragment of sprang.[2] In 1970 there were further finds from the fort, from a second century AD pit which may have been a refuse pit or a latrine.[3] These are all wool 2/2 twills in different qualities, with 8–12 threads per cm.

To these may be added four further finds from settlements, two of which are from recent excavations near Zürich. The first is a fragment of metal-replaced textile from an upper layer of the villa at Dietikon, Zürich,[4] although this fine cotton 2/2 twill adhering to a bracelet was found above the Roman layers and may not be reliably dated. Another textile, found in a pit at Winterthur (*Vitudurum*), Zürich, and dated to the second or third century AD, is made from a plant fibre, and is coarse and loosely woven in tabby.[5] A small imprint on a wall painting from Avenches (*Aventicum*), Vaud, shows how another method of preservation can reveal information on textiles. Here, even the spin is visible in some of the thread imprints.

The threads of 0.5 mm diameter are spun Z × ?Z and the weave is probably tabby.[6]

Finally, a carbonised basket weave (tabby with paired warp and weft) from Chur-Welschdörfli (*Curia*), Graubünden, found in 1963 and published by J. P. Wild,[7] has recently had a more complete fibre analysis. The fragment in the Swiss National Museum in Zürich was being re-mounted between two new glass plates, which provided an opportunity to take samples (Fig. 10.1). Scanning-electron microscopy (SEM) revealed that this textile is made from hemp. The fibres are larger than flax (up to 30–50 microns diameter) and show finer nodes and more irregular cross-sectional shapes, with larger lumina (the lumen is the central air channel); and the fibres often appear in bundles (Figs. 10.2–10.3), which is frequently the case with hemp. Hemp could certainly have been grown in the region of Chur, where the climate is favourable and where hemp has been grown until this century. L.Bender Jørgensen has shown that this textile-type is rare in Europe and was probably a Mediterranean cloth type introduced by the Romans.[8] The Z × Z spin, however, points to local production, or at least production in the northern provinces.

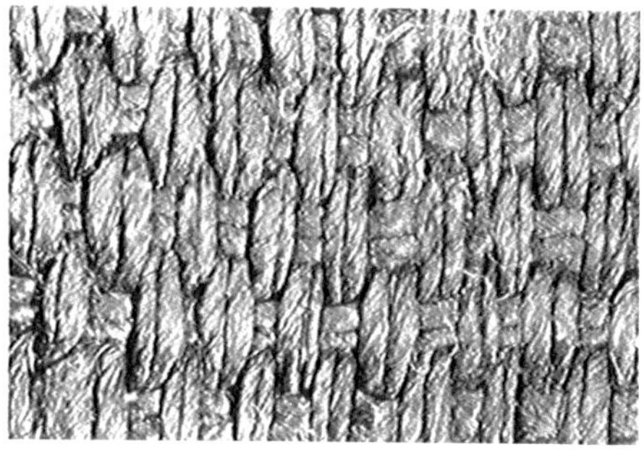

Fig. 10.1 Textile in basket-weave from Chur-Welschdörfli. Photo: A. Rast-Eicher.

Fig. 10.2 SEM photograph showing cross-section of hemp fibres in textile from Chur-Welschdörfli. Photo: A. Rast-Eicher.

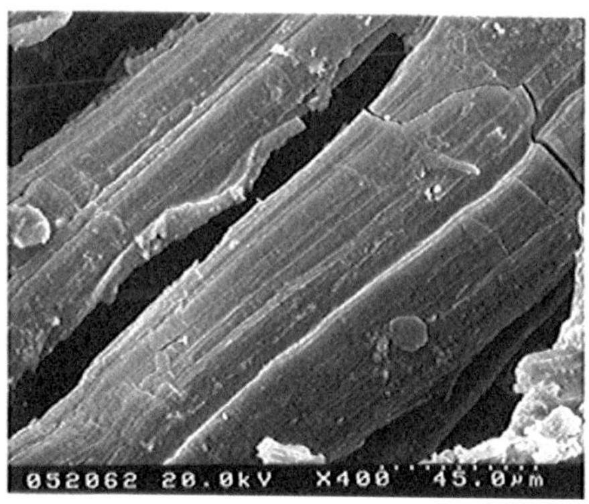

Fig. 10.3 SEM photograph showing longitudinal view of hemp fibres. Photo: A. Rast-Eicher.

Textiles from graves

In the Swiss Plateau, the tradition was for cremation burial, which usually leaves no textile remains. In Valais (see map, Fig. 10.4), however, which is the canton covering the upper valley of the Rhône in the Alps, with main settlements between Martigny (Fig. 10.4, site 1) and Brig (Fig. 10.4, site 2), inhumation continued to be practised. This Alpine region is an interesting area for the study of burial costume, as the Romanised settlement at Martigny may be

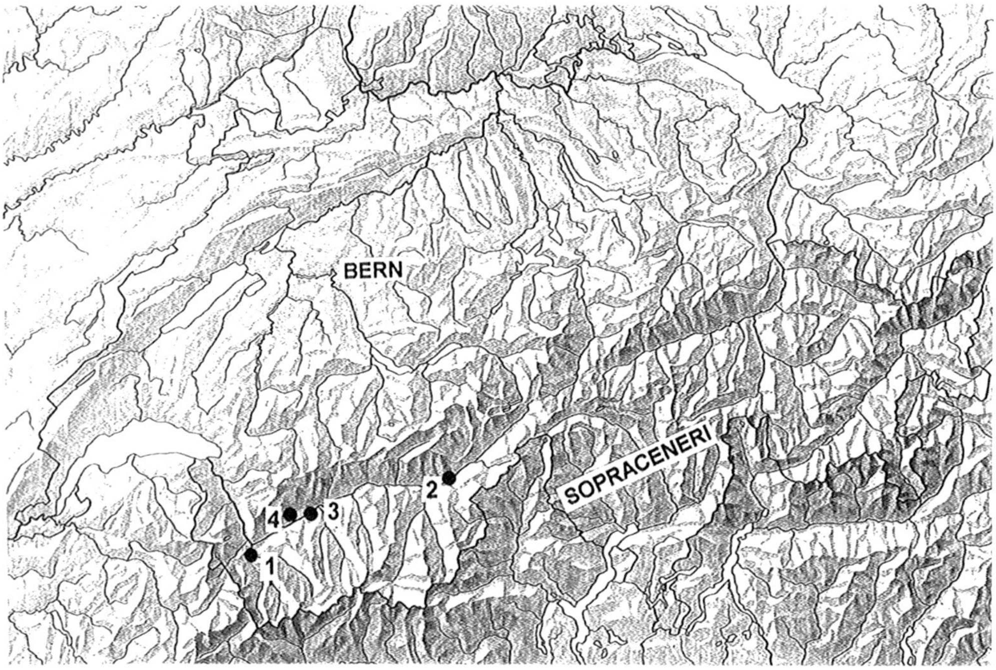

Fig. 10.4 Map of Switzerland, showing sites mentioned in the text.

contrasted with the continuity of the traditional 'peplos' costume at Brig. In the inhumations of Valais, metal objects sometimes preserve textiles by mineralisation (the replacement of textiles by metal salts), which allows the costume evidence to be studied. In addition, textiles from Pre-Roman Iron Age Sion (Fig. 10.4, site 3) have started to be analysed during recent years, and new excavations in Brig/Gamsen-Waldmatte (Fig. 10.4, site 2) have presented the opportunity to do the same with Roman graves. Even if the textile remains are small, each one provides further pieces for the puzzle. As with the carbonised material discussed above, SEM was a great help, as fibre identification of metal-replaced material is difficult without it.

The earliest signs of influence from the Roman world were found in 1998 in a woman's grave at La Matze in Sion (*Drusomagus*), a town located between Brig and Martigny (Fig. 10.4, site 3). Two fibulae were found in this grave, both variants of the 'Alesia type' and dated to the second half of the first century BC.[9] The woman had one fibula on either shoulder, as if wearing a 'peplos' (the 'peplos' is a tubular gown fastened at the shoulders with brooches). A purse with Celtic coins and traditional leg-rings confirm her origin in the region of Sion. The textile on the shoulder-brooches is a type which has not previously been found in Pre-Roman graves in that town. Whereas wool tabby was usual for the 'peplos' in La Tène C and D1 graves from Sous-le-Scex, Sion,[10] the woman from La Matze, Sion, wore a

Fig. 10.5 A diamond twill from La Matze, Sion. Photo: A. Rast-Eicher.

diamond twill (Fig. 10.5). The same textile, a 2/2 diamond twill, Z × S-spun, yarn diameter 0.5 mm, has been found on both fibulae and, under the fibula on the left shoulder, there are the remains of tabby repp, which, I think, must belong to a selvedge. This shows that the peplos was not worn like the classical Greek peplos, pinned on a large fold, but was clasped at the starting border or selvedge of the textile, in the manner of the so-called 'costume of Menimane' (a style of clothing illustrated by the funerary sculpture of Menimane, wife of Blussus, at Mainz[11]). Diamond twill woven with single, Z × S yarn is known from the Hallstatt period,[12] but has not yet been found in Swiss graves of the La Tène period; it is also rare in early La Tène graves throughout Europe. The few known examples come from Sonnenburg, Germany, Dürrnberg Grave 72, Austria, and Burton Fleming, England (UK). During the first, and especially the late first and second century AD, diamond twills become common in military contexts. With time they become more uniform in their pattern repeats and by the early medieval period, the 20 × 18 pattern is very frequent among diamond twills.[13] Was the woman from La Matze, Sion, wearing an especially rich garment, or perhaps a soldier's *sagum*? The fibulae, which seem to be a 'military' type, support this interpretation.

Martigny (Fig. 10.4, site 1)(*Octodorus/Forum Clausii Vallensium*) is a Roman site on the north–south trade route which was established in the middle of the first century AD, to link the region of Lake Geneva to Aosta in Northern Italy by way of the Grand Saint Bernard Pass.[14] The Romans introduced a new culture which left its traces in a large number of archaeological remains, such as stone buildings, Roman coins, stelae, ceramics and so on. These show the importance of Martigny as an administrative and cultural centre. In the late Roman period, Martigny remained important, while the former customs post of St Maurice (*Acaumus*) became a centre for the Christian church and, by the sixth century, had a famous monastery.

Textiles found in Martigny and its environs document this strong Roman influence. A small fragment on a coin of Tiberius (AD 22–30) represents traces of a linen textile woven in tabby. Because of the S-spin in both directions, it may be assumed that this textile was produced in southern parts of Europe, or in the Eastern Roman provinces, where S-spin was usual for linen textiles.[15] In 1900, at Plan-Conthey, between Martigny and Sion (Fig. 10.4, site 2), some very rich burials were found in the mausoleum of a villa-rustica, dated from finds of glassware to the fourth century.[16] The burials were in lead coffins, which are known to preserve textiles well, but only a few pieces have survived of what was probably excavated in 1900. These textiles are the well-known silk damask and the wool tapestry medallion.[17]

A completely different picture is presented by Gamsen-Waldmatte near Brig

(Fig. 10.4, site 4). This site was discovered in 1987 and is located on the route to the Simplon Pass. There was continuous settlement here from the Iron Age to the Late Roman period.[18] Houses were in most cases built of wood and the influence of Roman culture is modest. Bone remains show that the food supply largely came from sheep and goats, whereas in Martigny pork and later beef were dominant.[19] The village lived by farming, but had close contacts with southern valleys. The graveyard was placed outside the village and contains cremations dated to the second and third century, and inhumations of the early and late Roman periods; very small children were buried inside the houses. Strong links with the southern valleys of the Sopraceneri – the present-day Italian speaking part of Switzerland – are indicated by finds in the upper Valais of fibulae such as the 'Armbrustfibel', or Misox-type fibula (first century AD), a type which was not used around Martigny.[20] One cremation burial (Grave 9) contains four coins,[21] a large Misox-type fibula and a handle, and has been dated from the coins to the end of the second century AD. Remains of the same textile have survived on three of the four coins, on the fibula and on the handle. It is a Z × Z linen tabby (unlike the tabby from Martigny mentioned above, which was S × S), with 13 to 15 threads per cm (Fig. 10.6). It is clear that the well-preserved metal objects have been wrapped in this textile and added to the burial. This shows how, even in cremations, textile fragments can be preserved. Coins in general – including those from later graves – often seem to be wrapped in a textile and therefore merit special attention from archaeologists.

Fig. 10.6 Linen tabby on a coin from Brig-Glis/Gamsen-Waldmatte. Photo: A. Rast-Eicher.

Another inhumation from Gamsen-Waldmatte, Grave 98/1, contains four fibulae dated to the first half of the first century AD, one on each shoulder and two on the upper chest. All of them have remains of wool textiles preserved in association with them. On the left shoulder there were remains of a coarser garment (yarn diameter 1–1.2 mm, Z × Z, probably spin-patterned) together with a finer textile. The finer textile is a tabby with threads of 0.4–0.5 mm diameter. The wool in this textile could be analysed and proves to be relatively fine in quality, with a mean diameter of 21.6 microns and a maximum of 47 microns (Fig. 10.7).[22] A similar quality wool was found in the late La Tène textiles from Sous-le-Scex, Sion, and from Vidy near Lausanne.[23] I

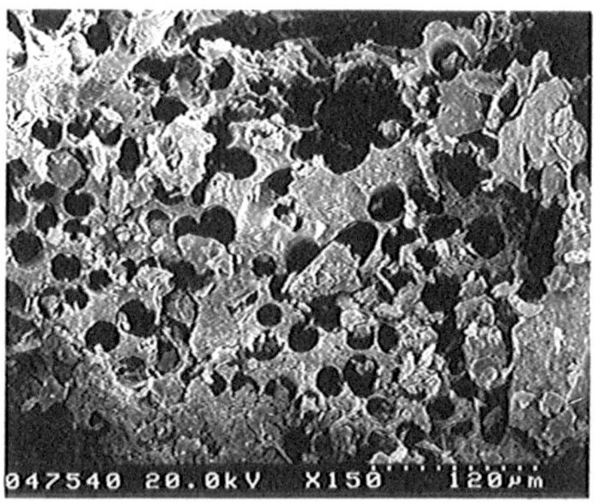

Fig. 10.7 Cross-sectional view of wool from textile in grave 98/1, Brig-Glis/Gamsen-Waldmatte. SEM photo: A. Rast-Eicher.

assume that the finer textile is part of the 'peplos', which was also fixed by one of the fibulae found on the chest, where threads of the same fine quality have also been found. The coarser quality may then be a second textile covering or wrapping the body and pinned by the same fibula. Spin-patterned twills of coarse quality have been found in pre-Roman burials, especially in southern parts of Switzerland.

Another inhumation at Gamsen-Waldmatte (Grave 89/21) is much later, being dated to the late fourth or early fifth century AD by a late type of Misox fibula and a coin.[24] The grave was found inside a stone building. The Misox-type fibula on the left shoulder fastened a 2/2 twill made of wool – as two folds directly by the pin show.[25] The pincer fibula on the right shoulder had unfortunately no textile remains. Broadly speaking, it is known that the peplos worn by women in the Pre-Roman Iron Age was still in use in the second century AD in the Swiss Plateau and even into the third century in Alpine regions.[26] It should not be forgotten, however, that the 'peplos' costume, with a pair of brooches on the shoulders, survived in other parts of Europe until the early medieval period.[27] The very large Misox fibulae were generally worn in pairs, as, for example, in the graves in Airolo-Madrano, Ticino, where they continued in use for women's dress until the third century.[28] Does this late grave from Brig/Gamsen-Waldmatte provide evidence for the 'peplos' even into the fourth century? Or was the peplos forgotten in the upper Valais by the end of the third century and does this burial with non-matching brooches on the shoulders represent a different style of costume? The pincer fibula could have fastened an outer garment such as a cloak, but the lack of textiles on this brooch means that there is at present no answer to these questions.

Conclusion

There are few textiles from settlements, and graves provide most of the new finds, especially in Valais (the upper Rhône valley). The different burial traditions, witnesses of cultural affiliations, are concentrated within this one valley. They are mirrored by textile remains and also in the costume style: the old-fashioned pre-Roman tradition in the upper valley around Brig and in the Alps, contrasts with the imported textiles such as rich silks, wool tapestry and foreign linens from the lower valley around Martigny.

Notes

1 J. P. Wild, *Textile manufacture in the Northern Roman Provinces* (Cambridge, 1970); for further discussion of the finds, see L. Bender Jørgensen, *North European Textiles until AD 1000* (Aarhus, 1992), pp. 108, 130

2 Wild 1970, *op. cit.*, table B, No. 31, 32, 47, 73, 93

3 Ch. Meyer-Freuler, *Vindonissa Feuerwehrmagazin* (Brugg, 1998), pit 3 of the 'Feuerwehrmagazin', FK 526, pp. 102–104. Detailed publication of the textiles in prep.

4 Ch. Ebnöther, *Der römische Gutshof in Dietikon* (Zürich/Egg, 1996), 120f.

5 A. Rast-Eicher, *Beiträge zum römischen Oberwinterthur – Vitudurum 5, Gewebe*, Beriche der Zürcher Denkmalpflege, Archäologische Monografien 10 (Zürich, 1991), p. 41. Textile: 6/Z/0.5–1.0 × 6/Z/0.5–1.0 per cm.

6 I should like to thank Michel Fuchs for the information. Avenches: No. 70/7865/1, Insula 10 East, room 15, excavated 1970. Further examples can be reported from France, from a painting in a bath: A. Barbet, *La peinture Romaine du peintre au restauranteur*, (Saint-Savin 1997), fig. 5

7 Wild 1970 *op. cit.*, table B, no. 37; plate VIIa.

8 Bender Jørgensen 1992, *op. cit.*, fig. 157.

9 A. Rast-Eicher, Les restes de textile, in: J. C. Moret and P. Taillard, Sion: Mystère autour d'une sépulture féminine, *Archäologie der Schweiz* 1 (2000). I should like to thank F. Wiblé (Office des recherches archéologiques) and the colleagues from the Bureau ARIA and Bureau TERA (Sion) for information concerning the grave finds from Valais.

10 J. P. Wild, 'Clothing in the North-West Provinces of the Roman Empire', *Bonner Jahrbücher*168 (1968), pp. 166–240.

11 A Rast-Eicher, 'Keltische Textilien der Schweiz', in L. Bender Jørgensen and C. Rinaldo (eds), *Textiles in European Archaeology*, report from the 6th NESAT Symposium, 7–11th May 1996 in Borås, Gotarc Series A, volume 1 (Göteborg, 1998), pp. 45–52.

12 Bender Jørgensen *op. cit.*, p. 124.

13 Bender Jørgensen 1992, *op. cit.* p. 133f.

14 F. Wiblé, 'Martigny/Forum Claudii Vallensium', in: Kantonales Museum für Archäologie (eds), *Vallis Poenina, Das Wallis in römischer Zeit, 1. Jh.-5. Jh. nach Christus*, Sitten, 1998, 166–174, with further literature.

15 A. Rast-Eicher, 'Kleine Fragmente – kleine Fundgruben', *Archaeological Textiles Newsletter* 28 (1999), p. 21.

16 F. Wible, 'Ein Mausoleum in Plan Conthey', in: Kantonales Museum für Archäologie (eds), *Vallis Poenina, Das Wallis in römischer Zeit, 1. Jh.-5. Jh. nach Christus*, Sitten, 1998, p. 185f.

17 J. P. Wild, 'Ein römischer Seidenstoff aus dem Wallis. Vallis Poenina an der antiken Seidenstrasse?' *Helvetia archaeologica* 18/70 (1987), pp. 59–73.

18 O. Paccolat, 'Le village gallo-romain de Brig-Glis/Waldmatte', *Archäologie der Schweiz* 20 (1997/1), pp. 25 –36.

19 C. Olive, 'Tradition und Wandel in der Walliser Viehwirtschaft', in: Kantonales Museum für Archäologie (eds), *Vallis Poenina, Das Wallis in römischer Zeit, 1. Jh.-5. Jh. nach Christus*, Sitten (1998), p. 91.

20 E. Ettlinger, *Die römischen Fibeln der Schweiz* (Bern, 1973), p. 46f.

21 The coins are published in: Suzanne Frey-Kupper/Oliver Frédéric Debuis (eds), *Inventaire des trouvailles monétaires Suisses* 1 (ITMS 1) (Lausanne, 1993), 140f., plate 25.

22 Total measurements 141; range 8.8–47.3μ; mean 21.6μ; standard deviation 6.6; medullas 7%; pigmentation not visible by SEM.

23 Rast-Eicher 1998, *op. cit.*

24 Paccolat 1997, op. cit. fig. 15; ITMS 1999, op. cit., 143.

25 Textile 3x1 cm, 2/2 twill, yarn Z-spun, 0.5 mm, in both directions.

26 S. Martin-Kilcher, 'Römische Grabfunde als Quelle zur Trachtgeschichte im zirkumalpinen Raum', in M. Struck (ed.), *Römerzeitliche Gräber als Quellen zu Religion, Bevölkerungsstruktur und Sozialgeschichte*, Internationale Fachkonferenz vom 18–20 February 1991 im Institut für Vor- und Frühgeschichte der Johannes Gutenberg-Universität Mainz (Mainz 1993), pp. 181–203.

27 M. Martin, 'Tradition und Wandel der fibelgeschmückten frühmittelalterlichen Frauenkleidung', *Jahrbuch des Römisch-Germanischen Zentralmuseums (JbRGZM)* 38 (1991/2), pp. 629–680.

28 E. Ettlinger, *Die Römischen Fibeln der Schweiz* (Bern, 1973); S. Martin-Kilcher, *op. cit.*

Chapter 11

BEYOND THE EMPIRE: AN IRISH MANTLE AND CLOAK

Elizabeth Wincott Heckett

Introduction

The two garments discussed here have recently been dated for the first time by the carbon-14 method, to the second to fourth centuries AD.[1] This sets them firmly into the period of the Roman Iron Age, from a find-spot outside the Roman provinces and within the area of traditional Celtic influence. The garments are a wool mantle and a leather cloak from Baronstown West, County Kildare, and they are at present the only pieces of clothing known in Ireland from the period. They seem to represent two different kinds of outer wear, the mantle being square or rectangular, and the cloak semi-circular. The Baronstown wool textile may be an all-purpose garment used as needed, as mantle, blanket, tunic/dress or shroud. It is a happy accident that much of the source material for setting these garments into context was written by John Peter Wild, and so it is a particular pleasure for the present author to offer this paper as her contribution to his *Festschrift*.

Technical details of the garments

The body of a man, twenty-five to thirty years old, was found in Clongownagh Bog, Baronstown West, County Kildare in 1953.[2] The remains are now about 1.35 metres in height, reaching from the shoulders to the extended feet. He appeared to have been wrapped in an inner covering of a wool textile[3] and an outer one of leather. Parts of the wool cloth protruded from under the left and right sides of the body and passed below it. It covered the upper part of the body and extended to the feet, being wrapped around the left foot and as far as the instep of the right. During the excavation of the body, the wool and leather garments were considerably damaged, and some pieces lost. The original description of the find records that the textile on the body seemed to consist of 'two main pieces' which overlapped and were held in place along the back of the body with small wooden pegs or twigs.[4] At least one wooden pin survives.

The leather garment, though more difficult to distinguish at the time, is described as covering the arms, body and legs, and also lying beneath it. It is clear from these remarks that both pieces were of considerable size and represent large garments. The leather cloak as reassembled measures approximately 1.75 m along the upper edge, and 1.10 m at the bottom of the rounded lower edge. It is of interest that the early Irish word for shroud is *geimnen* which is related to *gemen* or 'hide.' This usage dates to AD 668, when the Annals of Ulster record that a local prince 'was taken in his shroud to Daire (Derry).[5]

The wool mantle

The wool cloth of the mantle is 2/2 chevron twill, woven with a warp which is tight Z spin, diameter *c.* 1mm, 6–7 threads per cm; and a weft which is medium Z spin, *c.* 1.85 mm, 6 threads per cm; the thickness of the cloth is 1.4 mm, and it is two-tone in colour. The textile was well spun from combed wool and well woven, and must have been worn before its final use, since it was both darned and pieced together. Fourteen pieces remain, of which the two largest are (1) 435 mm, with a fringe 70–80 mm long, × 1160 mm; and (2) 390 mm, with a fringe 45 mm long, × 1100 mm. Pieces (1) and (2) are the 'two main pieces' described earlier. The fringe on (1) is an extension of the weft system, the fringe on (2) an extension of the warp. A roughly triangular piece, (3), measures 120 mm × 90 mm and is folded over, with wool stitching defining the fold.[6]

The weave is regular and balanced, with considerably thinner warp ends, which are more tightly spun than the weft picks. Part of piece (1) is composed of two layers of cloth, the larger overlaid on the smaller and sewn into place with Z-spun wool thread *c.* 2 mm diameter, of a darker colour than the weave yarn. The edges of both pieces have been turned under so that no raw edges are showing. Piece (2) is darned with thicker wool (Z medium spun, diameter 1.97–2.85 mm).

The edges of pieces (1) and (2) represent respectively one selvedge and one starting/finishing border, which overlapped on the body. This must mean they were contiguous in the original loompiece (Fig. 11.1). It then follows that the cloth was folded around the body in a cone (Fig. 11.2) leaving one corner lying above the head, until it was folded downwards. It may be deduced that piece (3) was part of this area of the textile (Fig. 11.1). It seems the fold was sewn down to be used by a living person, and not solely as a shroud. For that, simply making a fold would have sufficed.

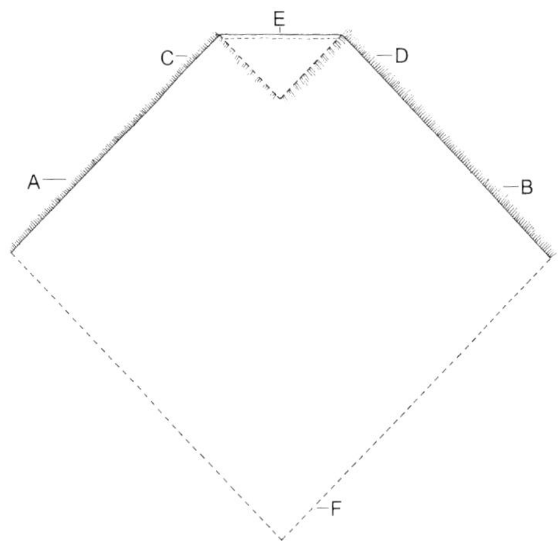

Fig. 11.1 Diagram of the wool mantle/cloak from Baronstown. A–C = fringe of warp ends, c.45 mm deep; B–D = fringe of weft threads, 70–80 mm deep; E = stitched fold; F = reconstructed areas of cloth.

Although in death the cloth was pinned at the back of the corpse, in life it would, of course, be turned to the front or side. This is a practical way to wear a square or rectangular textile as a cloak, since pinning the two contiguous sides together, and folding down the top corner make for a more generous wrap-around. The remaining corner hangs down at the back or side, giving considerable coverage. The cloth is worn on the bias which affords more stretch and comfort. The arms take up a goodly amount of the cloth so the long 'tail' is somewhat shortened (Fig. 11.3). This shape is seen on a mounted horseman at the back of a Pictish stone at Meigle, Perthshire,[7] and on female cloaked figures in soumak tapestries from the early ninth century Oseberg ship burial.[8]

There is an interesting parallel for the Baronstown find in the burial of a woman at Borremose, Denmark, which has recently been carbon-14 dated to 2380±100 BP.[9] She was wrapped in a wool blanket, transverse edges 1.17 m and 1.21 m, with lengthways selvedges 1.77 m and 1.83 m.[10] The cloth was 2/2 twill, S/S spun, warp 5/6, weft 4/5 threads per centimetre, with looped fringes on the transverse edges. It was folded crosswise with a flap approximately 0.8 m deep, over an underlying piece of 1.0 m. In two groups of holes near the folded edge were 'traces left by something which fastened the blanket round the deceased', perhaps thongs.

John Peter Wild discussed northern European cloaks in the paper given at the second North European Symposium on Archaeological Textiles.[11] Seventeen rectangular wool cloaks found in Free Germany were of larger dimensions and

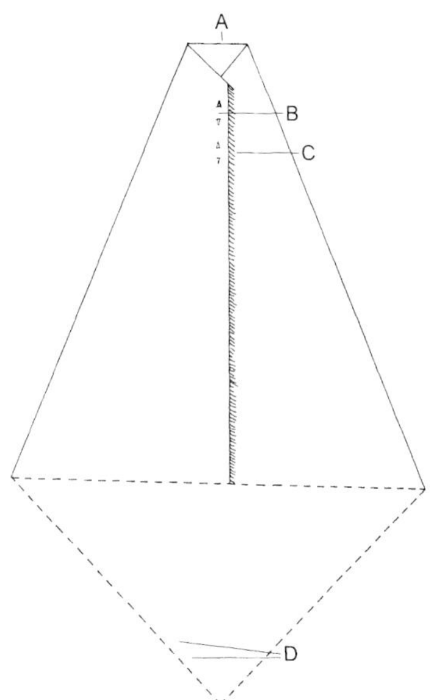

Fig. 11.2 Diagram of the mantle/cloak from Baronstown when worn. A = stitched fold (E of Fig. 11.1); B = wooden pins; C= warp fringe; D = reconstructed areas of cloth.

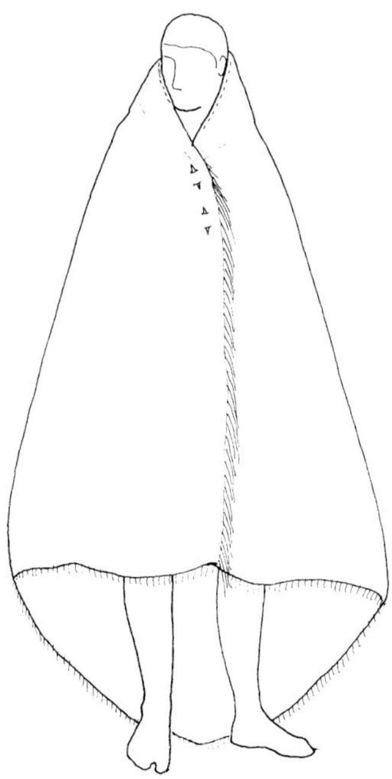

Fig. 11.3 How the Baronstown mantle may have looked when worn.

grander type than the Baronstown cloth. An impressive feature was the wide tablet-woven decorative borders on at least two sides of the cloaks: these do not exist on the Irish piece. It seems inappropriate here to make a sharp distinction between a cloak/mantle, blanket, shroud, or indeed skirt/tunic, since the basic square or rectangular loompiece would be used as the occasion demanded. Certainly, in historic Ireland and Scotland the mantle was also used as blanket. It is well-known that the belted plaid was worn in Scotland at least from the seventeenth century. This was arranged so that part was folded and belted to form a skirt and another part thrown over the head and shoulders, so creating the one-piece kilt and shawl which later divided into two separate items of dress. Again, the cloth was used as a blanket.[12] A French traveller in Ireland in 1644 commented that Irish women in the North 'have for dress a rug doubled and belted round the body and fastened to their neck.'[13] This may reflect an interesting survival of much earlier types of dress. The use of small wooden pins on the Baronstown mantle also has Scottish parallels. Martin Martin's account of the *Western Islands,* 1703, included the following: 'When they Travel on Foot, the *Plaid* is tied on the breast with a Bodkin of Bone or Wood, (just as the *Spina* wore by the *Germans*, according to the description of *C. Tacitus*).'[14]

The leather cloak

The leather cloak has overall dimensions of approximately 1.75 m × 1.10 m and is made in three segments, being semi-circular with one larger central, and two smaller matching side sections (Fig. 11.4). The former is composed of several pieces whose edges were pinched together from the underside, and top-stitched. Some small, regular stitches of excellent quality, using two S-plied fine strands of gut, have survived. The cloak is illustrated from the outer sides of the hides, which still retain hair.

The garment seemingly was worn with the long straight edge placed around the neck, so that two equal lengths fell down in front; these were then overlapped in a cone shape (Fig. 11.5a–b). In five places twin holes have been made, through which ties could be threaded. A small square area beneath each of the double holes was reinforced with stitching and perhaps an extra layer of skin. Further back at the bottom edge of the garment, remains of gut thread are knotted on to the leather.

The overlapping edges protected the wearer from bad weather, and the grouping of the three fastening

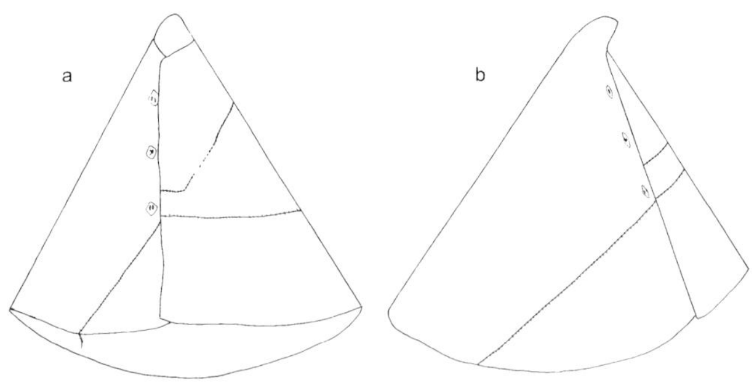

Fig. 11.5 Leather cloak from Baronstown viewed from (a) front and (b) side.

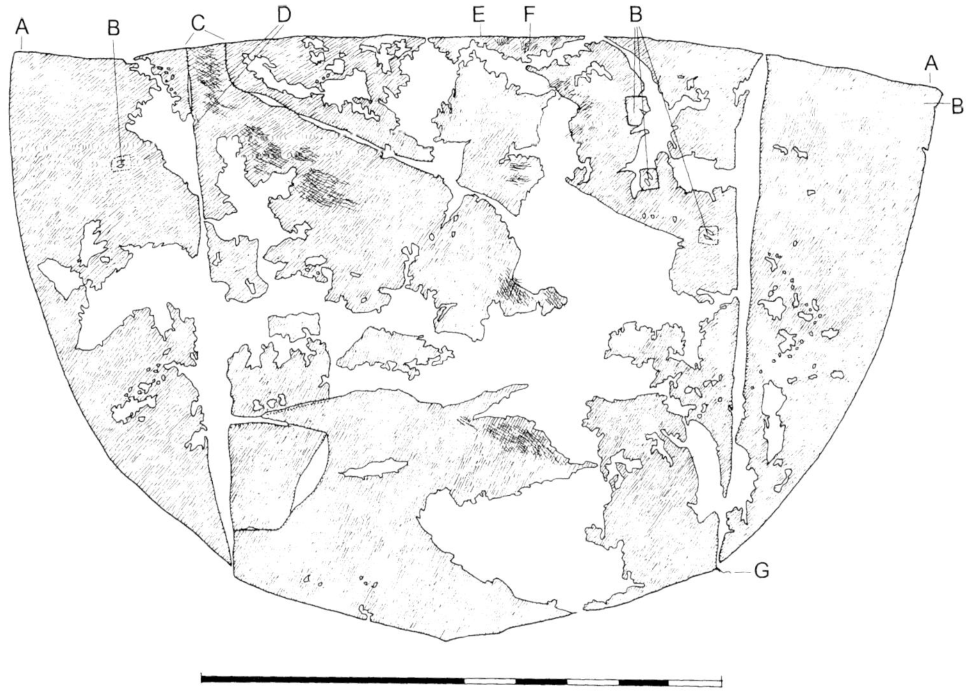

Fig. 11.4 Reconstruction of the leather cloak from Baronstown. A = bottom front; B = reinforced tie-spot; C = 2 S-plied gut stitching; D = piece inserted to form fold for neck/head; E = point to be centred at back of head; F = hairs on hide; G = remains of gut thread.

spots ensured that the overlap was well to one side of the body so the cloak would not blow open. The fourth, at the base of the cloak would also have secured the opening. The fifth, on the other side front, is more enigmatic since it is difficult to say how it was used. The cloak length of about 1.10 m would perhaps reach the knees or mid-calf; it could equally be worn pulled over the head (Fig. 11.6).

This garment brings to mind the hooded cloaks of the *genii cucullati* from Housesteads, Northumberland,[15] and Cirencester, Gloucestershire,[16] discussed by Gabra-Sanders in relation to the Orkney hood (this volume, pp. 98–104). A cloak without a hood is carved on a wooden figure from the Gallo-Roman sanctuary of Sequana.[17] The Middle Bronze Age male bog burial from Emmer-Erfscheidenveen, Netherlands, included a leather cloak more shaped, shorter and narrower than the Irish example.[18] There is a

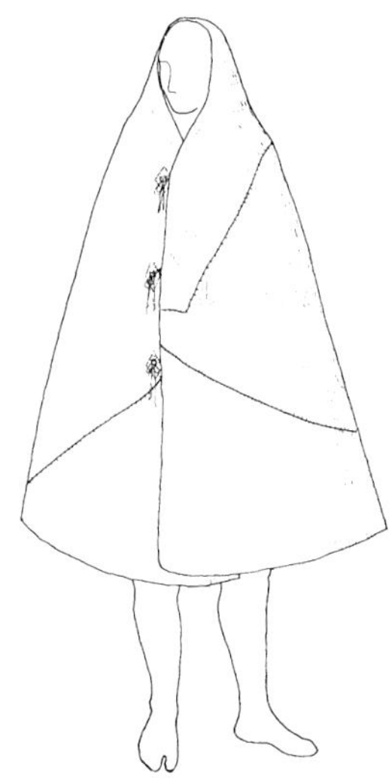

Fig. 11.6 How the leather cloak may have been worn.

wide range of skin capes from northern European Iron Age bog finds but these again are scantier and shorter; some were also fastened at the front with laces.[19] For example, Søgärds Mose man, who died about 2,000 years ago, was accompanied by three separate sheepskin capes.[20]

It must be noted that semi-circular garments can also be worn loosely around the shoulders. They are indeed the same basic shape as the Etruscan shawl[21] and Roman toga,[22] which look quite different because they are wrapped round the body.[23] It seems likely that the Baronstown cloak belongs in the family of leather or cloth garments known in the Roman world as *paenulae* or *casulae* (which later developed into the chasubles of the Christian church), and the *chlamys* or *paludamenti* worn by Roman officers.[24] John Peter Wild's discussion of the *byrrus* also referred to the leather *paenula* when quoting Martial's rhyme about the cloak 'which...will never let you down under a sudden shower of rain.' Also quoted is its proscription by Severus Alexander in Rome in the third century AD when only old men may wear it 'because of the cold', and both men and women on journeys 'since that sort of clothing has always been for journeys and wet weather.'[25] One can easily imagine that this type of leather cloak was highly necessary equipment for journeys in the Atlantic-influenced Irish climate. Just as Wild suggested the *byrrus* might have been a Gallic invention, so the *paenula* was perhaps current in northern and western Europe for many generations. It is pertinent here to recall the Danish Bronze Age coffin burials of *c.* 1200 BC, where the Muldbjerg and Trindhøj men wore semi-circular wool cloaks of somewhat larger dimensions.[26]

The title 'Beyond the Empire' echoes the notion of *Ultima Thule* and the remoteness of these outer isles. However, the movement of people, ideas and goods in the early centuries of the first millennium has been well documented so that it is not surprising that, even at the edges of the then known world, clothing should exist that is familiar in the wider European context.

Acknowledgments

I would like to thank Ragnall Ó Floinn and the National Museum of Ireland for allowing me to study the garments from Baronstown West, for permission to use the diagram of the leather cloak, and to draw upon unpublished material from the Museum's archives. I also wish to thank Rhoda Cronin for her illustrations.

Notes

1 A bone sample submitted for carbon 14-dating to the Archaeological Institute, Groningen, the Netherlands was dated to 1725±30BP (GrN-14758). A. L. Brindley and J. N. Lanting 'Irish bog bodies: the radiocarbon dates' in R. C. Turner and R. G. Scaife (eds.) *Bog Bodies – new discoveries and new perspectives* (London: British Museum Press, 1995). p. 134.

2 Máire Delaney, Ragnall Ó Floinn and Elizabeth Heckett, 'Bog body from Clongownagh,

Baronstown West, County Kildare, Ireland', in Bryony Coles, John Coles and Mogens Schou Jørgensen (eds), *Bog Bodies, Sacred Sites and Wetland Archaeology* (Exeter: Wetland Archaeology Research Project, 1999), pp. 67–68.
Ragnall Ó Floinn, 'A prehistoric bog burial at Baronstown West', *Journal of the County Kildare Archaeological Society and Surrounding Districts,* XVII (1987–1991) pp. 148–50.

3 In 1954 Dr. A. T. Lucas, then Director of the National Museum of Ireland sent Audrey Henshall a photograph of the textile which Dr. Henshall identified as good quality 2/2 herringbone (chevron) twill of slightly uneven stripes.

4 As described by Dr. Lucas in the account now held in the Museum's files.

5 Susan Leigh Fry, *Burial in Medieval Ireland 900–1500* (Dublin: Four Courts Press, 1999), p. 124.

6 Dimensions of other eleven pieces in millimetres: 4): 400 × 100, 5): 120 × 160, 6): 300 × 100, 7): 245 × 100, 8): 160 × 110, 9): 120 × 25, 10): 90 × 80, 11): 70 × 40, 12): 245 × 170, 13): 100 × 55, 14): 300 × 230.

7 Cecil L. Curle, 'The chronology of the Early Christian monuments of Scotland' *Proceedings of the Society of Antiquaries of Scotland*, vol. LXXIV (1939–40), plate XXXI.

8 The tapestries are held in the Viking Ships Museum, Oslo, Norway.

9 Wijnand van der Sanden, *Through nature to eternity – the bog bodies of northwest Europe* (Amsterdam: Batavian Lion International, 1996), p. 195.

10 Margrethe Hald, *Ancient Danish Textiles from Bogs and Burials* (Copenhagen: National Museum of Denmark, 1980) p. 20.

11 Lise Bender Jørgensen and John Peter Wild, 'Clothes from the Roman Empire – Romans and barbarians' in Lise Bender Jorgensen, Bente Magnus and Elisabeth Munksgaard eds, *Archaeological Textiles – NESAT 2* (Copenhagen: Arkaeologisk Institut, Kobenhavns Universitet, 1988), pp. 74–98.

12 H. F. McClintock, *Old Irish & Highland Dress* (Dundalk: Dundalgan Press, 1943), pp. 123–140.

13 Ibid., p. 74.

14 Ibid., p. 131.

15 Proinsias Mac Cana, *Celtic Mythology* (London: Chancellor Press, 1996), pp. 70–71.

16 Miranda Jane Green, *Celtic Myths* (London: British Museum Press, 1993), p. 11.

17 Susan Sievers, Radomir Pleiner, Natalie Venclova and Udo Geilenbrugge, 'L'artisanat' in Sabatino Mascato, Otto Hermann Frey, Venceslas Kruta, Barry Raftery and Miklos Szabo eds, *Les Celtes* (Milan: Bompiano, 1991). p. 437.

18 W. van der Sanden, pp. 152, 157, 162–3, in R. C. Turner and R. G. Scaife (eds), *Bog bodies – new discoveries and new perspectives* (London: British Museum Press, 1995). Margrethe Hald, *op. cit.*, pp. 313–322.

19 W. van der Sanden 1996, pp. 120–134.

20 W. van der Sanden 1996, p. 125.

21 Francois Boucher, *Histoire de Costume en Occident de l'Antiquite a nos jours'* (Paris: Flammarion, 1965), pp. 114, 119.

22 Hero Granger-Taylor, 'Weaving cloths to shape in the ancient world', *Textile History*, XIII, vol. 1, (1982), pp. 10–22.

23 Raymund James, *The Origin and Development of Roman Liturgical Vestments* (Exeter: Catholic Records Press, 1934), p. 6.

24 John Peter Wild, 'The *Byrrus Brittanicus*', *Antiquity*, XXXVII, (1963), pp. 193–202.

25 Wild, *op. cit.*, p. 194.

26 H. C. Broholm and M. Hald, *Costumes of the Bronze Age in Denmark* (Copenhagen: Nyt Nordisk Forlag, 1940), pp. 42, 60.

Chapter 12

THE ORKNEY HOOD, RE-DATED AND RE-CONSIDERED

Thea Gabra-Sanders

Introduction

A unique wool hood with shoulder cape, the Orkney Hood (Fig. 12.1), was dug up from a bog in St Andrew's Parish, Orkney, some time before 1867.[1] A. S. Henshall reported her findings on this hood in 'Early Textiles found in Scotland'[2] and M. L. Ryder identified the fleece types in the wool;[3] M. Findlay then published a report on its conservation.[4] The hood is made up of three separate woven pieces, the cloth of the hood itself, woven in 2/2 broken chevron (herringbone) twill with a paired weft (Fig. 12.2); a narrow tablet-woven band sewn along the bottom edge; and a broader tablet-woven band with a deep corded fringe sewn to the first tablet band (Fig. 12.3). The corded fringe is formed by an extended weft thread, a method similar to that used in the Danish Bronze Age corded skirts.[5] Another wool fabric with a fringe of knotted corded ends similar to the Orkney hood was found on a woman buried in peat at Haraldskjær Mose in Jutland, and recently re-dated to 450 BC.[6] Of interest is the resemblance of an undated fringed tablet-woven band in the Ulster Museum, Belfast,[7] to that on the Orkney hood. The technique used for these bands was in use from the Iron Age to the Viking Age, as was the chevron (herringbone) twill of the wool cloth.

Fig. 12.1 The Orkney Hood. Copyright: National Museums of Scotland.

Just below the shoulder level of the Orkney Hood is the broad tablet woven band, with at

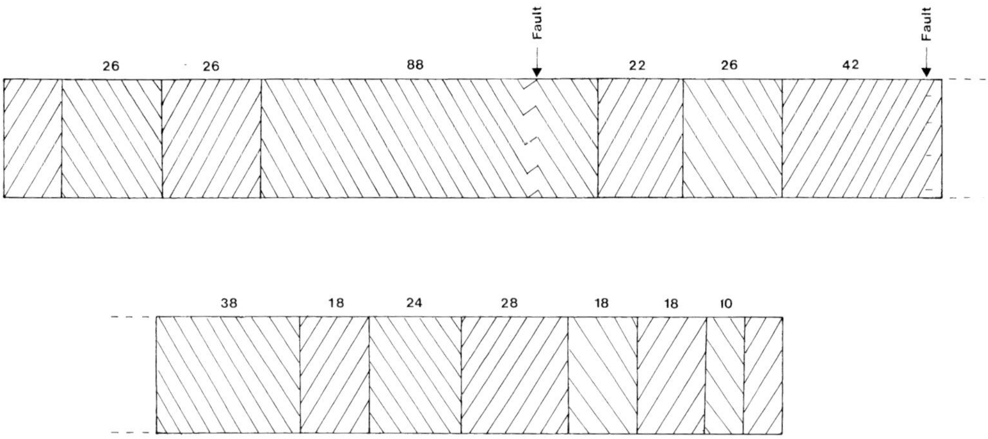

Fig. 12.2 A block diagram of the weave of the main cloth of the Orkney Hood (diagram by Penelope Walton Rogers, re-drawn by Rhoda Cronin). The weave is a 2/2 broken chevron (herringbone) twill with paired weft, yarn Z×Z+Z.

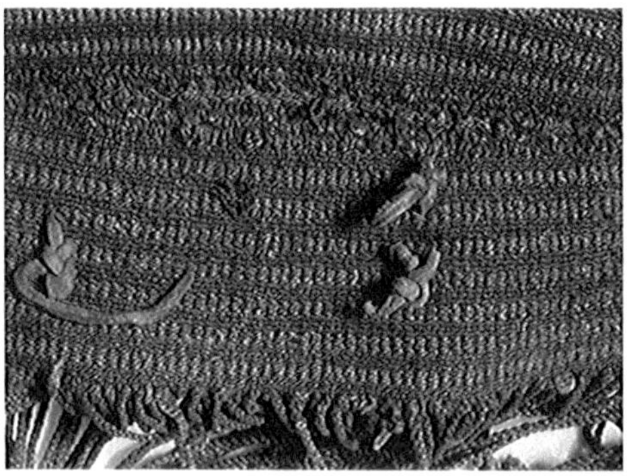

Fig. 12.3 Broad tablet-woven band showing the remains of the leather thongs and holes for the thongs. Copyright: National Museums of Scotland.

least eight pairs of holes, arranged more or less regularly on either side of the face opening. A few holes still contain leather thongs of which some are knotted (Fig. 12.3), but when the hood is hanging naturally these are concealed. It is not clear what they were used for, but they may have been either to fasten the hood to a cloak or dress or else for housing a draw-string.

In 1991, a wool sample from the Orkney hood was submitted to the Oxford University Radiocarbon Accelerator Unit, which produced a date of 1595±80 BP (OxA-3535), calibrated (to 2 sigma), which gives a calendar date of AD 250–615.[8] The closest parallel to the hood is a short hooded cape, which covers head and shoulders, from Krogens Mølle Mose, Denmark, made from fragments of brown sheepskin (the hair side inwards). Hald considered it to date from the early Iron Age, but it has now been carbon-14 dated to 80 BC.[9] Hooded capes were also widely worn in various other countries. An interesting example is the one from Russian Karelia where the hood continues into a cape, falling in a point reaching to the waist at the front and the back. Each point has a strap through which a belt passes to fasten the cape.[10] The Orkney Hood, however, is unique in many respects and its background and social milieu are as yet unknown. This paper is a brief overview of hoods which are known from other parts of Europe.

Celtic myth

There are various monuments in Britain with hooded deities, *genii cucullati*, 'hooded gods', which have associations with fertility and healing waters. These deities appear either singly or in triplets. A relief from Housesteads, on Hadrian's Wall in Northumberland, shows a trio of hooded deities, front facing, wearing heavy hooded cloaks. It is likely that these were made from wool. As Professor Piggott remarks: 'the high quality of British woollen cloaks attested by Diocletian's Edict of Prices a little earlier may owe something to the cloth industry in the north... Northerners knew the need of these things, and the three cloaked and hooded figures on the relief from the Housesteads *vicus* may in more ways than one be symbolical of the British herdsmen and the shepherds whose chariot driving ancestors, *pollentes nobilitate,* had counted their wealth in cattle and sheep'.[11] Another relief retrieved from a well at Lower Slaughter, Gloucestershire, shows a war god in his capacity as a healer standing beside three *genii cucullati*, suggesting a connection with healing.

Roman Gaul – sculptured reliefs

Cucullati are also known on the Continent and were very popular in the period of the Roman Empire. A small bronze statuette of a ploughman, in the Historical Museum in Trier, depicts a typical *cucullus*.[12] Reliefs carved on sarcophagi also show this type of garment. A sarcophagus at Déols (France) shows a hunting scene, where one of the hunters wears a *cucullus* with a braided border. The sarcophagus at Alliscamps Arles (France), shows another hunter wearing a *cucullus* which may be leather. These hoods were no doubt worn during the hunt to protect their owners from the weather or branches of trees. In the Archaeological Museum of Sens (France) is a fragment of a *stela* which has a representation of a shop selling *cuculli*. The shop-keeper has hung the *cuculli* like hams from the ceiling![13] Ancient Gaul was especially rich in sacred springs which had therapeutic powers. Wooden sculptures of humans, wearing hooded cloaks, have been recovered from the marshes at Source-de-la-Seine (source of the Seine) in a valley north-west of Dijon. This was one of the most important sites in the vicinity of the Gallo-Roman sanctuary of Sequana, the goddess of the source.[14]

The byrrus

Fig. 12.4 The Andrews Diptych, showing the miracle of the healing of the blind man, who is wearing a long, hooded cape; V & A, A47a-1926. Copyright: the Board of Trustees of the Victoria and Albert Museum.

According to written sources, the *byrrus* was a long, hooded, voluminous cape of heavy wool, or occasionally of skins, commonly worn outdoors in all kinds of weather (Fig. 12.4). It had a hood but was sleeveless.[15] Unfortunately there is only textual evidence for the existence of the *byrrus britannicus*. John Peter Wild quotes a papyrus letter from Terentianus, as the earliest known reference to the *byrrus*, in which Terentianus writes home with a request for various articles including a *byrrus*.[16] Wild continues with the association of the hooded *byrrus/paenula* with the law. Artemidorus of Ephesus is quoted as saying that under the Antonines' justice system, the accused was required to wear the *byrrus* when appearing in court to signify condemnation,[17] perhaps an antecedent of the black cap which British judges used to place on their head before pronouncing the death penalty.

It would appear that the hood played a considerable role in different areas of society, from Church dignitaries to jesters. In ecclesiastical life the hooded cope was worn in processions and at solemn ceremonies. The jesters on the other hand tended to attach bells to their hoods. There was another type of wool cape, the *paenula*, which was also very common in Italy, although the *byrrus* was more popular. Like the *byrrus*, the *paenula* was made as a half-circle and draped round the shoulders and neck.[18] It was tied with thongs inside high on the chest or by clasps on the outside, with the hood sewn on separately. Like the *byrrus*, this garment could be worn outside other garments, which was not very satisfactory, due to the method of fastening at the top in the front.

The Picts

The Picts were first recorded by the name *Picti* or Painted People in a Latin poem in AD 297. They were native people who lived in Scotland north of the Forth/Clyde valley for nearly six hundred years. They are best known for their carved stone monuments, the earliest dating from the mid-sixth century. A large cross-slab from St Madoe's on display in Perth Museum, depicts on one side (the reverse) three hooded horsemen each wearing a *cucullus*. This garment also appears on Pictish stone carvings with a religious theme, as on the reverse of St Vigean's cross slab, where two monks are wearing decorated vestments under their copes/cloaks. There is a little figure below the enthroned monks wearing a hooded cloak and short trousers.[19] A free-standing cross of a purely Irish type, at Papil, Shetland, represents the temptation of St Anthony by women disguised as birds, who whisper in his ear. Above the lion are two hooded monks with staffs facing each other.[20]

Buried Norsemen at Herjolfsnes, Greenland

Around AD 1300, Herjolfsnes in Greenland was a settlement of people descended from the Norse. Due to erosion by the sea it became necessary to exhume the cemetery at Herjolfsnes and in 1921, 110–120 burials were excavated by the Danish archaeologist Poul Nørlund.[21] Clothing for men, women and children, including seventeen hoods, was recovered. One of the garments for a male has been carbon-14 dated to AD 1350. The hoods were made to pull over the head and fitted closely around the neck, and have either a short cape or a longer one falling over the shoulders. These hoods differ from the earlier ones, as they have a liripipe at the back which could vary in length and width. In 1936, a body of a man was discovered in a peat bog at Bocksten, Sweden. The Bocksten Man was wearing a complete costume including a hood with a liripipe, dated to the early fourteenth century, which closely resembles the Greenland hoods.[22]

Fig. 12.5 Fresco, AD 1437, in the cathedral of Notre-Dame-de-Valère in Sion, Valais, Switzerland, showing Count Guillaume III (kneeling) wearing a hood with a shoulder cape made of fur. Copyright: Thea Gabra-Sanders.

Summary

Hoods with big shoulder capes have been known in Europe from Roman times. They could be made of various materials (Fig. 12.5) and could be lined with silk or fur. The hood, popular among the peasantry during the twelfth century, was by the end of the thirteenth century taken over by the gentry. The reason for this was an extension to the back of the hood called the liripipe, which made the hood fashionable. With the passage of time the liripipe became ever longer and in 1337 The Synod of Cologne banned the clergy from wearing hoods with liripipes of exaggerated length.

Hoods have shown themselves to be a very useful item of clothing and we should perhaps not be surprised that we have evidence for them from prehistoric times right up the present day.

Acknowledgements

I am grateful to Dr D. H. Caldwell for reading the draft of this paper. My thanks are due to Marjory Findlay, to Sarah Foskett for providing information on the Hood; to the Board of Trustees of the Victoria & Albert Museum and the Trustees of the National Museums of Scotland for providing photographs; and to Textile Research in Archaeology, York, for the weave diagram, Fig. 12.2.

Notes

1 J. Anderson, 'Notes on the contents of two Viking graves in Islay, discovered by William Campbell, Esq., Ballinaby; with notes of the burial customs of the Norse sea-kings, as recorded in the sagas and illustrated by their grave-mounds in Norway and in Scotland', in *Proceedings of the Society of Antiquaries of Scotland*, (1879), no. 14, pp. 51–89, NMS cat no.NA 3, pp. 51–89. J. Anderson, *Scotland in Pagan Times: The Iron Age* (Edinburgh, 1883), p. 103.

2 A. S. Henshall, Early textiles found in Scotland: Part 1 – Locally made, in *Proceedings of the Society of Antiquaries of Scotland*, (1951–2), no. 86, pp. 1–29.

3 M. L. Ryder, 'The Evolution of Scottish Breeds of Sheep', *Scot. Studies* (1968), 12, 139.

4 M. Findlay, 'Report on the conservation of the Orkney Hood', in *The Laboratories of the National Museum of Antiquity of Scotland*, no date, volume 2, pp. 95–102.

5 H. C. Broholm, *Bronzealderens Dragt*, (Nationalmuseet, Copenhagen, 1961), p. 62.

6 J. Anderson, *op. cit.*, (1879), pp. 80–81. For the C14 date of the Haraldskjær burial, see Wijnand van der Sanden, *Through Nature to Eternity – the Bog Bodies of North-West Europe* (Amsterdam: Batavian Lion International, 1996), pp. 194–5.

7 Accession no. A 34. 1911, Ulster Museum, Belfast. The band was found in 1893 between Moyarget and Ballintoy, Co. Antrim.

8 R. E. M. Hedges, R. A. Housley, C. Bronk-Ramsey and G. J. van Klinken, Radiocarbon dates from the Oxford AMS system: Archaeometry datelist 16. *Archaeometry*, (1993), 35, pp. 147–167.
T. Gabra-Sanders, 'An Update on the Orkney Hood', in *Archaeological Newsletter* (1997), 24, pp. 19–20.

9 Margrethe Hald, *Ancient Danish Textiles from Bogs and Burials* (Copenhagen: National Museum of Denmark, 1980) pp. 320. E. Munksgaard, *Oldtidsdragter* (1975), 127

10 U. T. Sirelius, 'Über einige Traggeräte und Umslagetücher bei den finnish-urrischen Vökern' *Finska fornminnesföreningens Tidskrift*, XXVI (1916), fig. 40.

11 S. Piggott, 'Native economies and the Roman occupation of North Britain', in Richmond (ed), *Roman and Native in North Britain* (1958) pp. 1–27, Edinburgh.

12 G. Roche-Bernard et A. Ferdiere, *Costumes et Textiles en Gaule Romaine* (Paris, Editions Errance, 1993) 35–36, 139.

13 Lloyd and Jennifer Laing, *Art of The Celts* (London: Thames and Hudson, 1996) p. 83, fig. 74.

[14] J. P. Wild, 'The Byrrus Britannicus', *Antiquity*, XXXVII (1963), p. 200.

[15] Ibid., p. 193.

[16] H. C. Youtie and J. G. Winter, 'Papyri and Ostraca from Karanis', *Michigan Papyri*, VIII, 1951, no. 467, 18ff.

[17] Artemidorus, *Oneirocritica*, II, 3.

[18] L. M. Wilson, *The clothing of the ancient Romans* (Baltimore, 1938), 87ff.

[19] E. Sutherland, *In Search of The Picts* (London: Constable, 1996), p. 90.

[20] C. L. Curle, 'The chronology of the early Christian Monuments of Scotland' *Proceedings of the Society of Scotland*, 1939–40, no. 84, pp. 60–115.

[21] P. Nørland, *Buried Norsemen at Herjolfsnes* (Copenhagen, 1924), pp. 151–173.

[22] M. Nockert, *Bockstenmannen och hans dräkt* (Hallands Ländsmuseer, Museet i Varberg, Borås, Sweden, 1997), p. 149.

Chapter 13

RECENT TEXTILE FINDS OF THE ROMAN PERIOD IN POLAND

Jerzy Maik

Introduction

To trace the beginnings of the study of archaeological textiles in Poland, one has to go back to the time of extensive excavations connected with preparations for the celebrations marking the one thousand years anniversary of the founding of the Polish State – or more exactly the Christianisation of the country – in 1966. It was then that the first studies of textiles discovered during excavations in Gdańsk, Opole and Wolin were published.[1] Prehistoric textiles were known mainly from impressions found on clay, but a few original textile finds dating back to the beginning of the Iron Age came from Lusatian Culture inhumations in Silesia and further textiles were found in Roman period cemeteries in Silesia and Pomerania. Such fabrics were discovered by German archaeologists as early as the 1930s, but we are only familiar with them from studies published by G. Sage and W. von Stokar, as the finds were lost during the war.[2]

Other textile finds dating from the Roman period come from the cemeteries at Węsiory and Kościelna Jania and have been published by A. Nahlik.[3] In the 1960s the present author was asked to examine textiles found during the excavation of a large burial site in Odry, Pomerania, and this research was subsequently published in an article on archaeological textiles of the Roman period on Polish territory.[4] This led to further work on the textiles discovered in burial sites in Gronowo[5] and Leśno,[6] Pomerania, and the current state of knowledge of Roman period textiles was then summarised in a book on textiles in Pomerania.[7] Further information concerning fabrics of the Roman period in Poland can also be found in L. Bender Jørgensen's publication on textiles from Northern Europe.[8]

Since then, a number of Roman period cemeteries, situated mainly in Pomerania, have been excavated and about 150 further pieces of textile have been found. All of these have now been examined, but not yet published. The present article is an attempt to answer questions concerning the significance of this recent work, namely whether they support previous theories and reinforce our knowledge of Roman period textiles, or alter our view. The latest fabrics come from burial grounds in Babi Dół-Borcz and Kamienica Szlachecka, Gdańsk province, Grzybnica, Nowy Łowicz and Szczypkowice, Szczecin province, Wyszembork, Olsztyn province,

Jartypory, Warsaw province, Masłomęcz and Gródek Nadbużny, Lublin province, Zawada, Kielce province and Zawieścice, Wrocław province (Fig. 13.1). Nearly all of the textiles come from inhumation graves, where they have survived because of their association with metal elements in the costume.

The Cemeteries and textiles

1. Babi Dół-Borcz, Gdańsk province, a Wielbark culture cemetery

Some pieces of cloth were found in a grave dated to the early Roman period (phase B2, according to Eggers' chronology). They were fragments of two wool textiles woven in 2/2 twill. One of them was made with yarn spun Z × S (ZS), the other Z × Z (ZZ).

2. Gródek Nadbużny, a Masłomęcz group cemetery

Two fragments, probably of the same linen textile, woven in 1/1 tabby with ZZ spin and three fragments of completely mineralized remains also woven in ZZ tabby, in

Fig. 13.1 Map of sites: 1. Babi Dół-Borcz, 2. Gródek Nadbużny, 3. Grzybnica, 4. Jartypory, 5. Kamienica Szlachecka, 6. Masłomęcz, 7. Nowy Łowicz, 8. Szczypkowice, 9. Wyszembork, 10. Zawada, 11. Zawieścice (drawn by E. Etorkiewicz-Marosik).

a very poor state of preservation, were found in a later Roman period grave (phase C2).

3. *Grzybnica, Szczecin province, a Wielbark culture cemetery*

Some wool textiles were found in four graves dating from the early Roman period (phase B2); in three graves dating to the close of the early Roman period or the beginning of the later Roman period (phase B2/C1); and in one grave of the later Roman period (phase C1) and a grave of the late Roman period (phase C2).

Of the eleven early Roman textiles found on the site, eight fragments are woven in 2/2 twill with ZS spin. Tablet-woven edges have survived on two pieces, one a starting border and the other a selvedge. The rest of the textiles (three pieces) are also woven in 2/2 twill, but they are made with ZZ spin. Four fragments woven in 2/2 twill with ZS spin and two similar pieces with ZZ spin date to the close of the early or the beginning of the later Roman period. One textile woven in 2/2 twill with ZS spin can be dated to the later Roman period and has a surviving tablet-woven selvedge. Finally, one piece of cloth woven in 2/2 twill with ZS spin dates from the late Roman period. This is the latest Roman period textile known to me from Polish territory.

4. *Jartypory, Warsaw province, a Wielbark culture cemetery*

A piece of carbonized textile and an impression of another on coal have survived in a cremation urn dated to the later Roman period (phase C1). Both the fabrics are woven in 1/1 tabby with ZZ spin.

5. *Kamienica Szlachecka, Gdańsk province, a Wielbark culture cemetery*

The earliest textiles from this burial site were found in 15 graves dated to the end of the early Roman period (phase B2/C1). The other fabrics come from nine graves dated to the later Roman period (phases C1 and C2). Only one phase C1 textile is made of flax, the rest are bits of wool cloth.

Four textiles of phase B2/C1 are tabbies. One of them is made with ZZ spin, another with ZS spin, and the rest have stripes of Z and S yarn in the warp or the weft, which results in a light-reflecting pattern of stripes ('spin-patterning'). The textile made from ZS yarn has a starting border in repp weave. The other textiles dating from this phase are fabrics woven in 2/2 twill or 2/2 diamond twill (one example). Five textiles woven in 2/2 twill are made with ZZ spin, six fabrics with ZS spin and three have Z and S stripes in both warp and weft, giving spin-patterned checks.

The textiles which are dated to the later Roman period (phase C1–C2) are also woven in 1/1 tabby or 2/2 twill. Of the three fragments of tabby, one was so poorly preserved that it was impossible to establish the yarn twist, but the second piece has ZZ spin and the third one has both Z and S yarns in the warp and the weft, giving a spin-patterned check. Among the fabrics made in 2/2 twill, two fragments have ZZ spin, eight pieces have ZS spin and two fragments have spin-patterned checks. One of the textiles of the later Roman period is woven in 2/2 diamond twill with ZS spin (the repeat is 20Z × 22S). There is also a piece of linen textile, a 1/1 tabby with ZZ spin.

6. Masłomęcz, Lublin province, a Masłomęcz group cemetery

Some small pieces of completely mineralized 1/1 tabby weave with ZS spin were found in a grave dated to the later Roman period (phase C2).

7. Nowy Łowicz, Szczecin province, a Wielbark culture cemetery

The wool textiles from this burial ground were found in eight graves dated to the close of the early or the beginning of the later Roman periods (phases B2/C1 and B2/C); one grave was from the later Roman period (phase C1); and one grave was only broadly dated to the Roman period.

One textile dating from the turn of the early Roman period is a 1/1 tabby with ZZ spin. The rest are woven in 2/2 twill or 2/2 diamond twill. Only three textiles in 2/2 twill are made with ZZ spin, the rest (23 fragments) being ZS spin-patterned checks. The borders and selvedges of some textiles have survived, all of them, except for one border from a sack, being made by tablet-weaving. Two textiles from this phase are woven in 2/2 diamond twill with ZS yarn and a tablet-woven starting border and selvedge have survived on one of these. One textile, from a later Roman period grave, was woven in 2/2 twill and has spin-patterned checks.

8. Szczypkowice, Gdańsk province, a Wielbark culture cemetery

A piece of wool cloth woven in 2/2 twill with Z and S spin in warp and the weft (a spin-patterned check) was found in a grave dated to the early Roman period (phase B2).

9. Wyszembork, Olsztyn province, a west-Baltic culture cemetery

A piece of completely mineralized textile woven in 2/2 twill weave with ZZ spin has survived on an iron object in a grave broadly dated to the Roman period.

10. Zawada, Kielce province, a Przeworsk culture cemetery

A mineralized fragment of textile was found on an iron buckle in an inhumation grave. The textile is a tabby made with ZS spin.

11. Zawieścice, Wrocław province, a Przeworsk culture cemetery

Some carbonized fragments of cloth woven in 1/1 tabby with ZZ spin were discovered in two cremation burials dated to the turn of the early Roman period (phase B2/C1) and the later Roman period (phase C1).

Conclusions

This survey shows that most of the more recent textile finds come from Wielbark culture cemeteries in Pomerania and in this respect the situation has not changed much since the earlier studies. This is probably the result of the practice of two different burial rites. In the Przeworsk culture, which was the other great culture of the Roman period within the area of present-day Poland, cremation was the dominant rite and consequently textile finds are scarce. Nevertheless, a few fabrics were recently found in cremation burials and although they were carbonized, they provide at least some information concerning the textiles of the Przeworsk culture. They are all woven in 1/1 tabby (Fig. 13.2), but the small number of finds and lack of information about the fibre they were made from makes it impossible for a researcher to draw any firm conclusions.

Fig. 13.2 Weaves of textiles: 1. tabby, 2. 2/2 twill, 3. 2/2 diamond twill (drawn by E. Etorkiewicz-Marosik).

As a result, we still know much more about the textiles of the Wielbark culture and the discovery of new samples did not bring about a fundamental change in the picture of those textiles. The fact that most of the fabrics are made in 2/2 twill or 2/2 diamond twill (Fig. 13.2) seems to suggest that the most popular weaving equipment was the loom with four heddle rods, or rather three heddle rods and one natural shed. This must have been a vertical warp-weighted loom, because the starting borders and selvedges were usually made with tablets. Plain 2/2 twill is typical of Roman period textiles and 2/2 diamond twill, characterized by repeats of various sizes, is also very popular. Fabrics of this type were found in Kamienica Szlachecka and Nowy Łowicz.

The starting border, by which the warp threads are suspended from the beam of a warp-weighted loom, was sometimes woven by simple band-weaving. This was the case with a 1/1 tabby-weave textile from Grave 62 in Kamienica Szlachecka, which had a border in repp weave (Fig. 13.3). Tablet-woven starting borders were, however, more

Fig. 13.3 Starting border of textile from Kamienica Szlachecka (drawn by E. Etorkiewicz-Marosik).

numerous. The number of tablets used for weaving the borders varies from textile to textile. For example, the border from Barrow 33, Grave 1, in Nowy Łowicz was made with seven tablets, and twelve were used to make the border found in Grave 62 at Kamienica Szlachecka (Fig. 13.4). The method employed to make the latter border was quite unusual. All the other borders known to me were made together with the warp so that the starting border was part of the product: the warp of such a textile is the weft of the starting band. In this case, however, the starting border was woven so as to be a separate ribbon and the warp was simply tied to it. Unfortunately, only the border and the warp loops of this fabric have survived, which renders a full reconstruction impossible. A similar border from Vrangstrup, Denmark, has been described by Lise Raeder Knudsen.[9]

While the textiles discussed here were being examined, it became clear that the selvedge was a different type of edge. In textiles dating from the Roman period the cloth edges were often strengthened or were the decorative part of the fabric. To strengthen the cloth edge, a hollow selvedge was woven, as in the textiles from Grave 43 at Babi Dół-Borcz and Barrow 3, Grave 2 at Nowy Łowicz. The selvedge of the fabric from Nowy Łowicz was woven round a cord which was 2 mm thick, a technique which was probably intended to give additional strength to the border. Decorative edges, by contrast, were made with tablets hung on the outermost warp threads, sometimes using several dozen tablets. It seems that selvedges of this type were part of textiles intended to be worn whole, for instance, as ornamental cloaks. The selvedge of the textile found in Barrow 58, Grave 2, however, was atypical (Fig. 13.5). Its weft turns back as usual and encircles the outermost thread of the warp. Then it runs the width of the selvedge again and is cut off at its inner edge. This piece of cloth might be a starting border or a closing border. However, a greater density of threads running across

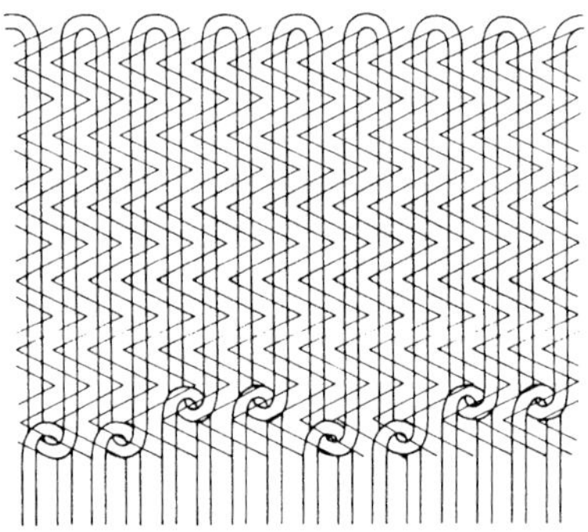

Fig. 13.4 Starting border of textile from Kamienica Szlachecka (drawn by E. Etorkiewicz-Marosik).

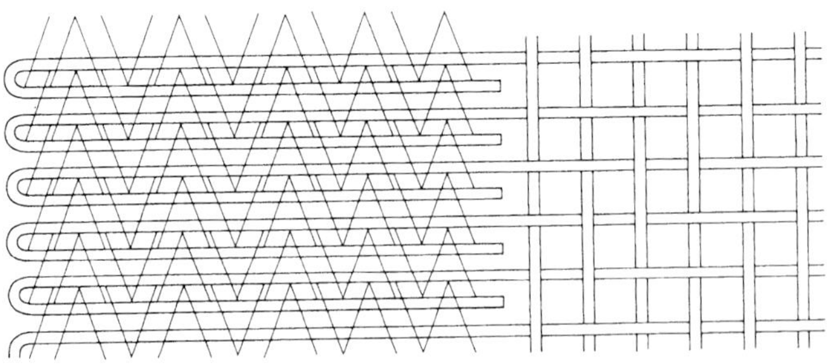

Fig. 13.5 Selvedge of textile from Nowy Lowicz (drawn by E. Etorkiewicz-Marosik).

the edge (20 threads per cm) than alongside the edge (16 threads per cm) suggests that this is a selvedge.

This border is on a textile woven in 2/2 twill and has Z and S yarns in both warp and weft (spin-patterned checks), in the following sequence: 2S-2Z-3S-1Z-3S-1Z-14S in the warp and 8Z-34S-5Z-3S in the weft. The use of this method resulted in a check which appeared differently as it caught the light. In my opinion this textile is a remnant of an ornamental cloak. The textile discovered in Barrow 33, Grave 1, in Nowy Łowicz may have also been part of such a cloak. The latter example was woven in 2/2 diamond twill and had a starting border worked on at least 25 tablets.

The textiles found in inhumation graves can hardly ever serve as a basis for the full reconstruction of garments. Only tiny fragments of cloth are found in association with metal objects and then only rarely. In some cases, however, two or three different textiles may be discovered next to one object and in such a situation an attempt can be made to establish the kinds of garment the textiles belong to. The large number of textiles found in Barrow 55 at Nowy Łowicz made it possible tentatively to reconstruct the clothes of the person buried in the grave. The woman may have been dressed in a shift with sleeves and a sleeveless dress with shoulder-straps. She probably had an ornamental cloak, which was used as the winding-sheet (Fig. 13.6). Similar outfits are known from Roman period representations of Germanic people, such as those illustrated on the column of Marcus Aurelius. I once reconstructed a set of such clothes based on the finds from Odry and Gronowo.[10]

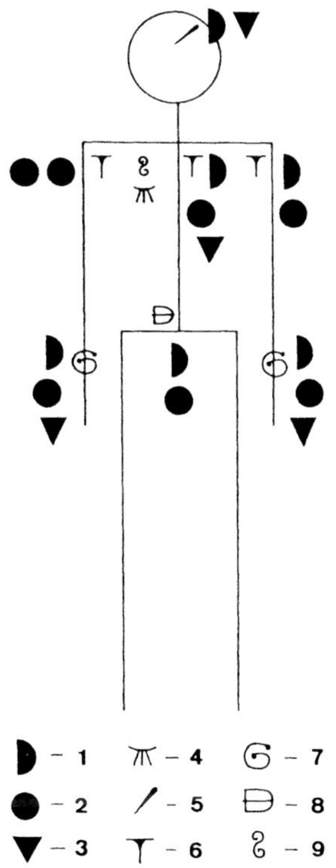

Fig. 13.6 Textiles in Barrow 55 in Nowy Łowicz: 1. shift, 2. dress, 3. cloak, 4. fringes, 5. needle, 6. fibula, 7. bracelet, 8. buckle, 9. S-shaped clasp (drawn by E. Etorkiewicz-Marosik).

The Roman period textiles of the most recent study and the textiles of the earlier work, together with other archaeological finds, such as loom weights and spindle whorls, will form the basis of a monograph on the textiles of this period, exclusively in the Wielbark culture. Such a study should show whether there were any changes in textiles in particular phases of the Roman period and should help to establish the character of those changes, since the previous picture was rather static. Using analyses of the wool fibre and comparative studies between samples from this territory and the Roman provinces, the monograph will also discuss the issue of textiles which may have been imported, mainly from the Roman Empire.[11] The present article may be regarded as an introduction to further, more comprehensive studies.

Translated by Zuzanna Poklewska-Parra

Notes

1 J. Kamińska, A. Nahlik, *Włókiennictwo gdańskie*, Łódź 1958, W. Hołowicz, *Opole w wiekach X–XII*, Katowice 1956, pp. 189–216, A. Nahlik, 'Tkaniny wykopaliskowe z wczesnośredniowiecznego Wolina', *Materiały Zachodnio-Pomorskie*, V (1959), pp. 257–276.

2 G. Sage, 'Gewebereste auf vorgeschichtlichen Eisengeräten in Schlesien', *Altschlesien*, IV (1932), pp. 69–82, G. Sage, 'Die Gewebereste aus Fürstengräbern von Sakrau' *Altschlesien*, V (1934), pp. 272–284, W. v. Stokar, *Die Gewebefunde von Luggewiese (Ein Beitrag zur germanischen Trachtenforschung*, manuscript in the National Museum in Szczecin.

3 A. Nahlik, 'Analiza tkanin', in J. Kmieciński, M. Blombergowa, K. Walenta, 'Cmentarzysko kurhanowe ze starszego okresu rzymskiego w Węsiorach, w pow. kartuskim, *Prace i Materiały Muzeum Archeologicznego i Etnograficznego w Łodzi*, Seria Archeologiczna, XII, 1966, pp. 114–115, A. Nahlik, *Analizy tkanin z Kościelnej Jani*, manuscript in the Archaeological Museum in Gdańsk.

4 J. Maik, 'Tkaniny wykopaliskowe z okresu rzymskiego z terenu Polski', *Pomorania Antiqua*, VII, 1977, pp. 77–145

5 Ibid.

6 T. Grabarczyk, J. Kmieciśski, J. Maik, K. Walenta, 'Période Romaine en Poméranie', *Inventaria Archaeologica*, Pologne, fasc. XLIII, (1979), pl. 27–272.

7 J. Maik, *Wyroby włókiennicze na Pomorzu z okresu rzymskiego i ze średniowiecza*, Wrocław-Warszawa-Kraków-Gdańsk-Łódź, 1988

8 L. Bender Jørgensen, *Forhistoriske textiler i Skandinavien (Prehistoric Scandinavian Textiles*, København 1986, pp. 333–334, L. Bender Jørgensen, *North European Textiles until AD 1000*, Aarhus 1992, pp. 86–90, 246–251.

9 Lise Raeder Knudsen, 'An Iron Age cloak with tablet-woven borders: a new interpretation of the method of production, *NESAT IV*, p. 83, fig. 5.

10 J. Maik, 'Zastosowanie tkanin w odzieży ludności kultury wielbarskiej', in *Problemy kultury wielbarskiej*, Słupsk 1981, pp. 217–233.

11 J. P. Wild, *Textile Manufacture in the Northern Roman Provinces*, Cambridge 1970.

Chapter 14

THE EARLY ALAMANNI: THE START OF A NEW TEXTILE PROJECT

Johanna Banck-Burgess

A *Festschrift* provides one with the pleasant opportunity to choose a topic relatively freely. This is especially the case when the person to be honoured has dealt with a wide and interesting area of research. When I was considering which contribution would most please John Peter, a letter he wrote to me came to mind. In this letter, John Peter suggested that he considers the publication date of a *Festschrift* to be the endpoint in the career of its recipient. The authors of this *Festschrift*, however, do not see it this way; with this volume we intend to pay tribute to John Peter Wild's work up to the present and we also look forward to many studies from him in the future. In this spirit, my contribution intends to raise questions rather than to give answers, in the hope that the future research of John Peter Wild can contribute to the solutions of these problems.

As part of a research project for the Deutsche Forschungsgemeinschaft, I am working on questions such as, what are the distinguishing features of Alamannic textiles, that is, what was the state of the art, which traditions came into play, and to what extent were textiles produced as a craft and possibly as a trade. Historically speaking, the Alamanni were Elb-Germanic tribes that settled in areas east of the upper Rhine as far as the Donau during the Migration Period.[1] At the end of the fifth century they came under Frankish rule, which was led by the Merovingian dynasty.

Our knowledge of Alamannic textile crafts is restricted mainly to the Merovingian period. From this period there exist *Reihengräberfelder* (row-grave cemeteries), which present good preservation conditions for textiles, and most of these finds have been examined and published by H.-J. Hundt.[2] Even at the beginning of his research dealing with Merovingian textiles, Hundt was able to determine that the Alamanni used not only the usual early medieval weaves such as herringbone, lozenge and diamond twill, but that they had a special preference for rich weaves. The variety of patterns that, according to Hundt, were characterized by patterns in both weave and colour, can be found as early as the sixth century. The textile finds from the burial field at Sirnau are characteristic of this style.[3]

The present article, however, deals with the early Alamanni and their textile crafts, of which we have very little knowledge. For better understanding of the questions that arise in this context, a few historical details may be outlined. After AD 260, the Roman Empire was forced by the Teutons to give up the Neckar *limes* line and to establish a new line of defence on the Rhine and the Danube. The lands that were given up, including that of the Decumates, were taken over by the Alamanni. This was 200 years before the Alamanni were forced to join the Frankish Empire at the end of the fifth century. Within this time-frame various Germanic tribes were unified. The translation of the name Alamanni as 'Alle Männer' (all men) is taken as a sign of the open nature of this tribe. Juthungs and Bucinobantes, for example, are still named as tribes in their own right around AD 270, but by the middle of the fourth century they are seen as being part of the Alamanni.[4]

One of the most intriguing topics in this period, which for the most part falls within the Migration Period, involves the formation of the extended tribe of the Alamanni and the way they saw themselves. Questions surrounding this topic must be formulated with discrimination, as the development of this tribe during the tension-filled times of sharing borders with the Romans was extremely varied. Certain groups of Alamanni acted as border-patrolling *foederati* and thus had ties to the Roman Empire. This was especially the case in the late fourth century and the first half of the fifth century, when the Roman occupiers were increasingly pulling out from the border zones and border security was taken over by the Teutons. The economic advantages that these contractual agreements with the Romans brought the Alamanni can be seen clearly in burial fields such as that in Wyh,[5] but the extent to which these *foederati* distanced themselves, or were kept at a distance from, the other Alamanni can only be guessed at.

Just as the varied development of the Alamanni is important for understanding how they saw themselves, it is also important in this context to consider their descent from the Elb-Teutons and their development from the middle of the third century onwards. Roman texts tell us that the Teutonic 'Neckarsueben' lived on the upper Rhine as early as the first century AD.[6] It will be useful at this point to glance at a problem in current research: the Teutons, who in the second half of the third century settled in the border areas that had been abandoned by the Romans, are said to have been culturally relatively underdeveloped. However, it is remarkable that the Teutons did not make full use of the partially preserved Roman infrastructure, preferring to use their own traditional building style.[7]

Evaluating early Alamannic culture is difficult and to what extent settlement site conditions have led to misinterpretation of the finds is, likewise, difficult to determine. To put it rather pointedly, the relatively poor (or lack of) material remains is all too quickly interpreted as a lack of cultural expression. This rash assessment surely derives in part from the contrast of these sites with the much better conditions at Merovingian and neighbouring Roman sites, that reflect the high cultural level of those peoples. In contrast with the *Reihengräberfelder*, an Eldorado for textile finds, there are very few known burial sites from the third and fourth centuries. The predominant funeral custom is thought to have been cremation burial without burial gifts, which would be very difficult to analyse archaeologically. To the extent that any bodies were actually interred, the practitioners were predominantly members of the upper classes who had begun burying their dead under the influence of Christianized Romans. In the area settled by the Alamanni, the archaeological source conditions for the Migration Period have improved greatly thanks to intensive research,[8] and also to settlement archaeology.[9] It must be assumed that the lands just beyond the border of the Roman Empire were fairly densely settled in late antiquity.[10]

Textiles, besides fulfilling a practical function, are a very important means of social expression, through which differences in status, sex, or age can be expressed. Textiles are an important means of interpersonal communication that can signal group membership or division. In this context, costume of course come to mind first, and yet, there is a wide spectrum of textiles besides clothes that play an equally important role in secular and religious life. Take, for example, the lavish and complicated twill and tablet weaving in the wall hangings from the grave of the early Celtic prince in Eberdingen-Hochdorf.[11]

The state of preservation of archaeological textiles is only rarely good enough to make possible a reconstruction of the artefact – this deficit distinguishes textiles from other types of artefacts and thwarts attempts at developing a textile typology. Be that as it may, details of production techniques can furnish important information about the procedure and the traditions involved in production. The analysis of early Celtic textiles, for example, has shown that the weavers in the Hallstatt and early La Tène cultures worked strictly according to their indigenous traditions but at the same time were quite open for influences from southern Alpine cultures.[12] Here I have reverted to Celtic finds in an article dealing with Alamanni only in order to show that textiles can be a sensitive indicator of traditions and innovations in archaeological cultures or groups. If we see textiles not only as a necessary utilitarian object in everyday life, but also as a social and group-indicating means of expression with enduring traditional features, then the question arises, which direction did the development of the early Alamannic textile crafts take, or what was the creative fashioning of textiles during the Migration Period? To what extent was the Alamannic textile handicraft shaped by the heritage of the Germanic settlers? In what way can original and independent characteristics be recognized in the textile crafts of Alamannic groups? One part of the research project on Alamannic textiles will deal with exactly these questions.

It seems reasonable to assume that Alamannic textile crafts were a melting pot for Germanic, Celtic and Roman traditions. These traditions are to some extent already known. The Thorsberger *Prachtmantel* stands as an excellent example of textile crafts in Free Germany and, in the context of a discussion between L. Bender Jørgensen and J. P. Wild over the export of Roman weaving to Teutonia, J. P. Wild has described weaves from the West Roman province.[13] Furthermore, remains of Celtic handicraft techniques were surely preserved in the weaving of the Romanized population.

After all this theoretical exposition, the readers of this contribution will be asking themselves where the finds are that form the basis for questions and research proposals of this kind. This will be a difficult task, and one which will involve searching countless storerooms for badly preserved, old and new finds, until it is eventually possible to provide a foundation of facts.

Notes

1 H. Schach-Dörges, 'Zusammengespülte und vermengte Menschen' in *Die Alamannen, Begleitband zur Ausstellung 'Die Alamannen' vom 14. Juni 1997 bis 14. September 1997 in Stuttgart* (Archäologisches Landesmuseum Baden-Württemberg: Stuttgart 1997), p. 79.

2 See part of the bibliography in I. Bollbuck, *Studien zu merowingerzeitlichen Textilien* (dissertation, University of Hamburg, 1987).

3 H. J. Hundt, 'Die Textilfunde (Sirnau und Oberesslingen)' in R. Koch, *Katalog Esslingen, Teil II. Die merowingischen Funde. Veröffentlichungen des Staatlichen Amtes für Denkmalpflege Stuttgart, Reihe A, Vor- und Frühgeschichte,* Heft 13/II (Stuttgart 1969), pp. 71–79.

4 *Lexikon des Mittelalters* 1980, 264. H. Schach-Dörges, 'Zu süddeutschen Grabfunden frühalamannischer Zeit, Versuch einer Bestandsaufnahme', *Fundberichte aus Baden-Württemberg,* Bd. 22/1 (Stuttgart 1998), pp. 627–654.

5 G. Fingerlin, *Frühalamannische Grabfunde aus Wyhl am Kaiserstuhl, Kreis Emmendingen. Archäologische Ausgrabungen in Baden-Württemberg* (Stuttgart, 1982) pp. 159–162.

6 I. Jensen, 'Erste Germanen am Oberrhein', in E. Sanmeister (ed.) *Zeitspuren, Archäologisches aus Baden* (Freiburg 1993), p. 126.

7 Schach-Dörges 1998, *op. cit.* (note 4), p. 639

8 Schach-Dörges 1998, *op. cit.*

9 C. Bücker, 'Frühe Alamannen im Breisgau, Untersuchungen zu den Anfängen der germanischen Besiedlung im Breisgau während des 4. und 5. Jahrhunderts n. Chr. Archäologie und Geschichte', in H. U. Nuber *et al.* (eds) *Freiburger Forschungen zum ersten Jahrtausend in Südwestdeutschland* IX (Sigmaringen 1999).

10 G. Fingerlin, 'Brisigavi im Vorfeld von Breisach. Archäologische Spuren der Völkerwanderungszeit zwischen Rhein und Schwarzwald', *Archäologische Nachrichten aus Baden,* XXXIV (Freiburg 1985), p. 44.

11 J. Banck-Burgess, *Hochdorf IV, Die Textilfunde aus dem späthallstattzeitlichen Fürstengrab von Eberdingen-Hochdorf (Kreis Ludwigsburg) und weitere Grabtextilien aus hallstatt- und latènezeitlichen Kulturgruppen, (Forschungen und Berichte zur Vor- und Frühgeschichte in Baden-Württemberg,* LXX (Stuttgart 1999), pp. 120–123.

12 Banck-Burgess *op. cit.*, pp. 127–129. J. Banck, 'Prähistorische Textiltradition' in B. Fritsch *et al.* (eds), *Tradition und Innovation, Prähistorische Archäologie als Historische Wissenschaft: Festschrift für Christian Strahm (Internationale Archäologie, Studia Honoraria* III (Rahden/Westfalia 1998).

13 L. Bender Jørgensen and J. P. Wild, 'Clothes from the Roman Empire: Barbarians and Romans' in L. Bender Jørgensen, B. Magnus and E. Munksgaard (eds) *Archaeological Textiles: Report from the 2nd NESAT symposium 1.–4. V. 1984* (*Arkaeologiske Skrifter* 2) (Copenhagen 1988), pp. 65–98.

Chapter 15

RECENT ANALYSES OF THE TEXTILES FROM BÖKENER MOOR AND VAALER MOOR, GERMANY

Klaus Tidow
with a contribution from Penelope Walton Rogers

Part 1. The textiles, by Klaus Tidow

Introduction

The Neumünster Textile Museum's collection includes textiles from bogs in Schleswig-Holstein and North Saxony, the most remarkable ones being those excavated from Bökener Moor and Vaaler Moor in Schleswig-Holstein. Karl Schlabow described them in detail in his book *Textilfunde der Eisenzeit in Norddeutschland,* but until now we have not had any more precise dating than 'Iron Age textile finds'. A re-design of the Museum's 'Early History of Weaving' section offered the opportunity to do additional wool and dye analyses. These were carried out by Penelope Walton Rogers and the results form the second part of this article.

Sites and circumstances of the excavations

The origin of the finds from Bökener Moor and Vaaler Moor and their long journey to the collections of the Neumünster Textile Museum have been described by Karl Schlabow in his book.[1] Bökener Moor is situated west of the town of Neumünster, whilst Vaaler Moor is in the Dithmarschen area in the south-west part of Schleswig-Holstein. The textiles were not excavated by archeologists, but were discovered while digging peat. The textiles from Vaaler Moor were excavated in 1888, those from Bökener Moor in 1936. Both groups were salvaged by teachers who perceived the value of such finds for research into prehistory. In an indirect way these finds came to the Neumünster Textile Museum and were catalogued and analysed by Karl Schlabow in 1954. The results are summarised in Table 15.1, with a few corrections made through more recent analyses. Most of the finds are remains of larger pieces, the rest probably having been destroyed by the peat-cutting. Today they are surprisingly well preserved, even though some of them have been displayed in show-cases for the last 40 years.

The textiles from Bökener and Vaaler Moor have been catalogued as 15 different numbered items, and there are also two unnumbered items. Most suitably, the textiles have been classified as broad or narrow textiles.

No.	Weave	Colour	Yarn diam.	Spin	Thread-count per cm	Comments
Bökener Moor						
28	2/2 plain twill	light and dark brown	0.5–1.0 mm	Z × Z	12 × 10	Striped: 3 bands of light brown yarn, 14 threads each
29	2/1 plain twill	mid brown	1.0 mm	Z × Z	7 × 7	
30*	2/1 plain twill	red-brown	1.0 mm	Z × Z	9 × 8	42 fragments and one felt
31*	2/2 diamond twill	mid and light brown	0.5–0.8 mm	Z × Z	10 × 10	Tablet-woven selvedge and end-border (six tablets); pattern repeat 24Z × 24Z threads
32	2/2 diamond twill	light brown	0.5 mm	Z × S	10 × 12	In weft, a stripe in Z-spun yarn, 4.5 mm diameter; pattern repeat 20Z × 18S threads; fringe
33	2/2 plain twill	red-brown	0.5–0.8 mm	Z × Z	10 × 9	
Vaaler Moor						
20	2/2 diamond twill	mid and red brown	0.5–0.8 mm	Z × S	12 × 11	Tablet-woven starting border (four tablets); pattern repeat 20Z × 18S threads
21	2/2 diamond twill	mid and dark brown	0.8 mm	Z × Z	10 × 10	Two tablet-woven selvedges (six tablets); pattern repeat 24Z × 24Z threads
22	tablet-weaving	light brown and greenish	1.0 mm	S-ply	–	Band, 35 mm wide; 38 tablets
23	tablet-weaving	light brown and greenish	1.0 mm	S-ply	–	Band, 20–45 mm wide; 20 tablets
24	tablet-weaving	light brown	1.0 mm	S-ply	–	Band, 15–25 mm wide; 24 tablets
25*	1/1 tabby	red brown and	1.0–2.0 mm	Z × Z	? × 5 weft	Band, 39 warp threads; 35 mm black-brown wide; three fragments; sheep's wool in warp, goat hair in weft
26a*/b	2/2 plain twill	mid and light brown	0.8 mm	Z × Z	10 × 9	Two separate textiles
27	2/2 diamond twill	mid brown	0.5 mm	Z × S	18 × 18	Pattern repeat; 20Z × 18S threads
36*	2/2 diamond twill	mid and light brown	0.5–0.8 mm	Z × Z	–	Tablet-woven selvedge and starting border; pattern repeat 20Z × 26Z; seven fragments
No.1	2/2 diamond twill	red-brown	0.5 mm	Z × S	12 × 12	Simple selvedge and tablet woven starting border (4 tablets)
No.2	2/2 diamond twill	dark brown	0.5–0.8 mm	Z × S	11 × 12	Three fragments

*Table 15.1 Technical details of the textiles from Bökener Moor and Vaaler Moor, Germany. All are made from wool, unless otherwise stated. * indicates selected for wool and dye analysis.*

The broad textiles

2/1 TWILL

Textile no. 29 is a 2/1 twill of coarse quality, without any special characteristics such as selvedges, patterns or cut edges. In contrast, selvedges, cut edges and also folded edgings have been preserved on several fragments of another 2/1 twill, textile no. 30. This also has felted patches on one face and an obvious reddish-brown colour. This textile has been dyed with madder and the wool analysis has shown that the fleece type is Hairy Medium in one direction and Generalised Medium in the other (see below). These remains are probably parts of one or several tunics. The subject of costume, however, is still to be addressed.

2/2 TWILL

Textiles nos. 26a, 26b, 28 and 33 are 2/2 twills of medium quality. As no selvedges (or starting borders) have been found, warp and weft cannot be determined with certainty. Textiles nos. 26a and 26b are sewn to each other, and no. 26b has an edging which is stitched to the textile with a plied (S2Z) wool yarn. Wool and dye analyses have been performed only on textile no. 26a. In this textile, one system consists of Hairy Medium wool, the other of Medium wool. The textile was dyed red, but the dye could not be determined.

Textile no. 28 is noteworthy for its stripe pattern. Three stripes of 14 light brown threads each can be detected on a dark ground.

Diamond twill without selvedges

The two 2/2 diamond twills, no. 27 and unnumbered item 2, are of different quality, the former fine and the latter of middling quality. No analytical work has been carried out on these two.

Diamond twill with fringe

Textile no. 32 is a 2/2 diamond twill of medium quality made with Z-spun yarn in the warp and S-spun yarn in the weft. It has a simple selvedge and an end-border of plied and knotted threads forming a fringe. A stripe in the weft, about 45 mm wide and consisting of Z-spun, rather than S-spun yarn, has also been observed. It is not clear whether this is deliberate patterning or the use of a wrong weft bobbin.

Diamond twill with tablet-woven selvedges

Four 2/2 diamond twills with tablet-woven selvedges have been found, nos. 20, 31, 36 and unnumbered item 1. Textile no. 20 also has a tablet-woven starting border worked on four × four-hole tablets. The Z-spun threads of the starting border are actually red-brown and probably dyed. Only dye analysis could show if this is also true for the partly red-brown and medium-brown warp and weft threads of the diamond twill.

No. 31 is a textile of medium quality with medium brown warp and light brown weft (Fig. 15.1). The selvedges are woven of greenish-brown threads (Z-spun, S-plied) with four × four-hole-tablets. Four × four-hole tablets have also been used for the end-border, although this one is of plain Z-spun, light brown threads. The warp of this diamond twill is a naturally brown wool, Medium fleece type, while the weft is white wool, Hairy Medium fleece type. The dye analysis did not yield results, but dyed wool in the tablet-woven borders cannot be excluded.

Textile no. 36 represents the remains of a *Prachtmantel*. There are seven fragments, two of them with a selvedge and an end-border, one with an end-border only. Joined together, they form a width of 1. 30 m, but we can assume that the textile was originally far wider. The selvedges are woven with 20 tablets in one and 24 in the other; the end-border has 42 tablets. Karl Schlabow has comprehensively described the technical properties of this *Prachtmantel* elsewhere.[2] He points out that the selvedges have not been woven simultaneously with the diamond twill, but have been added to the main textile subsequently in a second working process.

Samples from the warp and the weft of the diamond twill were analysed for wool quality and possible dye. The diamond twill is woven from naturally pigmented wool (originally light brown and white), and has Hairy Medium fleece-

Fig. 15.1 Textile no. 31, from Bökener Moor: a wool 2/2 diamond twill with tablet-woven selvedge and end-border (fringed); pattern repeat 24 × 24; the warp is pigmented wool (brown) and the weft non-pigmented.

type in the warp and the weft. As no dye analysis has been performed on the tablet-woven selvedges, it must remain uncertain as to whether they consist of naturally pigmented wool as well, but in the end-border of this *Prachtmantel*, a narrow stripe of dark brown can still be seen.

The unnumbered textile 1 is of middling quality and now of a red-brown colour. It is assumed to be another dyed diamond twill. The preserved starting border has been woven with four × four-hole-tablets.

Narrow bands

Band in tabby (Fig. 15.2)

Band no. 25 consists of a yellow-brown to red-brown warp and black-brown weft. The analysis by Penelope Walton Rogers found that the warp is spun from sheep's wool (Medium fleece type), the weft of goat hair. The warp has been dyed red, although the dye could not be identified. The band is of a coarse quality.

BAND IN DIAMOND TWILL AND TABLET WEAVING

The surviving fragment of this band has a central area woven in diamond twill and two selvedges in tablet weaving. The selvedges have been woven with six × four-hole-tablets each. The warp of the diamond twill is lighter coloured than the weft.

TABLET-WOVEN BANDS

As with the previous example, only small pieces have survived from the three tablet-woven bands, nos. 22, 23 and 24, the remaining lengths being 300, 330 and 370 mm respectively. The technique of these tablet bands has been comprehensively discussed by Karl Schlabow, to which reference may be made.[3]

These three bands are clearly different from each other. no. 22 is a simple band, although patterned with coloured threads, six tablets threaded with light brown, four tablets with dark green, twenty tablets with greenish and eight tablets with light grey threads. No. 23 is narrow at the start, then broadens to show a weft-float pattern between stripes of three to five tablets each. In band no. 24 there are patches where the weft is not preserved any more. In these areas the weft was probably spun from a different material (perhaps flax), which has not survived burial in the bog. These bands have not yet been subject to wool or dye analysis, so that they are not considered in the following discussion.

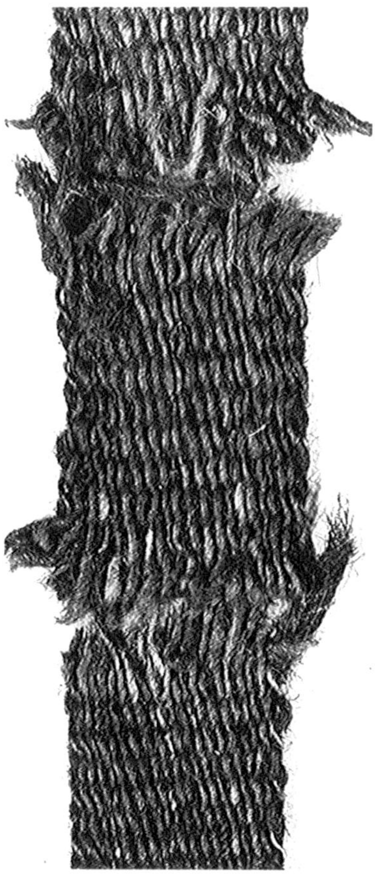

Fig. 15.2 Textile no. 25, from Vaaler Moor: a tabby-woven band with white sheep's wool in the warp and pigmented goat hair in the weft.

Discussion

Research into prehistoric textiles from Northern and Central Europe has in recent years focused on questions of origin and distribution.[4] This caused us to reinvestigate the well known wool textiles from the *Wurtensiedlungen* (marsh settlements) of the Dutch and German coast of the North Sea in a comprehensive manner, making comparisons between sites. In addition to the traditional textile analysis – that is, determination of raw material, binding system, yarn type and count – we had the opportunity to do quite numerous wool and dye analyses. From this, it was possible to distinguish several textile qualities.[5]

Other new impulses for research into prehistoric textile techniques and clothing came from the carbon-14 dating of almost all bog burials from North Saxony and Schleswig-Holstein. Some have proved to be considerably older, some younger than assumed before.[6] Finally, the remains of a Jutland *Prachtmantel* were re-examined from the textile technology point of view, inducing a new debate about the origin of such clothing.[7]

In this context, the textile finds of Bökener Moor and Vaaler Moor, which are not as yet precisely dated, are of special interest, because they are well preserved and can therefore be subjected to wool and dye analysis. This led to the selection of five textiles, among them the remains of another *Prachtmantel* (listed below). Comparison with the wool textiles from Thorsberg and Feddersen Wierde (Table 15.2) shows that the four broad textiles (2/1 twill, 2/2 twill and the two diamond twills) may well date from the late Roman Iron Age, although the 2/1 twill could just as easily date from the early medieval period. The fifth textile, a narrow tabby-weave band, cannot be dated.

Part 2: The raw materials, by Penelope Walton Rogers

The five textiles selected from the collection for analysis of the raw materials were a 2/1 twill (no. 30) and a diamond twill (no. 31) from Bökener Moor; and a narrow woven band (no. 25), a 2/2 twill (no. 26a) and a diamond twill (no. 36) from Vaaler Moor. The aim was to identify the nature of the fibres and the dyes, and to look for any diagnostic features which might help fix the date of the textiles.

Weave	Very Coarse			Coarse		Medium–fine				Fine		Very fine		
	ZS	ZZ	SS	ZS	ZZ	ZS	ZZ	SS	Z/Z+S*	ZS	ZZ	ZS	ZZ	Z+S/Z+S*
Feddersen Wierde (settlement), third century AD														
1/1 tabby	–	–	–	–	4	1	10	–	–	–	1	–	–	–
2/1 plain twill	–	–	–	–	1	–	–	–	–	–	–	–	–	–
2/2 plain twill	–	–	–	–	4	2	15	–	1	–	4	–	–	–
2/2 chevron twill	–	–	–	–	–	–	–	–	–	–	1	–	–	–
2/2 diamond twill	–	–	–	–	–	–	–	–	–	1	–	–	–	–
Thorsberg (peat bog), third/fourth century AD														
1/1 tabby	–	–	2	–	–	–	–	–	–	–	–	–	–	–
1/1 tabby narrow band	–	–	–	–	–	–	1	–	–	–	–	–	–	–
2/1 lozenge twill	–	–	–	–	–	1	–	–	–	–	–	–	–	–
2/2 plain twill	–	–	–	1	–	8	–	–	–	–	–	–	–	1
2/2 plain twill band	–	–	–	–	–	–	–	1	–	–	–	–	–	–
2/2 diamond twill	–	–	–	–	–	2	–	–	–	9	–	1	–	–

* Spin–patterned fabrics

Notes: Very coarse = *c.*5x5 threads per cm; Coarse = *c.*8x8; Medium–fine = *c.*12x12; Fine = *c.*18x18; Very fine = >18x18

Table 15.2 Comparable wool textiles from Feddersen Wierde and Thorsberg, Germany.

Species identification

During analysis, warp and weft were regarded as separate samples. Fibres from each yarn were examined by transmitted light microscopy, at ×100 and ×400 magnification, using whole-mount preparations. Most of the fibres showed the typical irregular mosaic scale pattern of sheep's wool, but one yarn, the weft from the coarse woven band from Vaaler Moor, no. 25, was clearly different from the rest and was examined in more detail. In this sample, the cross-sections were round and oval in the finer fibres; and flat, elliptical, figure-eight and bean-shaped in the coarse ones. The scale pattern was irregular mosaic with smooth margins, changing along the length of the coarse fibres to waved with close crenate margins. These features identified the sample as goat hair.[8] The warp yarn from the band was then re-examined, but was confirmed as sheep's wool. The coarse fibres of goat hair have sometimes been used in the past for sackcloth, or for the warp yarns of clothing textiles, but the use of sheep's wool in the warp and goat hair in the weft is very unusual.

Fleece types

Fleece types are identified by measuring the diameters of 100 fibres. According to the range, mean and distribution of the measurements, the sample may be allocated to one of the seven fleece types outlined by Dr M. L. Ryder.[9] Of the nine wool yarns examined here, five are Hairy Medium (HM), one Generalised Medium (GM) and three Medium (M) (Table 15.3).

In evolutionary terms, the HM is the most primitive fleece type. In Danish textiles it can be seen emerging from the fleece of the wild ancestor during the Bronze Age and Pre-Roman Iron Age (and similar evidence is starting to appear for other North European countries); a coarsening of the undercoat can be observed by the Migration Period, a process which may have begun in the Roman Iron Age.[10] The undercoats of the HM fleece types in this sample are all relatively coarse, which suggests that they belong to the Roman Iron Age at the earliest.

The Generalised Medium (GM) came next in evolutionary terms. This first appears in Danish and German textiles of the Roman Iron Age, and an occasional GM fleece will often occur in a predominantly HM flock. These two can, then, be seen as related types.

The Medium fleece (M) is a more developed type, which evolved out of the GM type. It is only occasionally found as early as the Roman period and continued to be rare for the next five centuries, except in Norway, where the type seems to have been established by the Migration Period.[11] In England the M type does not occur in any numbers until the 10th century, when it may have arrived with the Vikings,[12] and there were few examples in the seventh- to ninth-century North German collection previously studied.[13]

There is, however, a problem in distinguishing the HM from M types in this collection. Some of the HM fleece types have – rather unusually – a symmetrical distribution (Table 15.3), which means that they are closer to the M types than is

Textile	Yarn	Range	Mode(s)	Mean±S.D.	Pearson Coeff. of Skew, distribution	Medullas	Pigment	Fleece type	Fleece colour
Bökener Moor									
No.30	close-set	11-106	20	31.5±18.2	+1.30, skewed positive	11% (4 kemp)	2%	Hairy Medium	white
	wide-set	10-51	21	27.5±9.3	+0.44, skewed positive	1%	none	Generalised Medium	white
No.31	dark warp	16-58	27	32.9±7.7	+0.14, symmetrical	4%	32%m	Medium*	light brown
	light weft	12-65	21	31.7±11.5	+0.57, skewed positive	1%	none	Hairy Medium	white
Vaaler Moor									
No.25	warp	16–60	32	35.9±10.0	+0.37, symmetrical	3%	1%	Medium	white
	weft	17–80	multi	48.1±14.6	–0.04, continuous	≥10%	50%d 40%m	GOAT HAIR	dark brown
No.26a	close-set	14–61	26,30	32.5±11.3	+0.65, skewed positive	0	1%	Hairy Medium	white
	wide-set	14–48	32	30.4±7.4	–0.17, symmetrical	0	none	Medium	white
No.36	dark	12–55, 70	34	33.7±9.3	–0.01, symmetrical	1%	34%m	Hairy Medium*	light brown
	light	12–55, 92	24, 31	32.0±12.4	+0.39, symmetrical	5%	2%	Hairy Medium*	white

Table 15.3 Fleece types of the wool textiles from Bökener Moor and Vaaler Moor, Germany. Statistics for each sample are based on the measurement of the diameters of 100 fibres. Measurements in microns (1 micron = 0.001 mm). Pigment: m = moderate; d = dense.

normal. In two cases, only the presence of one fibre over 60 microns diameter distinguishes the HM from the M. Therefore, although they are technically different fleece types, they originate in sheep with similar fleeces. The two diamond twills, Bökener Moor no. 31 and Vaaler Moor no. 36, are more alike than the exact fleece-type identifications (M × HM and HM × HM respectively) might suggest.

Natural pigmentation

Natural pigmentation in the fibre was identified by microscopy, from the presence and density of pigment granules. Both the diamond twills examined (no. 31 and no. 36) have one yarn made from a naturally pigmented fleece (Fig. 15.1). In both cases, moderate pigmentation was noted on approximately one-third of the fibres, indicating a light brown wool. The opposing yarns were made from a white fleece. The use of naturally pigmented fibres for colour patterning can be seen as early as the Bronze Age and continues into the tenth century, so that it does not offer any dating evidence. It does, however, highlight the similarity between the two diamond twills. The goat hair in the weft of the tabby band (no. 25) was also pigmented, dark brown to black, in contrast with the white wool in the warp (Fig. 15.2).

Dyes

Dyes were analysed by extracting any colorants present into a series of solvent systems and then using the extracts for absorption spectrophotometry and thin-layer chromatography.[14] All five samples were stained with an orange-brown substance which is assumed to be contamination from the peaty soil. This hampered the dye analysis, but red dyes have nevertheless been confidently detected in three textiles.

Madder dye was detected in the 2/1 twill from Bökener Moor. TLC revealed its chief chemical constituents to be alizarin and purpurin, which suggests that the dye has derived from the roots of Dyers' Madder, *Rubia tinctorum* L., rather than one of the wild madders or bedstraws. Evidence from Denmark, Britain and Germany suggests that Dyers' Madder came into use during the Roman occupation of north-west Europe.[15] It disappeared as the Romans left the north, and native wild madder and/or bedstraw took its place in the Migration Period.[16] Dyers' Madder re-appeared in the seventh-century royal site of Sutton Hoo, England, and from that point onwards it is more frequently detected in textiles, especially those from late Anglo-Saxon England.[17]

An unidentified red dye was detected in the narrow woven band, no. 25 and the plain twill, 26a from Vaaler Moor. It was present only in the warp of the band, which means that it cannot be contamination from the burial. On extraction, the dye was rich cherry red, whether in acid or basic conditions, although it was a more muted brownish red on the yarn. The colorant lacked diagnostic characteristics and it is therefore impossible to know its origin, although it may be noted that some of the lichen dyes, especially the 'crottles', which yield orange and golden shades, are similarly difficult to characterise.

Finally, when the peat stain had been removed from the diamond twill from

Bökener Moor, no. 31, the textile appeared a golden yellow. This yellow colorant disappeared in the test for mordant dyes, and, as with the reds, the colorant could not be characterised; it does not appear to be one of the flavonoid yellows, such as weld or greenweed. In this instance, because the colorant is present in both warp and weft, it is impossible to tell whether this is an unusual form of contamination, or else some unknown yellow dye.

Comment

The two diamond twills from Bökener Moor and Vaaler Moor are very much alike in terms of their raw materials. Both have been made with light brown wool in the warp and white wool in the weft, although the Bökener Moor example may have been dyed yellow as well. As noted, above, the quality of their wools is also similar, even though one has been identified as M × HM and the other as HM × HM.

The Vaaler Moor textile is thought to be an example of a *Prachtmantel*. Klaus Tidow has provided some records of measurements made by Schlabow of fibres from the *Prachtmantel* from second-century AD Vehnemoor. These appear to be GM or HM in the warp and HM in the weft. They are different from the Bökener Moor and Vaaler Moor diamond twills, in that they have a finer undercoat (modes 18–20 microns) than in the present specimens (see the modes in Table 15.3). This fine undercoat is typical of the pre-Roman Iron Age and the early Roman Iron Age.[18] If it is true that the coarsening of the undercoat in HM fleeces occurred in the late Roman Iron Age and the Migration period (see above), then the Bökener Moor and the Vaaler Moor diamond twills may be later than the Vehnemoor example – although more data are required before it is possible to be confident of this. This does not (yet) help with the debate over the place of origin of *Prachtmanteln*.

The narrow band from Vaaler Moor (no. 25), with red-dyed warp and dark brown goat hair weft, is an unusual piece which cannot be matched elsewhere. The red dye and the M fleece type in the warp, however, show a link with the red-dyed plain 2/2 twill with HM × M fleece types from the same site (no. 26a).

The ZZ 2/1 twill from Bökener Moor is similar to a seventh- or eighth-century ZS 2/1 twill from Hessens, HE4. Both are made from white wool, a feature which was not especially common in the Hessens collection;[19] both have been dyed red with Dyers' Madder, which is also unusual for early medieval Germany; and the Hessens example has been made with HM in warp and weft, while the Bökener Moor example is HM × GM. As described above, the GM evolved from the HM and both could occur in the same flock. Both the Hessens and Bökener Moor textiles have kemp fibres present (kemp are short fibres with a wide latticed medulla which occur in certain types of primitive fleece).

Summary, *by Klaus Tidow and Penelope Walton Rogers*

The new analyses which have been carried out in recent years on wool textiles from settlements (Hessens, Oldorf and Niens) and from bogs (Böken and Vaaler, as described here) have shown that the wools used for the common textile types were carefully chosen. In addition, the palette of dyes is proving to be more extensive than was originally thought.

As to the original question asked of the present study, whether the textiles of Bökener Moor and Vaaler Moor can be dated more precisely on the basis of these new facts, we have no definite answer. The wools used would fit most readily in the late Roman Iron Age or Migration Period, but there is such a similarity between the 2/1 twill from Bökener Moor and that from seventh/eighth-century Hessens that some sort of connection between the two seems likely.

While it has not been possible to give dates for the textiles, based on their raw materials, some groupings of material have been made (see above, *Comment*), which may in the future prove useful. It must be hoped that, as more work is carried out into this particular aspect of textile studies, and more carbon-14 dates become available, a clearer pattern does in time emerge. In that context, it would be of especial interest to carry out dye and wool analyses on the well known cloaks and cloths from Germania Libera which John Peter Wild has already analysed and compared.[20] We may then be able to look back at the information gathered from the Bökener Moor and Vaaler Moor textiles and understand where exactly they belong in the history of German textile production.

Notes

1 K. Schlabow, *Textilfunde der Eisenzeit in Norddeutschland,* Göttinger Schriften zur Vor- und Frühgeschichte XV (Neumünster, 1976), p. 16 and 23.

2 K. Schlabow, *op. cit.*, p. 68ff.

3 K. Schlabow, *op. cit.*, p. 91ff.

4 L. Bender Jørgensen, *Forhistoriske Textiler i Skandinavien: Prehistoric Scandinavian Textiles* (Nordiske Fortidsminder, IX, Copenhagen 1986). L. Bender Jørgensen, *North European textiles until AD 1000* (Aarhus, 1992).

5 K. Tidow, 'Textiltechnische Untersuchungen an Wollgeweben aus friesischen Wurtensiedlungen von der Mitte des 7. bis zur Mitte des 13. Jahrhunderts und Vergleiche mit Grab- und Siedlungsfunden aus dem nördlichen Europa' in *Probleme der Küstenforschung im südlichen Nordseegebiet* XXIII (1995), pp. 352–87. P. Walton Rogers, 'The raw materials of textiles from northern Germany and the Netherlands', in *Probleme der Küstenforschung im südlichen Nordseegebiet* XXIII (1995), pp. 389–400.

6 W. van der Sanden, 'C14-Datierungen von Moorleichen aus Niedersachsen und Schleswig-Holstein', in *Die Kunde* N. F. XLVI (1995), pp. 137–155.

7 L. Raeder Knudsen, 'An Iron Age cloak with tablet-woven borders: a new interpretation of method of production', in: *Textiles in European Archaeology* (Report from the 6th NESAT Symposium, 7–11th May in Boras, Göteborg, 1998), pp. 79–84.

8 A. B. Wildman, *The Microscopy of Animal Textile Fibres* (WIRA, Leeds, 1954). H. M. Appleyard, *Guide to the Identification of Animal fibres* (WIRA, Leeds, 1978).

9 M. L. Ryder, 'Changes in the fleece of sheep following domestication' in P. J. Ucko and G. E. Dimbleby (eds), *The Domestication and Exploitation of Plants and Animals* (London, 1969), pp. 495–521.
For definitions of individual fleece-types, see the Glossary in Walton Rogers 1995 *op. cit.*

[10] P. Walton, 'Dyes and wools in Iron Age textiles from Norway and Denmark', *Journal of Danish Archaeology* VII (1988a)(pp. 144–158), pp. 146–7.

[11] Ibid. 149–152

[12] P. Walton, *Textiles, Cordage and Raw Fibres from 16–22 Coppergate* (The Archaeology of York XVII, no. 5, 1989), p. 307

[13] Walton Rogers *op. cit.* (1995).

[14] P. Walton and G. W. Taylor, 'The characterisation of dyes in textiles from archaeological excavations', *Chromatography and Analysis* XVII, p. 5–7

[15] Walton *op. cit.* (1988a), pp. 154–5.

[16] Ibid. Walton and Taylor *op. cit.* (1991).

[17] P. Walton, 'Dyes of the Viking Age: a summary of recent work', *Dyes in History and Archaeology* VII (1988b), pp. 14–20. P. Walton *op. cit.* (1989), pp. 400–1. P. Walton Rogers *Textile Production at 16–22 Coppergate* (*The Archaeology of York* XVII no. 11, 1997), p. 1769.

[18] Walton *op. cit.* (1988a), pp. 144–7.

[19] Walton Rogers *op. cit.* (1995).

[20] L. Bender Jørgensen and J. P. Wild, 'Clothes from the Roman Empire, Barbarians and Romans', in *Archaeological Textiles* (NESAT II) Copenhagen 1988 (pp. 65–98), 65ff. and especially fig. 5.

Chapter 16

A TYPICAL COSTUME OF THE NORTH GERMAN IRON AGE? SOME OBSERVATIONS DURING CONSERVATION OF THE BERNUTHSFELD 'PLAID'

Heidemarie Farke

Introduction

In May 1907, a man's body was found in the bog of Hogehahn near Bernuthsfeld (Kreis Aurich, Germany),[1] at a time when the water table in the bog was still high. A number of items were found with the body and among them were a fringed blanket or cloak,[2] a pair of puttee-like leg-bindings,[3] a man's kirtle (full tunic),[4] and a cloth or plaid.[5]

The turbulent circumstances of the excavation and its later treatment have been described in earlier publications. Without much hesitation, the wool textiles and garments were attributed to the Roman period and to the Germanic culture contemporary with the Roman Empire. As recently as 1976, the Bernuthsfeld find was dated to the Iron Age of northern Germany, on the merit of having been found in a North German bog.[6] The clothing style corresponded well with the general idea of German costume at that time. This was based on sculpted stone monuments in Romania and on the columns of Trajan and Marcus Aurelius in Rome (Fig. 16.1). Tacitus' account of the Germans contributed further to this image, together with archaeological finds from that period: a range of textiles and garments, providing direct evidence, have been preserved in the bogs of northern Europe, including an almost complete male costume from the sacrificial bog at Thorsberg, and several garments from the bogs of Damendorf and Obenaltendorf, to name but a few.

Fig. 16.1 Reconstructed costume of the Bernuthsfeld bog find after Girke.

The Bernuthsfeld garments

Cloaks were a major feature of men's costume, often made as large fringed rectangles. The cloak from Bernuthsfeld fitted nicely into this, being almost 2.0 m by 1.7 m. It was woven in herringbone twill (2/2 chevron twill) with tight tubular selvedges and, like the other bog garments, is made from wool. The leg-bindings, which were evidently worn as puttees (spirally wrapped) are made from two similar pieces, put together in the same way. Both are approximately 3.60 m long and have a variable width of around 0.25 m. They have been woven in tabby, as long bands with simple, non-reinforced selvedges. The uneven width probably derives from both the weaving process and from later wear.

All parts of the costume show clear signs of wear and damage. They are patched and mended and have presumably been used for a long time. The tunic, or kirtle, is made from no less than 45 separate pieces stitched together like a patchwork, and looks rather like a carter's smock. It is a shirt-like overgarment, cut in a simple, loose style, with inset sleeves, and a round neckline with an asymmetrical front slit. This kind of tunic can be found in illustrations of the early ninth century, in excavated garments of the tenth century, and also in High Gothic art.

The man's kirtle has already been discussed at the sixth NESAT (North European Symposium on Archaeological Textiles) meeting in Borås. In the present paper, the smaller cloth, or plaid, which also counts as part of the garment suite of this bog find, is to be described. After being on display in the museum's exhibition for many years, this item needed fresh conservation, along with other parts of the Bernuthsfeld costume (Fig. 16.2). The plaid has preserved dimensions of 0.92–0.94 m by 1.40–1.42 m, and it turns out to be made from several different pieces. Textile 1 is plain, and has been made into a complete rectangle with the help of Textile 2, which is striped and preserved in several fragments. The two pieces are not evenly put together or made to match, but rather seem to come from a collection of worn, but still usable pieces. From these 'second-hand textiles', good pieces have been selected and sewn together as a plaid. This is evident on Textile 1, which is cut along the line of the threads and obviously derives from a former outer garment. The signs of wear-and-tear in the worn and felted areas, which cannot be explained by use as a plaid, also support this theory.

Textile 1

This once very woolly textile is a plain twill. The yarn used for the weft is thick and loosely spun; after weaving the web was 'raised' (brushed) so that a layer of wool and hair covers the surface of the weave, perhaps in imitation of an animal pelt. For this effect, long-staple wool must have been used. Analysis of the fibres in the weft yarn shows a preserved fibre length of 150–200 mm. In its present state of preservation, the weave is loose, even and rather coarse. Originally, it must have been very soft, woolly, full and draping. Now, the wool pile is worn, broken, chemically and physically degraded, so that the original, unique charm and character of this warm fabric is mostly lost (Figs. 16.3 and 16.4).

Fibre: sheep's wool, mixed quality, long-staple (Fig. 16.5)
Weave: plain 2/2 twill

Fig. 16.2 The plaid after conservation. Photo: H. Farke.

Fig. 16.3 Textile 1, close-up, showing the weave and the typically damaged Hairy Medium wool. Magnification: approx. 2.5×, photo: H. Farke.

Fig. 16.4 Textile 1, close-up, showing a well preserved area, and the long wool fibres. Magnification: approx. 1×, photo: H. Farke.

Warp: Z-spun yarn, diameter 0.8 to 2.8 mm, unevenly spun
Weft: S-spun yarn, diameter 2.0 to 4.0 mm, loose and evenly spun
Count: 5–6 warp threads per cm × 3 weft threads per cm.

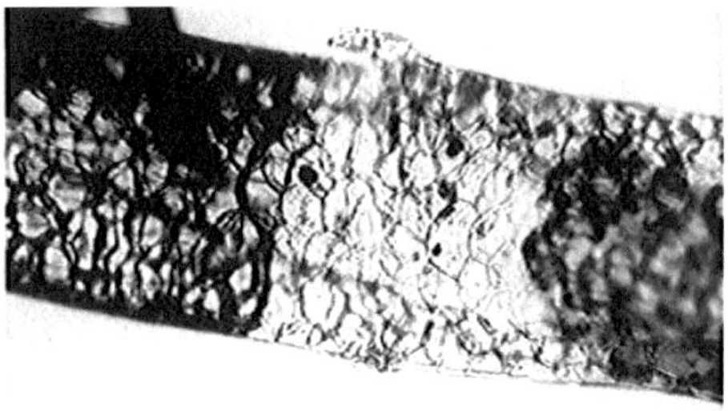

Fig. 16.5 Textile 1. A wool kemp (short, coarse fibre) from the weft. Magnification: approx. 125×, photo: H. Farke.

Textile 2

Textile 2 is a striped L-shaped weave that has been added to Textile 1 in order to fill out the rectangular shape of the plaid. It has been stitched along the length and width of the irregular shape of Textile 1, the cut or torn edges turned in as an overcast seam. The joining of the two pieces appears in some places to be butted, while in others they partly overlap each other. The surviving width of this striped tabby textile is about 0.9 m, but it may very well have been woven to double that width. As with Textile 1, this textile has also been used for a second time.

The warp is a natural-coloured Z-spun yarn. The colour of the individual fibres varies from light to dark brown. Light and dark yarns have been spun from this combination and set up as warp on the loom without any obvious regularity or continuity, as, for example, in the sequence 4 dark threads, 4 light threads, 2 dark, 2 light, 2 dark, 2 light, 4 dark, 4 light, 2 dark, 4 light, 2 dark, 5 light, and so on. Often, a yarn which began with dark fibres ends with light. This produces an uneven quality along the stripes, but at the same time has a lively and agreeable effect (Fig. 16.6).

One strip of the striped textile, Textile 2, exists only as a starting border. Although the border itself is well preserved, the corner where it would have joined the

Fig. 16.6 Textile 2, close-up, showing the light and dark warp threads. Magnification: approx. 1.6×, photo: H. Farke.

Fig. 16.7 Textile 2, close-up, showing the starting border. Magnification: approx. 1.6×, photo: H. Farke.

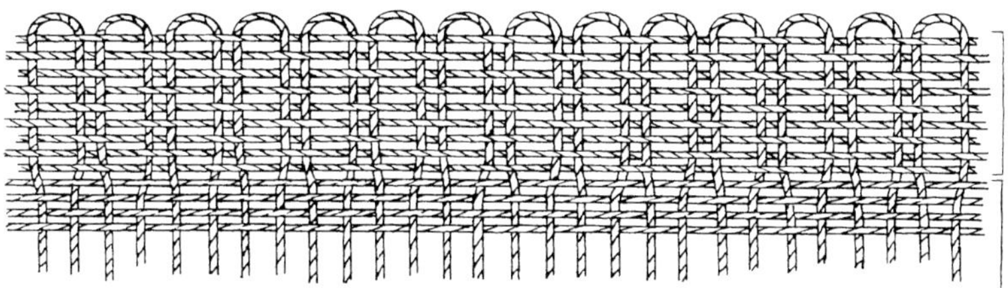

Fig. 16.8 Diagram of the starting border of textile 2 (see Fig. 16.7). Drawing: H. Farke.

Fig. 16.9 Textile 2, close up, showing a detail of the selvedge. Magnification: approx. 1.6×.

selvedge has unfortunately been destroyed. The starting border is about 90 mm wide and has been woven in tabby repp on nine warp threads. The warp and weft yarns of the border are similar and correspond with the warp yarns in the striped weave. Two weft threads lie in one shed and separate after the starting border, becoming the warp of the tabby weave (Fig. 16.7, Fig. 16.8). The wool chosen for the warp of the starting border is mainly dark.

The selvedge is an integral part of the tabby weave of the main body of the cloth; the selvedge cord is constructed from six warp threads. The weaving was with two threads (that is, two bobbins). In other words, a weft yarn reaching the selvedge does not turn back into the textile until after the next return (Fig. 16.9, Fig. 16.10). This points to the production of a large textile and to an attempt to weave evenly with a strong selvedge.

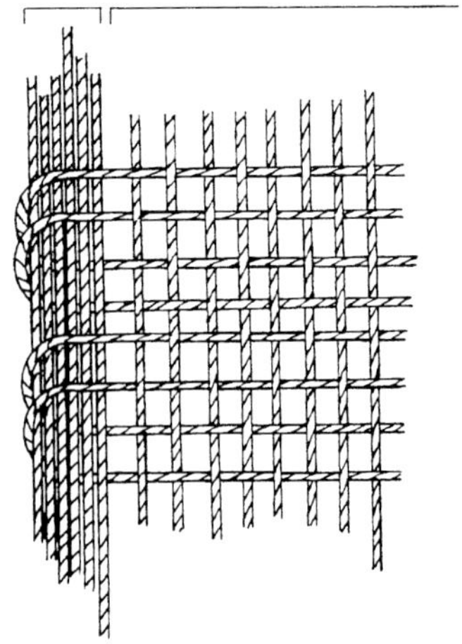

Fig. 16.10 Diagram of the selvedge on Textile 2. Drawing: H. Farke.

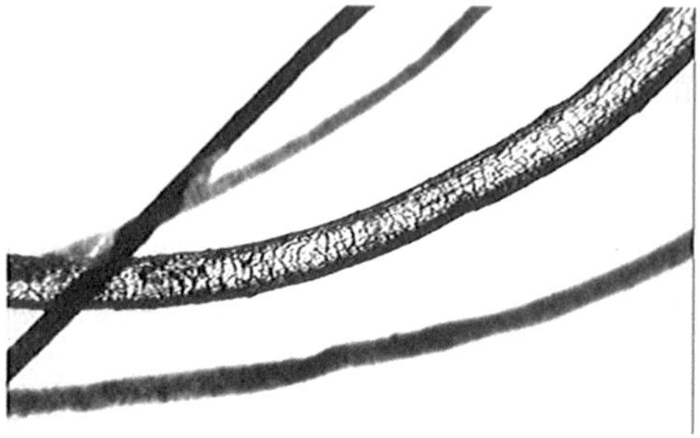

Fig. 16.11 Textile 2. The dark (pigmented) wool from the warp. Magnification: approx. 125×, photo: H. Farke.

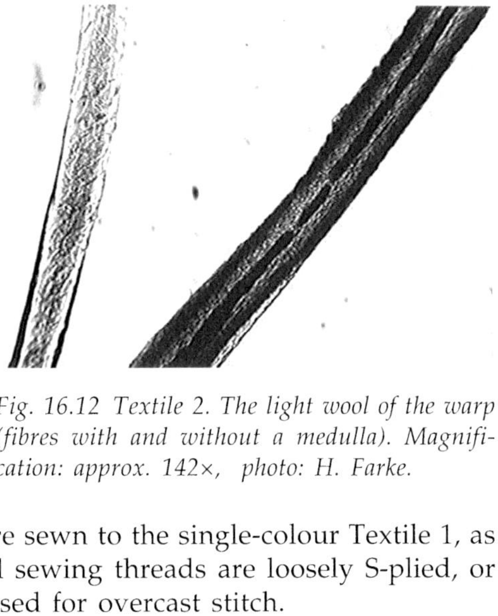

Fig. 16.12 Textile 2. The light wool of the warp (fibres with and without a medulla). Magnification: approx. 142×, photo: H. Farke.

Fibre: sheep's wool, mixed quality, light to dark brown
Weave: tabby
Warp: Z-spun yarn, diameter 0.8–2.0 mm (Fig. 16.11, Fig. 16.12); arrangement of colour in warp as described above
Weft: S-spun yarn, diameter 0.9–5 mm, dark brown with a few light fibres
Count: 5 warp threads per cm × 0.75 weft threads per cm (i.e. 7.5 weft threads per 10 cm)

Two further pieces of the striped textile were sewn to the single-colour Textile 1, as patches over old, worn-out parts. The wool sewing threads are loosely S-plied, or Z-spun yarn used double, and have been used for overcast stitch.

Thread 1: sheep's wool, S-plied, diameter 1.3–1.6 mm
Thread 2: sheep's wool, Z-spun yarn, diameter 0.8–1 mm

Conclusion

The Bernuthsfeld 'plaid' was – like the man's kirtle – made from re-used textiles. It is obvious that the striped Textile 2 was adapted to fit into the single-colour twill, Textile 1. The previous use of these textiles is not clear, but it is highly likely that they derive from two outer garments. The striped textile may have been part of a woman's gown (*Frauenrock*).[7] The piled Textile 1, made from long-staple wool to look like an animal pelt, may have been a cloak. The preserved garment parts may suggest a jacket, kirtle or something similar, although, sadly, no remains of seams have survived from this first use. All the wear damage shows intense use of the original garment. Only when really worn out, were the parts which were still in good condition re-used for the present plaid-like textile. The way in which they have been joined, and the stitching, indicate that the 'plaid' was made for functional rather than an aesthetic purposes. Furthermore, it is not certain that the object is preserved in its full original size.

According to Hahne,[8] Mestorf[9] and Schlabow,[10] the textiles from Bernuthsfeld were dated to the North German Iron Age, and yet, this clothing is obviously different from the Iron Age textiles found so far. In that period, garments were usually woven to shape on the warp-weighted loom. Although the 'plaid' undoubtedly was produced on the warp-weighted loom, various technical details lead me to assume that it does not belong to the Iron Age, but to the medieval period[11] – just as the Bernuthsfeld kirtle has been shown to be. Even though the individual pieces may be fitted into the shape of Germanic costume, they do not seem to me to belong to it. All the textiles are typically medieval, for example in the character of the yarn (warp and weft), the selvedges, the weave structure and – last but not least – the width. The seams observed as 'unusual' by Mestorf[12] do not match those of the Roman period, such as the so-called 'Thorsberg seam'. Furthermore, details of the cut, such as the asymmetrical front slash on the kirtle, and the shape of the sleeve parts (possibly re-used from a shawl) have not been found among Roman textiles and costumes. This man's clothes are distinct from the relatively homogeneous costume group we know from, for example, Obenaltendorf, Hunteburg, Damendorf, Dätgen, Rendswühren, Thorsberg and Vehnemoor.

While the analysis presented here was being carried out, further research into the bog finds from North Saxony and Schleswig-Holstein has produced new evidence for the dating of the Bernuthsfeld find. A C-14 date of 1290±45 BP (AD *c.* 660) has shown that the Bernuthsfeld man lived in the early medieval period.[13] If the bog find from Bernuthsfeld must be re-dated as early medieval, it means that what is traditionally seen as the typical Iron Age costume in northern Germany continued into the Middle Ages, seemingly without important change or sizeable foreign influences. Whether the Bernuthsfeld find should be seen as an independent costume, a step into a new period remains for the present uncertain. To clarify this, more research and analyses are needed.

Dear John Peter, unfortunately this means that I cannot present you with a textile of the Roman period from Germany. It is, however, of considerable importance for the following period and the corrected dating of the Bernuthsfeld bog find has now given us a more complete view of German dress in general.

Notes

1 H. Hahne, *Vorzeitfunde aus Niedersachsen* VI: *Moorleichen* (Hanover, 1915). J. Mestorf, *Moorleichen* (*Bericht über das Museum vaterländischer Altertümer*, XLIV(Kiel, 1907). K. Schlabow, *Textilfunde der Eisenzeit in Norddeutschland* (Neumünster, 1976).

[2] Hahne, *op. cit.*; Schlabow *op. cit.*

[3] Hahne *op. cit.*

[4] H. Farke, *Der Männerkittel aus Bernuthsfeld. Beobachtungen während einer Restaurierung*, in L. Bender Jørgensen and C. Rinaldo, *Textiles in European Archaeology, Sixth NESAT Symposium, 7th–11th May 1996 in Borås* (Gotarc Series A, Göteborg, 1998), pp. 99–106. H. Farke, 'Patchwork aus dem frühen Mittelalter. Konservierung eines Moorfundes', *Arbeitsblätter für Restauratoren* II (Mainze 1998), pp. 258–261. Hahne *op. cit.* Mestorf *op. cit.* Schlabow *op. cit.*

[5] H. Farke and A. Corbacy, 'Moorfund aus Bernuthsfeld, Tuch' (Schleswig 1995: unpublished manuscript. Hahne *op. cit.*

[6] G. Girke, *Die Tracht der Germanen in der vor- und frühgeschichtlichen Zeit* (Leipzig, 1923).

[7] Hahne *op. cit.*

[8] Hahne *op. cit.*

[9] Mestorf *op. cit.*

[10] Schlabow *op. cit.*

[11] K. Tidow 'Hoch- und spätmittelalterliche Woll- und Leinengewebe aus Ausgrabungen in Norddeutschland', *Der Sachsenspiegel* II (Oldenburg 1995)

[12] Mestorf *op. cit.*

[13] W. van der Sanden, 'C14-Datierungen von Moorleichen aus Niedersachsen und Schleswig-Holstein', *Die Kunde* New Series XLVI (1995), pp. 137–156

Chapter 17

FROM THE ROMAN HORIZONTAL LOOM TO THE 3/1 TWILL DAMASK LOOM OF THE EARLY MEDIEVAL PERIOD

Daniël De Jonghe

Silk 3/1 twill block damasks of the Roman period have been the subject of several different studies by De Jonghe, and De Jonghe and Tavernier.[1] Referring to this work, John Peter Wild has named the loom on which they were woven, 'the Roman horizontal loom'.[2] In the following study, the characteristics of this loom will be considered, with the intention of making a comparison with the loom used to weave the 3/1 twill damask, inv. Tx 601, from the Royal Museum of Art and History in Brussels. This fabric is one of a group of 3/1 twill silk damasks, with well-defined characteristics, which have mostly been found in treasuries of West European churches. They are dated between the fourth and the seventh century, and are attributed to the eastern Mediterranean area.

Technical characteristics of Roman silk block damasks

This group contains only the following examples:[3]

* two fragments from third-century Palmyra, Syria
* two fragments from end of third-century Trier, Germany
* one fragment from later third-century Holborough, Kent, England
* three fragments from third/fourth-century Cologne, Germany
* four fragments from third/fourth-century Ribeauvillé, France
* one fragment from fourth-century Conthey, Kt Wallis, Switzerland
* one fragment from the second half of the fourth century, from Jovia, Hungary

In these silks, the warp is Z-twist and the weft without apparent twist, except for fragment S38 from Palmyra, where both warp and weft do not have apparent twist. They are treated separately from the wool damasks of the Roman period (see Cardon this volume, pp 12–20).

All the fabrics of this silk group have a simple rectilinear pattern of alternating warp-faced and weft-faced zones, but through the period of their use there is an evolution in both pattern and technology. The damasks of the earliest period have only chequered patterns, as exemplified by the Palmyra damasks. The blocks are based on multiples of four warp threads and an odd number of picks (weft threads)(Fig. 17.1). The twill direction remains the same vertically, but horizontally it reverses in alternate blocks. At the edges of the blocks all the binding points are in opposition.

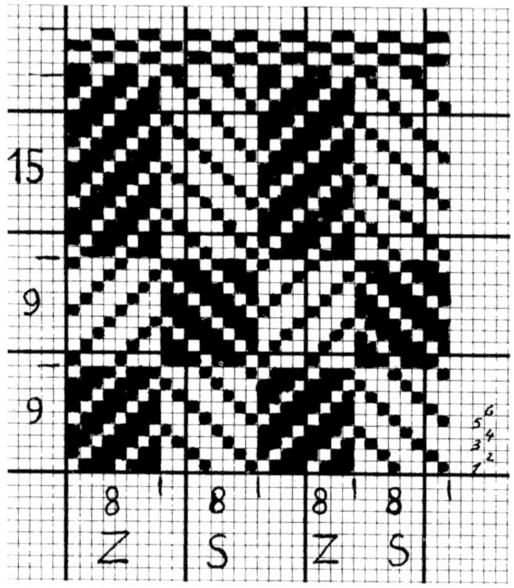

Fig. 17.1 Weave diagram of a Roman block damask from Palmyra (S38), Syria.

In damask of the intermediate period, represented by the purple silk from Trier, the geometric pattern is constructed from five vertical sections. The blocks consist of eight warp threads and both odd and even numbers of picks. The twill direction of the odd vertical sections does not change, but the twill direction of the two even vertical sections alters, depending on the binding effect (warp-faced or weft-faced) of the next adjacent block to the left. Where the binding effect is the same, the twill takes the direction of the adjacent block, but where the binding effect is different, the twill direction is opposite. With this procedure it is impossible to have all the binding points in opposition at the edges of the blocks.

In the final period, the damasks have both chequered patterns and patterns constructed from three or four vertical sections, as illustrated by the fragments from Cologne, Ribeauvillé, Jovia, Conthey and Holborough, and the yellow fragment from Trier. In these, all the warp-faced blocks have a Z-twill direction while all the weft-faced blocks have an S-twill direction. The blocks are based on multiples of two warp threads and two weft picks. At the edges of the blocks all the binding points are in opposition.

In these Roman damasks, the warp count varies from 45 to 60 threads per cm and the weft count from 30 to 60 picks per cm, the ratio between warp and weft in the different fragments being close to 1:1.

The technology of weaving Roman silk block damasks

As a result of the study of the technological characteristics described above, and a study of the weaving faults, it has been possible to identify the weaving procedure and the essential characteristics of the loom which was used to make Roman silk block damasks.[4] Because of the rather high number of heddle-rods (twenty for the purple silk from Trier, for example) and the rather complicated weaving procedure, we may assume a horizontal loom with a simple construction and without any superstructure. This loom cannot have had a reed and the heddle-rods probably rested on the warp-sheet when not in use. The threading of the warp threads must have been executed on two to five sets of four heddle-rods. The warp threads would have been connected one by one to the rods by means of separate cord loops and each warp thread would have been attached to only one rod. The number of heddle-rods for the different patterns was therefore between eight and twenty and the selection of the heddle-rods must have been done by hand. In order to open a particular shed, the weaver would have to raise various heddle-rods simultaneously and to accomplish this he must have been aided by an assistant-weaver, who worked the heddles in groups, by means of auxiliary rods.[5]

Technical characteristics of early medieval twill damasks

The 3/1 twill silk damasks of the early medieval period include the following:

- Silk, inv. Tx 601, from the Royal Museum of Art and History in Brussels (Fig. 17.2). I. Errera calls it an Egyptian or Byzantine product of the sixth–seventh century.[6]
- Two fragments from the Museum of St Ambrose in Milan, of which the most important is the lion-hunt silk.[7] According to Hero Granger-Taylor,[8] there are firm indications that this silk should not be dated later than the silks from Trier, which means that it must be dated to the fourth century. She thinks that this silk could have been woven in Italy.[9]

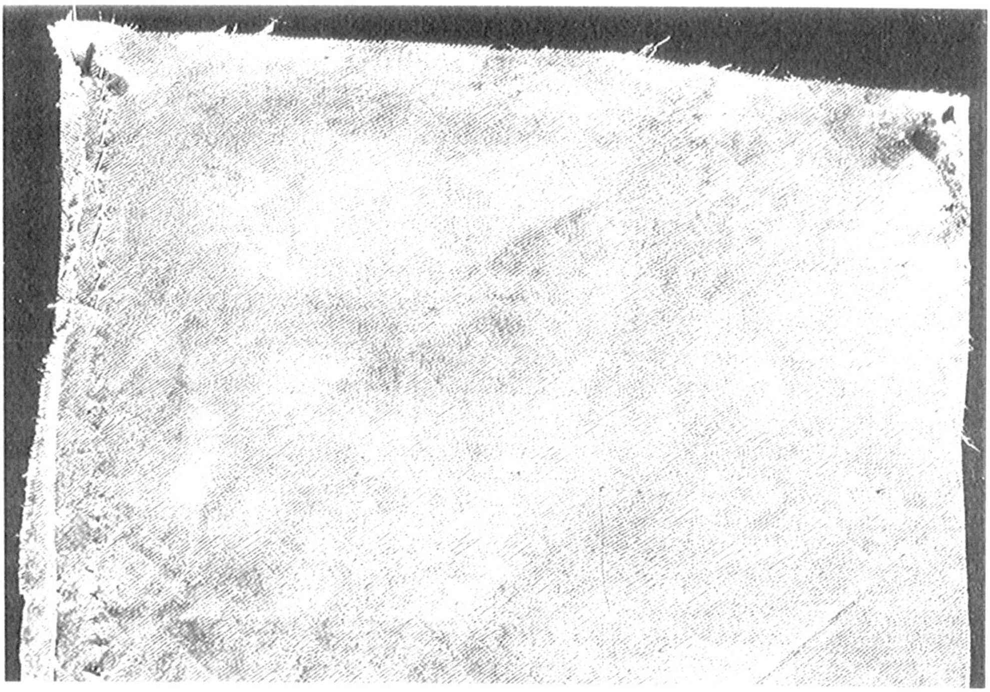

Fig. 17.2 An early medieval 3/1 twill silk damask, Brussels, Royal Museum of Art and History, silk inv. Tx 601 (Copyright Institut Royal du Patrimoine Artistique).

- Three fragments from the cathedral at Chur, Switzerland. No. s 23 and 24, as described by Emil Vogt,[10] appear as No. s 48 and 49 in Brigitta Schmedding's publication.[11] Schmedding puts the origin of these pieces in the eastern Mediterranean area, in the sixth or seventh century.
- One fragment (Vogt No. 6) from the abbey at St Maurice, Wallis, Switzerland. The pattern can be compared with the lion-hunt silk from the Museum of St Ambrose in Milan. According to Vogt, this silk is to be dated to the fifth century.[12] Schmedding (No. 120) attributes this silk to the Mediterranean area, in the fifth–sixth century.[13]
- Two fragments from the church of St Lorentz bei Paspels, Graubünden, Switzerland,[14] which, according to Schmedding (No. 186), are dated to the sixth or seventh century.[15]
- One fragment from the treasury of the church of St Servatius at Maastricht.[16] This two-coloured silk is dated by A. Stauffer to the sixth–seventh century.

Some of these silks allow us to establish that the pattern was woven at right angles to the warp. This applies to the silk inv. Tx 601 from Brussels, the silks from the Museum of St Ambrose in Milan, the abbey of St Maurice (Vogt No. 6) and the treasury of the church of St Servatius at Maastricht.

In all these fabrics the warp is Z-twist silk and the weft is silk without apparent twist. The technological characteristics may be summarised as follows. The ornament is sometimes geometric, sometimes floral or figurative. The warp decoupure (the decoupure is the smallest unit from which the design is built up) is not constant and can vary within the same fragment, from four to five, or from five to six warp threads.[17] Similarly, the weft decoupure varies within a single fragment, from three to four picks or from four to five picks. The twill direction is the same for the two binding-effects. On the edges of the pattern the binding points are never in opposition.[18] The warp count of the different fragments varies from 50 to 84 threads per cm and the weft count varies from 40 to 60 picks per cm. The ratio between the warp count and the weft count of the different fragments is between 1:1 and 3:2.

The two most striking differences between this group and the block damasks of the Roman period are as follows. Firstly, the twill direction of early medieval 3/1 twill damasks is always the same in both warp- and weft-effect sections, but in Roman silk block damasks the twill direction of the two effects is the same or opposed in the earliest two periods, and opposed in the final period. Secondly, on the edges of the pattern the binding points are never in opposition in early medieval damasks, while in Roman block damasks they are always in opposition, with the exception of the single intermediate fabric (the purple silk from Trier).

The technology of weaving early medieval twill damasks

As a result of the study of the technical characteristics described above and examination of the weaving faults,[19] the essential characteristics of the loom (Fig. 17.3) and a procedure for weaving the early medieval silk 3/1 twill damasks may be proposed. First of all, the loom must have been a drawloom with heddle-rods or shafts. For the silk from Brussels, inv. Tx 601, the simple (the part of the drawloom which controls

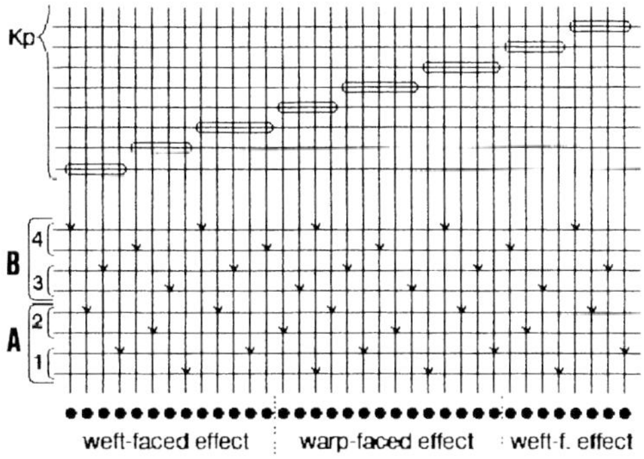

Fig. 17.3 The drawloom tie-up necessary to weave the early medieval 3/1 twill damasks; Kp = pattern harness; 1, 2, 3, 4 = the four paired heddle-rods of the lifting harness; note the displaced threading.

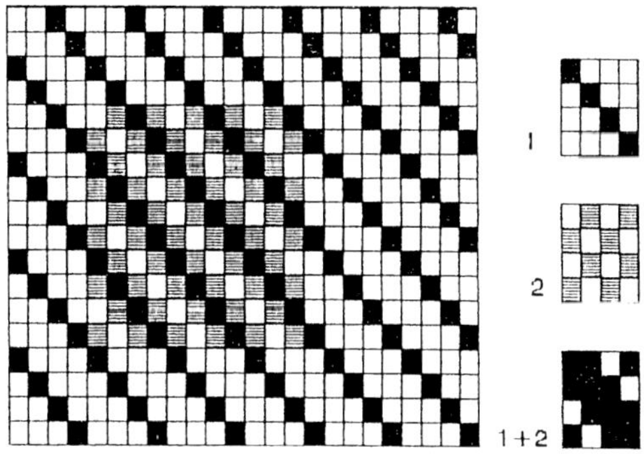

Fig. 17.5. The superimposition of weft-faced 3/1 twill weave upon tabby weave, in order to obtain warp-faced 3/1 twill weave.

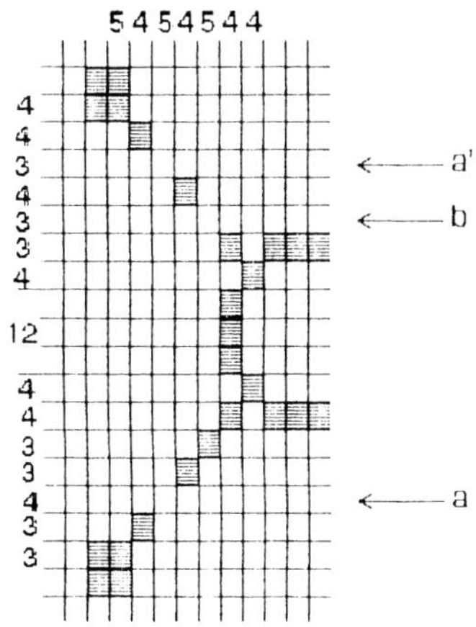

Fig. 17.4. Errors in the weaving of 3/1 twill damask Tx 601. Three warp and weft decoupures are missing: the elements indicated by (a) and (a') are reproduced in all the pattern repeats, in both vertical and the horizontal directions.

the design) must have contained 112 to 140 draw cords.[20] In contradiction of our earlier publications,[21] new research has established that the loom of silk Tx 601 was equipped with a 'permanent memory', so that the pattern and weaving faults repeat at regular intervals (Fig. 17.4). The loom did not have a depression harness. It was equipped with a pattern harness (pattern-making device) and a lifting harness (binding device) composed of only four pairs of heddle rods or shafts.

The warp threads were threaded on the two harnesses, thread by thread on the lifting harness (Figs. 17.3 and 17.7: 1234), but in groups of four, five or six threads on the pattern harness (Figs. 17.3 and 17.7:kp). They were threaded on the lifting harness by a displaced threading (Fig. 17.3). Warp-faced 3/1 twill was obtained by superimposing weft-faced 3/1 twill upon tabby (Fig. 17.5), probably by the following procedure (Figs. 17.3, 17.6–17.7):

- stage 1 (F1). Pull lash 1 and move the shed-lath (Ls) into the shed beyond the lifting harness; let go lash 1.
- stage 2 (F2). Lift the group of heddle-rods (B) and move rod (a) into the shed. Rod (a) now carries two out of four warp threads.
- stage 3 (F3). Turn the shed-lath (Ls) on its edge, push lightly on rod (a) and move rod

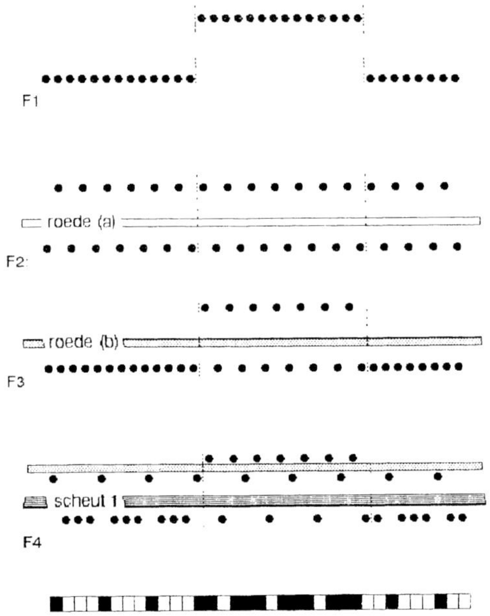

Fig. 17.6 Weaving procedure for 3/1 twill damask in four stages; roede = rod (a); Scheut = weft pick.

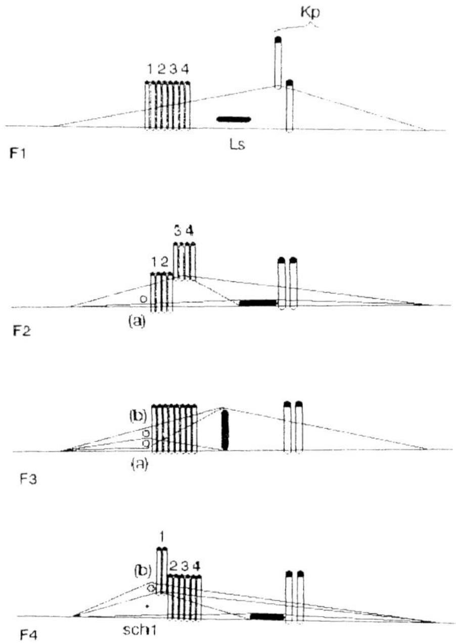

Fig. 17.7 Weaving procedure for 3/1 twill damask, showing the opening of the shed for the first pick in four successive stages.

(b) into the upper shed. Extract rod (a). Rod (b) now carries only two out of four of the warp threads separated out by lash 1(kp): this gives warp-faced twill.

- stage 4 (F4). Turn the shed-lath (Ls) back down and lift the nearest group of heddle-rods (1). Now one in four of the warp threads are raised, as well as rod (b), so that three in four of the warp threads separated out by lash 1 (kp) are raised for warp-faced twill, and one in four of the other parts for weft-faced twill. Pass the pick through this final shed (pick 1) and extract rod (b).

The shed-lath (Ls) must be used for two, three or four successive picks. For weaving these picks, the procedure restarts from stage 2 (F2). Stage 1 (F1) must be restarted at the point where the decoupure is finished. The advantage of the procedure is that a lash has to be pulled only once per decoupure (the lashes are the cords which operate the simple and thus the design). The disadvantage is that a fault made when pulling a lash or when introducing the shed-lath (Ls) is reproduced for all the picks of the decoupure.

During this procedure, the groups (A and B: Fig. 17.3) of two paired heddle rods must be lifted alternately at stage 2 (F2) for the insertion of the shed rod (a), and the groups of paired heddle rods, 1,2,3,4, must be lifted in the order 1–3–2–4 at stage 4 (F4), as described below for a weft decoupure of only three picks.

Pick 1

- Pull lash 1 and enter the shed-lath (Ls); release lash 1.

- Lift group (B) of the lifting harness and enter rod (a).
- Turn the shed-lath (Ls) on its edge, enter rod (b) and extract rod (a).
- Turn back the shed-lath (Ls), lift group (1) of the lifting harness, enter pick 1 and extract rod (b).

Pick 2
- Lift group (A) of the lifting harness and enter rod (a).
- Turn the shed-lath (Ls) on its edge, enter rod (b) and extract rod (a).
- Turn back the shed-lath (Ls), lift group (3) of the lifting harness, enter pick 2 and extract rod (b).

Pick 3
- Lift group (B) of the lifting harness and put rod (a) into the shed.
- Turn the shed-lath (Ls) on its edge, enter rod (b) into the shed and remove rod (a).
- Turn back the shed-lath (Ls), lift group (2) of the lifting harness, enter pick 3 and extract rod (b).

Pick 4 (first pick of the next decoupure)
- extract shed-lath (Ls), pull lash 2 and enter the shed-lath (Ls).
- Lift group (A) of the lifting harness and enter rod (a).
- Turn the shed-lath (Ls) on its edge, enter rod (b) and extract rod (a).
- Turn back the shed-lath (Ls), lift group (4) of the lifting harness, enter pick 4 and extract rod (b).

For the next four picks the two groups (A) and (B), and the four groups, 1,2,3,4, of the lifting harness must be treated in the same way. In the above example we supposed a decoupure of three picks. Indeed, the number of picks per decoupure is independent of the number of picks per cycle. After the entering of any weft-pick, the shed-lath (Ls) can be extracted and re-entered for the next decoupure. The choice of the number of picks in a specific decoupure depends on when the weaver or the assistant-weaver (drawboy) extracts the shed-lath (Ls). At this point, the end of the decoupure is realised and this signals that the drawboy must pull the next lash.

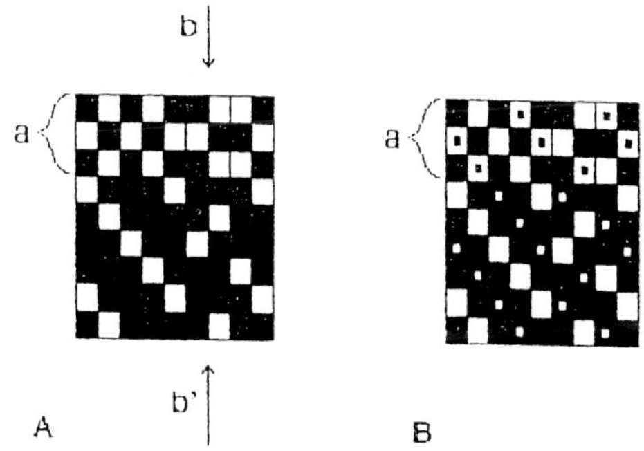

Fig. 17.8 How faults occur in 3/1 twill damask: A: Fault 1: two interchanged warp threads (line b–b). Fault 2: the three upper picks are executed in tabby weave (area a). B: The same faults with indication of the omitted binding points of weft-faced 3/1 twill weave.

Although it is impossible to prove irrefutably the complete procedure proposed here, we have found important indications that warp-faced 3/1 twill was realised by the principle of superimposing weft-faced 3/1 twill upon tabby weave (Fig. 17.5). It concerns a weaving fault found in the fragment Tx 601 from Brussels (Fig. 17.8) mentioned above. In addition, some selection faults, repeated in the complete decoupure, which were found in the same fragment, prove that the weaver(s) have used a shed-lath in order to save the shed, pulled by a lash, over three, four or five picks of the same decoupure (Fig. 17.9).

Fig. 17.9. Weave diagram for part of 3/1 twill damask, Tx601, showing a fault illustrated which has caused the right arm of the swastika motif to become shortened. This weaving fault occurs in one warp decoupure and two complete weft decoupures. It reappears on every repeat, but only in the weft direction.

Conclusion

The most striking differences between the weaving characteristics of the early medieval group and those of the Roman silk block damasks are as follows. First, warp-faced 3/1 twill was realised by superimposing weft-faced 3/1 twill on tabby weave, for the early medieval damasks. Second, the warp threads were no longer threaded on a limited number of sets of four heddle-rods. They were threaded on two harnesses, a lifting harness of four heddle-rods and a pattern harness of multiple heddle-rods. The warp threads were connected to the rods of the lifting harness, one by one, by separate loops. On the pattern harness the warp was threaded in groups according to the warp decoupure. The pattern-making device of the early medieval damasks was therefore totally different from the device which was used to realise the patterns of the Roman block damasks. We may suppose that the weavers of the medieval damasks adapted for their needs the principles of the drawloom of the contemporaneous weft-faced compound tabbies. In this context, it is interesting to mention the silk textile from the tomb of St. Paulinus in Trier, dated no later than AD 395, as published by John Peter Wild.[22] According to our analysis, this silk, which is decorated with circles and crosses, was woven by means of a loom equipped with a lifting harness consisting of two heddle-rods for the binding warp threads and a pattern harness consisting of 34 heddle-rods for the pattern-making warp (reverse threading).[23]

From the study of the 3/1 twill damask, Tx 601 from the Royal Museum of Art and History in Brussels, it may be deduced that this sort of damask was woven in a period when Byzantine weavers did not have at their disposal looms equipped with a combination of lifting, depression and pattern harnesses. The only lifting harness on their looms was composed of four heddle-rods (eventually doubled). These rods were manipulated so that it was possible to weave damasks. In contrast with the procedure used to weave Roman block damasks, this procedure, however laborious, allowed them to realise patterns with fluid outlines. Even so, the 3/1 twill damasks made by this procedure, are of an inferior quality compared with the 3/1 twill damasks made on fully developed drawlooms equipped with three harnesses, a lifting harness, a depression harness and a pattern harness. With the three-harness loom, one always obtains opposed binding points at the edges of the pattern, at the point that the warp and weft decoupure add up to a multiple of two threads. In contrast, the procedure used for early medieval 3/1 twill damasks never has opposed binding points. This disadvantage leads to deformation of the outlines. Additionally, in order to keep small details, it is necessary to work with a warp and weft decoupure of at least three threads, which means that the weft count must be relatively high. Since, on the one hand, the procedure is rather laborious, and, on the other hand, the weft count must be relatively high, the production of these 3/1 twill damasks demands a lot of effort. From this, one can see why the procedure for the early medieval 3/1 twill damasks would disappear as soon as it was possible to obtain the same effect with other constructions. Perhaps structures such as those of the monochrome weft-faced compound twills (*geritzter Samit*), monochrome lampas and the proto-lampas of the 10th–11th centuries, may be considered as products made in an attempt to replace the laborious procedure for weaving 3/1 twill damasks. At present, there is no indication that the Byzantine weavers worked with a lifting harness and a depression harness on the same warp.

Notes

1 D. De Jonghe and M. Tavernier, 'Die spätantiken Köper 4-damaste aus dem Sarg des Bishofs Paulinus in der Krypta der St.-Paulinus-Kirche zu Trier', *Trierer Zeitschrift*, Jhrg. 40/41, 1977–78, pp. 145–74; D. De Jonghe and M. Tavernier 'Les damassés de la proche-antiquité', *Bulletin de Liaison du CIETA*, NE 47–48, 1978-I & II, pp. 14–42; D. De Jonghe and M. Tavernier, 'Les damassés de Palmyre', *Bulletin de Liaison du CIETA*, NE 54, 1981-II, pp. 20–52; D. De Jonghe and M. Tavernier, 'De textielresten uit graf 6', in *Maria van Bourgondië, Brugge*, Brugge, 1982a, pp. 207–234; D. De Jonghe and M. Tavernier, 'Les damassés de Palmyre', *Annales Archéologiques Arabes Syriennes*, Vol. XXXII, 1982b, pp. 89–116; D. De Jonghe, 'Quatre types de damas sergé 3 lie 1 du 1er au 14ème siècle', *Compte-Rendu Symposium AEDTA*, Paris, 1983, pp. 48–62.

2 J. P. Wild, 'The Roman Horizontal Loom', *American Journal of Archaeology*, 91, 1987, pp. 459–471.

3 All of these fragments have been discussed in the publications listed in note 1, except for the piece from Brigetio (Szony) which is as yet unpublished; and the piece from Jovia, which appears in:
W. Endrei, 'Über Blöckchendamaste', in: *Opera Textilia Variorum Temporum; to Honour Agnes Geijer on Her Ninetieth Birthday 26th October 1988*, Stockholm 1988, pp. 23–26.

4 D. De Jonghe and M. Tavernier, 1981-II, art. cit.; J. P. Wild, 1987, art. cit.

5 D. De Jonghe and C. Verhecken-Lammens, 'Le vêtement damassé 4219 de la Fondation Abegg à Riggisberg', *Riggisberger Berichte, Band 2, Varia 1994*, Abegg-stiftung, Riggisberg, 1994, pp. 41–72; pp. 60–61. The construction of overturning handles which has been proposed as an alternative for the Roman horizontal loom, for the weaving of the wool block damask tunic from Riggisberg, is not taken into consideration here, because this construction cannot be used for block damasks, such as the silk block damasks, which have more than two sections (two sets of heddle-rods).

6 I. Errera, *Catalogue d'étoffes anciennes et modernes, 3e édition*, Bruxelles, 1927; p. 13, Nr 1.

7 A. de Capitano d'Argazo, 'Antichi tessuti della basilica Ambrosiana', in *"L'ARTE" rivista di storia dell'arte medioevale e moderna*, Milano, 1941, pp. 41–60.

8 H. Granger-Taylor, 'The two dalmatics of Saint Ambrose', in *Bulletin de Liaison du CIETA*, NE 57–58, 1983-I et II, pp. 127–173; p. 143. At Trier we found two block damasks, one purple, the other yellow. We have demonstrated that the yellow block damask must be considered a representative of the final period; D. De Jonghe and M. Tavernier, art. cit., 1978 I et II.

9 H. Granger-Taylor, 1983 I et II, art. cit., pp. 143–144.

10 E. Vogt, 'Frühmittelalterliche Seidenstoffe aus dem Hochaltar der Kathedrale Chur', in *Zeitschrift für Archaeologie und Kunstgeschichte*, 13, 1952, pp. 1–23, Taf. 1–10; Taf. 8, 1–2; 8, 3–4; 8, 5–6; Nrs. 22, 23 and 24.

11 B. Schmedding, *Mittelalterliche Textilien in Kirchen und Klöstern der Schweiz*, Abegg-Stiftung, Bern, 1978, pp. 58–59.

12 E. Vogt, '*Frühmittelalterliche Stoffe aus der Abtei St-Maurice*, Zeitschrift für Archaeologie und Kunstgeschichte', 18, 1958, H. 3, pp. 110–140, Taf. 27–38; pp. 121–123, Nr 6; E. Vogt, 'Die textilreste aus dem Reliquienbehalter des Altars in der Kirche St. Lorenz bei Paspels', *Zeitschrift für Archaeologie und Kunstgeschichte*, 2, 1963/64, pp. 83–90; Tav. 21–26; p. 85.

13 B. Schmedding, 1978, *op. cit.*, pp. 152–153.

14 E. Vogt, 1963/64, art. cit., pp. 84–85, Nrs. 2 and 3; Taf. 21 c, d; 21 e, f.

15 B. Schmedding, 1978, *op. cit.*, p. 204.

16 A. Muthesius, 'De zijden stoffen in de Schatkamer van de Sint Servaaskerk te Maastricht', in *Publications*, 1974, afb. 17; A. Stauffer, *Die mittelalterlichen Textilien von St. Servatius in Maastricht*, Maastricht, 1991, pp. 92–94.

17 According to A. de Capitano D'Arzago, the silk with the lion-hunt (S7) has a decoupure of four warp threads, but detailed examination of the photographs from A. De Capitano D'Arzago, by both H. Granger-Taylor and by myself, rather shows a decoupure of six warp threads.

18 A question mark must be placed beside the weave diagram of this fragment, fig. 25, Tav. XV, which has been published by A. De Capitano D'Arzago. According to this drawing, the two twill weaves would be used so that the binding opposition points are present at the lower and right-hand edges of the pattern. With the superimposition principle (see later) this is impossible.

19 D. De Jonghe, 'Een vroeg-middeleeuwse keper 4-damast uit de Koninklijke Musea voor Kunst en Geschiedenis', *Bulletin van de Koninklijke Musea voor Kunst en Geschiedenis, Brussel*, 69, 1998. pp. 115–232. The comments on all the weaving faults in silk Tx 601 can be found in this article.

20 H. Granger-Taylor, 1983 I et II, art. cit., p. 150: between 200 and 250 heddle-rods or cords (lion-hunt damask).

21 D. De Jonghe and M. Tavernier, 1982a, art. cit., p. 221; D. De Jonghe, 1983, art. cit., p. 54.

22 J. P. Wild, *Textile manufacture in the Northern Roman Provinces*, Cambridge, 1970, p. 53 and fig. 46 p. 169; J. P. Wild, 1987, art. cit., p. 467.

23 D. De Jonghe provides the following analysis of the fragment of the weft-faced compound tabby from Trier.

Repeat

Dimensions: 1,375 × 1,5 cm

Composition: repeat with horizontal and vertical symmetrical axes.

Warp
Material and count:
– Main warp: brown poil silk, light Z spun, thinner as the binding warp; 24–28/cm.
– Binding warp: brown poil silk, light Z spun; 24–28/cm.
Proportion: 1/1
Decoupure: 1 main warp thread.

Weft
Material and count:
– Ground weft: brown tram silk; 85–90/cm.
– Pattern weft: beige tram silk, thinner as the brown weft; 85–90/cm.
Proportion:
– 1 pick, 1st lat, brown
– 1 pick, 2nd lat, beige
Decoupure: 2 passes.

Weave construction
Weft-faced compound tabby. The threads of the main warp separate the wefts, making the colour required at that point appear on the upper face, and hiding the other colour on the reverse. The binding warp threads are worked in tabby in each pass.

Chapter 18

A PREVIOUSLY UNRECOGNISED LION SILK AT CANTERBURY CATHEDRAL

Anna Muthesius

Introduction

In Byzantium the lion was termed a 'fierce and imperial beast' and imperially inscribed silks with striding lion motifs acted as potent emblems of political authority.[1] Striding lion motifs had appeared widely in classical Greece, and so their 're-emergence' in Byzantium gives rise to some interesting questions.[2] Was there an unbroken tradition for the use of this motif? What was the role of such imagery in promulgating the classical tradition? How far did this imagery contribute to the definition of the relationship between divine and imperial authority? This paper is offered as a small tribute to John Peter Wild, whose dedication to the excavation, research and publication of early textiles is legendary.

The striding lion motif in Classical Greece

Writing in 1971, John Peter singled out a rare linen with an embroidered striding lion motif (Victoria and Albert Museum T220A,B-1953).[3] This classical piece had been discovered in a bronze urn at Koropi, outside Athens.[4] It is a Z-spun linen, first published in 1954 by John Beckwith, and assigned a late fifth century date.[5] Elizabeth Barber, writing in 1991, dated the textile more broadly to the first millennium BC, describing the find as a 'small swatch of Z-spun linen, embroidered with metallic thread'. The embroidered design Barber detailed as a diaper pattern with a tiny lion motif in lozenges, the lion shown 'walking with tail lifted and front paw raised'.[6] In 1997 Margaret Miller returned to this little published embroidery, to suggest that its lion motif reflected Achaemenid tradition.[7] She believed that the embroidery itself was perhaps Phoenician; and that the linen fell into the category of one of the many types of precious Eastern textiles which were imported and were evidently much in demand in Athens.[8] She suggested that the appearance of this imported linen in classical Athens, served to demonstrate the power of textiles as a medium for the transmission of cultural influences.[9] Today the lions of the once resplendent Koropi linen embroidery can be recognised only in outline, through a series of pin pricks (Fig. 18.1).[10] Only a few minute traces of the original silver-gilt embroidery remain.

Fig. 18.1 A classical Greek linen from Koropi, outside Athens; the outline of an embroidered striding lion is visible as pin pricks and some traces of silver-gilt threads (Victoria and Albert Museum T220 A,B-1953). Photograph provided by Linda Woolley and printed with kind permission of the Victoria and Albert Museum.

The striding lion, either with the animal shown in profile or with its head turned to the front to face the viewer, is well established upon early Greek vases. Both forms of striding lion are found, for instance, upon a Milesian (MWG) *oinochoe* from the Black Sea, now in Athens (Fig. 18.2).[11] The frontally facing lion there is actually shown attacking a stag, and as the body of this 'lion' is covered with decorative circle patterns, some prefer to term it not a lion but a panther/leopard. The other animal, another lion, is shown in profile, and this has a plain body. Both animals are depicted with a front paw raised. On a Chalcidian deep cup (Athens Goulandris 718, once at Castle Ashby), a plain frontally facing lion is depicted with all four feet firmly planted upon the ground.[12] There were evidently variations in detail in the depiction of these early Greek lion motifs. Boardman implies that

Fig. 18.2 A Milesian oinochoe, *from the Black Sea, showing a decorated, 'lion' (perhaps a panther or leopard) facing front and attacking a stag; and a plain lion in profile (Athens, previously Vlasto).*

the turning of the head to face the viewer was a late innovation in early Greek vase painting, of an 'orientalising' type produced in Corinth in the seventh century BC.[13]

The lion silk at Canterbury Cathedral

At Canterbury Cathedral Treasury a paired main warp twill silk (weft-faced compound twill), with striding lion motif, acts as an interesting foil to the classical examples.[14] It is one of an impressive series of silks used for seal bags at the Cathedral, and it was first noted by G. Robinson and H. Urquhart in an article of 1934.[15] At that time, bag 22 was no longer attached to any seal which might have helped with its dating. Robinson and Urquhart thought that the design on the silk was difficult to reconstruct, but the head of a 'large cat' was visible. They concluded that the motif was an Italian copy of a 'Chinese scaled dragon'.[16]

A closer examination of Canterbury silk no. 22, reveals the outline of an ornate lion motif, most clearly visible on the back of the piece (Figs. 18.3–18.4). The design is obscured on the face of the textile through excessive wear of its surface wefts. The whole silk measures 225 mm by 125 mm (maximum w. × h.); the face of the lion has a breadth of 65mm. The fragment shows part of a walking lion motif in the form of a frontally facing lion with ornate mane and with two striding front legs. Only the raised tail of another missing lion, which would have appeared in front, is visible. The body and the rear legs of the lion motif do not survive on the fragment, but there is sufficient of the design remaining to be able to recognise the survival into medieval times of a classical form of striding lion motif.

Canterbury lion silk no. 22, has a red-purple ground and a design in yellow and off-white with use of red-purple markings.[17] Technically and stylistically it can be

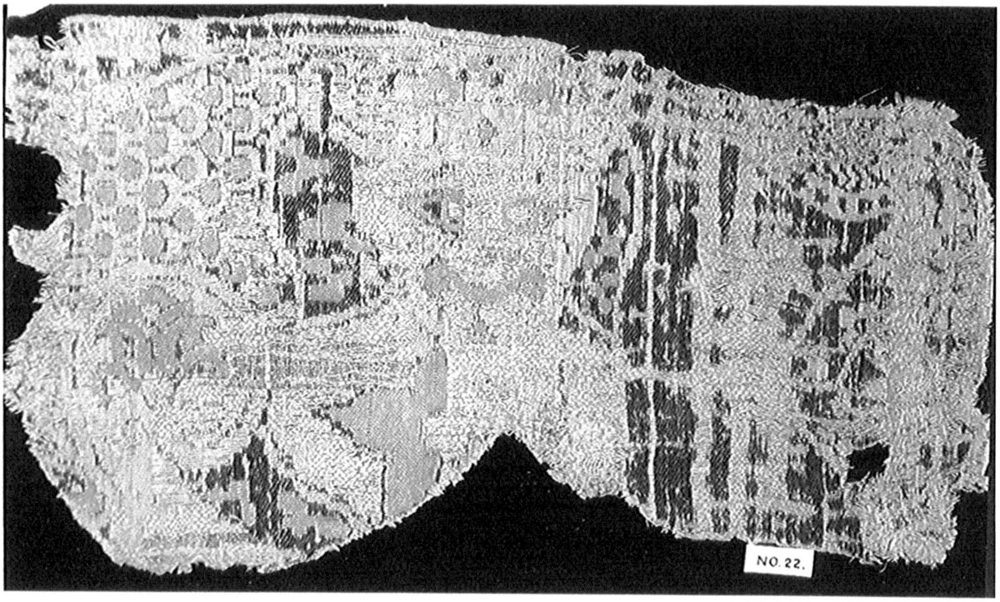

Fig. 18.3 Canterbury silk no. 22 (M660): the front. This and Fig. 18.4 kindly reproduced with permission of Canterbury Cathedral authorities (see Colour Plate VI).

Fig. 18.4 Canterbury silk no. 22 (M660): the reverse (see Colour Plate VII).

dated ninth to tenth century. It is a most interesting addition to a group of Byzantine striding lion silks, variously dated between the eighth and eleventh centuries.[18]

Comparative material

Several of the striding lion silks reached Europe as diplomatic gifts.[19] A number of these can be closely dated from evidence contained in their woven inscriptions[20] to dates between AD 869 and 1025.[21] These have been listed under the heading Group 1A in Table 18.1. Two related striding lion silks are no longer extant and these are categorised as Group 1B in the same table. A further group of five surviving striding lion silks do not bear any inscriptions and are listed under Group B (Table 18.1). The main characteristics of the groups are summarised in Table 18.2. The Canterbury Cathedral Lion silk no. 22, belongs to Group 2.

A striking difference between Group 1 and Group 2, concerns the degree of ornamentation employed upon the bodies of the animals. The most highly ornate creatures occur in Group 2, in examples i (Ravenna), ii (Berlin), iii (Berlin) and iv (Canterbury no. 22). Geometric or foliate motifs decorate the bodies of all the animals depicted on these silks, while Group 1 uses only undecorated lions. It is difficult to say for certain whether the Sens fragment with a lion's paw, here assigned to Group 2, example iv, did or did not bear ornament: it is possible that if more of the original silk came to light, this too might belong with the plain imperial Byzantine lion silks.

In general, the evidence suggests that highly decorated animals were in vogue in the ninth to tenth century, but that in the tenth to eleventh century plainer animals were preferred, perhaps under the influence of a change in imperial production. Certainly, the documented imperial lion silk from, St. Arnoul, Créspy, France (Group 1B, i), most plausibly dated to AD

Group 1A: extant, inscribed, imperial Byzantine lion silks

- i. Berlin, Schloss Köpenick (now St. Servatius, Siegburg): lion silk M52, AD 921–923[22]
- iia. Berlin, Schloss Charlottenburg: lion silk M615 (two fragments), AD 976–1025[23]
- iib. Krefeld, Kunstgewerbe Museum: lion silk M616 (several fragments), AD 976–1025.[24] (This silk has been misplaced and can no longer be located at the museum.)
- iic. Düsseldorf, Kunst Museum: lion silk M54 (six fragments): AD 976–1025.[25] (Silks M615, M616, and M54 were originally all joined and formed a single silk .)
- iii. Cologne–Deutz, St. Heribert: lion silk M53, AD 976– 025.[26]

Group 1B: inscribed imperial Byzantine lion silks, documented but now lost

- i. Créspy, St. Arnoul: lion silk, AD 869?[27]
- ii. Auxerre, St. Eusèbe: lion silk, AD 813–820?[28]

Group 2: non-inscribed lion silks, dated on technical and stylistic grounds

- i. Ravenna, Museo Nationale: lion silk M55, ninth to tenth century AD[29]
- ii. Berlin, Schloss Charlottenburg, Kunstgewerbe Museum, inv. 78.634: lion silk M56, ninth to tenth century AD.[30]
- iii. Berlin, Schloss Charlottenburg, Kunstgewerbe Museum, inv. 78.645: lion silk M57, ninth to tenth century AD.[31]
- iv. Sens, Cathedral treasury: lion silk M534 (fragment showing only the lion's paws); eighth to ninth century AD.[32]
- v. Canterbury Cathedral no. 22: lion silk M660, ninth to tenth century AD.

Table 18.1 Lion silks: their location and date of manufacture. M numbers are those allocated in Muthesius' registry of silks: see A. Muthesius, Byzantine Silk Weaving *(Vienna 1997).*

869, fits in with this chronology.[33] The lions of this lost silk bore red and green ornament across the body. The decorative nature of the piece contrasts with the plainer extant lion silks dated to the tenth to eleventh centuries (Group 1A, i and ii a–c). A noticeable feature of the later silks is also the use of a small tree motif behind the backs of the lions. This tree device in the context of striding lion motifs, finds a striking antecedent on a Roman pavement mosaic at Horkstow in Lincolnshire.[34]

The striding lion/panther-leopard motif

The discussion so far has aimed to place the Canterbury Cathedral lion silk (no. 22) in the context of Byzantine silk weaving. At this point it is necessary to pin down the silk's motif in greater detail. Earlier mention was made of the fact that two distinct striding animals appeared in antiquity: the lion and the panther-leopard. Strictly speaking, because of its decoration, the Canterbury piece could be viewed more as a panther-leopard than as a plain lion motif. Did the Byzantines know the difference between the plain and the decorated animal? In this context one has to remember that a distinction between the two 'families' of animals did appear to be known in the eighth to ninth century, judging from the appearance of both categories on the St. Ambrogio Hunter silk in Milan (M14 A,B).[35] The question is, did any classical distinction become blurred later on?

It is apparent that the plain lion motif (Athens, Goulandis 718 cup) and the panther-leopard motif (Milesian (MWG) *oinochoe*), were known in ancient Greece. During the tenth century in Byzantium a strong classical element appeared in both ivory carving and in manuscript illumination, under the influence of the Macedonian emperors. This revival was aimed to boost the image of the imperial house,[36] but scholars writing of this 'Macedonian Renaissance' have in general failed to notice Byzantine silks. The present study might suggest that a classical revival was evident there too, not least in the use of the striding lion/panther-leopard motifs. Not only that, but Byzantine silks would indicate a classical revival that was well under way as early as the ninth century. Indeed, even earlier, in the eighth to ninth century, Byzantine silk weavers were mixing classical and Sasanian motifs (consider the Dioscorides silk, M36, at St. Servatius, Maastricht).[37]

If striding lion/panther-leopard motifs were symbols from the past, how far did

Group 1A Paired main warp twills, extant, bearing woven imperial Byzantine inscriptions naming specific, datable rulers.
Group 1B Silks today lost, weaves unrecorded. Documentation shows that these were lion silks, with woven imperial Byzantine inscriptions also naming specific rulers.
Group 2 Nos (i), (ii), (iii) and (v) are paired main warp twills, without inscriptions. No. (iv) is a single main warp twill, a fragment without inscription. These silks are datable using technical and stylistic evidence.

Table 18.2: a summary of the main characteristics of the different groups of striding lion silks

they retain their original meaning? Did the images have a variety of meanings, or did they bear fixed messages? In any symbolism that Byzantium might have known, the issue of the relationship of divine to imperial authority would have been important. The immediate problem of transference of symbols from classical into Byzantine culture, would have concerned the 'Christianisation' of the image. In the case of our striding lion motifs there needed to be a link between a classical nature symbol and a sign of Christian belief. This process appears to have been encouraged in Byzantium between the fourth and sixth centuries in particular as a means of boosting imperial authority. A church of the period of Justinian in eastern Libya provides an excellent example of the process.[38] In the nave pavement at Qasr-el-Lebia within an Earth and Ocean composition, the striding lion occurs (third register down, second register across). The lion even has its front paw raised. The mosaic is datable to AD 539–540 and has been interpreted as an attempt by Justinian to imitate the acts of the Divine Creator. The emperor, God's representative on earth, acted as founder of cities and churches, in imitation of God's act of creation and of his establishment of a Kingdom in Heaven.

The depiction of animals and divinities was widespread from an early date and ancient nature cults developed imagery which left a strong mark on Byzantine silks. Both in ancient Greece and in the ancient Near East, lions and nature deities were often depicted together.[39] A distinction has been claimed between the traditions of Greek and of Minoan, or Mycenaean, art. The Greek goddess or 'mistress of the animals' held the beasts apart forcibly, but the Minoan or Mycenaean antecedents for the theme, Martinos claims, revealed a heraldic approach, with the goddess merely flanked by lions. This forceful goddess developed under North Syrian or Levantine influence, according to Martinos.[40] Martinos traced the Syrian goddess type to Crete and mainland Greece at a time when a class of warrior aristocrat was seeking to establish a special relationship with the divine.[41] One may enquire in this context, how far the warrior Macedonian emperors, perhaps unconsciously, were treading the same path. They certainly termed themselves the 'devout' emperors on the striding lion silks of the tenth to eleventh centuries, and these silks were used as diplomatic gifts to promote the image of the power and authority of the Byzantine imperial house.[42]

Not only the striding lion/ panther-leopard motifs of classical antiquity appear on Byzantine silks. Other ancient motifs, such as griffins, eagles, eagles attacking quadrupeds, and so on, occurred upon Byzantine silks of the tenth to eleventh century.[43]All these ancient images were absorbed into Christian allegory. The eagle rending a deer was interpreted as a symbol of the gathering of gentiles at the Body of Christ,[44] or of the faithful before the Body and Blood of Christ.[45] John Chrysostom associated the eagle and the carcass with communion and with the Resurrection of the Son of Justice.[46] Another commentator interpreted the image as Christ's Victory over Evil.[47]

Moralising Christian imagery made extensive use of classical motifs. At the same time, it appears that a secular tradition might have developed based on popular literature – a theme which has not been extensively researched in the field of Byzantine studies. In the context of this paper it is interesting to note, for instance, that both lions and panthers feature in the Byzantine romance of Digenis Akritis.[48]

Here the lion is seen as a wild beast. Human action aided by divine intervention, overcomes the beast. The conquest provides a medium for the demonstration of human bravery and devotion. The hero may slay the beast by the power of the sword but he could only do so with his bare hands provided God's power had been granted.[49] Twelve 'well proven hunting leopards' were the gift of Digenis' father-in-law to the hero, according to the legend.[50] It was also seen as a miraculous sign when wild beast and domesticated animal (lion and sheep) were found to be feeding together.[51] The imagery is secular but tinged with Christian morality.

Conclusion

A detailed study of the use of ancient motifs upon Byzantine silks has still to be undertaken. A preliminary study of one such motif, the striding lion/panther-leopard motif, presented here, suggests this field may prove a fruitful area for further consideration. Such a study may throw valuable light upon the nature of transmission of classical tradition and upon Byzantine understanding of classical heritage. Imperial authority in the context of divine grace was a major tenet of Byzantine civilisation. The striding lion/panther-leopard motifs appear to have provided an image for the authority and legitimacy of the imperial house.

A parting thought is provided with reference to a multi-bodied panther-leopard silk at Aachen Cathedral treasury. This amusing twelfth-century, paired main warp twill silk, depicts a single headed, spotted, multi-bodied quadruped in playful posture. Its closest parallel occurs in the form of a literary description of a pattern upon a Byzantine lady's dress in a popular romance.[52] Perhaps by the twelfth century a distinction had been drawn between the use of classical imagery in a Christian and in a secular context? The highly decorative panther-leopard motifs of the ninth to tenth century Byzantine silks (including Canterbury no. 22) may have paved the way for such a development.

Notes

1. A. P Kazhdan and A. M. Talbot (eds) *Oxford Dictionary of Byzantium*, II (Oxford, 1991), entry number 1231. Source *Migne, PG.* 54, p. 699, lines 10–11.
2. See for example, J. Boardman, *Early Greek Vase Painting* (London, 1998), illustrations on pp. 152 and 242.
3. J. P. Wild, *Textile Manufacture in the Northern Roman Provinces* (Cambridge: Cambridge University Press, 1970), pp. 45 and 132; Table H, no. 13.
4. I wish to thank Linda Woolley of the Textile Department, Victoria and Albert Musuem, for her kind assistance regarding the Koropi linen in her care.
5. J. Beckwith, 'Textile fragments from Classical Antiquity: an important find at Koropi, near Athens', in *Illustrated London News*, XXIII (January 1954), pp. 114–115.
6. E. J. W. Barber, *Prehistoric Textiles* (New Jersey, 1991), p. 206.
7. M. C. Miller, *Athens and Persia in the Fifth Century BC. A Study in Cultural Receptivity.* (Cambridge, 1997), p. 80, note 119.

8 Ibid., chapter 2, pp. 29–62, and figs. 7–9. The Achaemenid Persian lion in fig. 7 has one paw raised. This is on a cloisonné enamel excavated at the sanctuary of Zeus, Dodona. Figures 8 and 9 show two Achaemenid Persian lions excavated at the sanctuary of the great Gods, Samothrace. These do not have front paw raised. All three lions face forwards in profile, rather than having their heads turned towards the viewer. Figure 27 of Miller's book shows a dark picture of the Koropi linen.

9 Ibid., chapter 3, 63ff and especially pp. 75–81 with discussion of the Koropi linen on pp. 80–81.

10 Beckwith, *Textile fragments*, p. 114. Two plates include a total of five Koropi fragments. Three of the five bore lion embroidery. Measurements for two of the three embroidered fragments are given as 4 ¾ × 4 ¼ and 8 × 4 inches.

11 Boardman, *Early Greek Vase Painting*, fig. 286 on p. 152.

12 Ibid., p. 242, fig. 478.

13 Ibid., pp. 87 and 181.

14 This silk was examined by the present author in the 1980s and again last year. I am indebted to the Librarian of the Chapter House of Canterbury Cathedral for access to the piece. I also wish to thank Ann Oakley for her earlier assistance concerning access to all the seal bags.

15 G. Robinson, H. Urquhart, 'Seal Bags in the Cathedral Church of Canterbury' *Archaeologia* 84(1935) pp. 163–211; under seal bag no. 22.

16 Ibid., under the catalogue description for silk no. 22

17 For the chronology of weaving types consult A. Muthesius, *Byzantine Silk Weaving* (Vienna, 1997), chapter 16, pp. 145–148 and chart acting as fig. 15. For the dating of the single main warp twills in general see chapter 7, pp. 65–79.

18 Ibid., chapter 4, pp. 34–38 and notes 1–34 on pp. 40–41.

19 Ibid., pp. 37–38.

20 Ibid., pp. 34–37.

21 Ibid., pp. 34–36 and catalogue numbers M52, M53, M54 on pp. 180–182. Documented examples of lion silks with imperial inscriptions are discussed on pp. 36–37.

22 Ibid., pp. 180–181 with further bibliography. Also, figs. 1A, 1B, 2A, and 3A.

23 Ibid., pp. 35 and 220 and fig. 2B (there mislabelled as M52 instead of M615).

24 Ibid., pp. 35 and 220 and fig. 96B.

25 Ibid., pp. 35 and 181–182 and fig. 3B.

26 Ibid., pp. 181.

27 Ibid., pp. 36–37 showing eighteenth-century transcription of the inscription, with translation.

28 Ibid., p. 37.

29 Ibid., chapter 5, pp. 44–45, 182 and figs. 11A and 11B.

30 Ibid., pp. 47 and 182 and fig. 13A.

31 Ibid., pp. 47 and 182 and fig. 13B.

32 Ibid., pp. 46–47 and 217 and figs. 12A and 12B.

33 Ibid., pp. 36–37 and footnote 22 on p. 41 referring to C. Carlier, *Histoire du duché de Valois* I (Paris, 1764), pp. 268–269, where the copied inscription appears.

34 Muthesius, *Byzantine Silk Weaving*, p. 35 with footnote 16 on p. 40, citing F. Klingender, *Animals in Art and Thought to the end of the Middle Ages* (London, 1971), plate 74. This shows the lion mosaic motif with tree device at Horkstow in Lincolnshire, a Roman site.

35 Ibid., p. 169 and figs. 102A and 102B.

36 For the Byzantine Macedonian Empire see *Byzance* (Paris: Louvre, exhibition catalogue,

1992–1993), section 3, pp. 208–215. The classical revival manuscripts appear on pp. 342–352, and some relevant ivories are shown on pp. 242–244.

37 Muthesius, *Byzantine Silk Weaving*, p. 73 and catalogue number M36 with fig. 22B.

38 H. Maguire, *Earth and Ocean. The Terrestrial World in Early Byzantine Art* (Pennsylvania and London,1987), p. 45 and fig. 52, and pp. 48–49.

39 N. Martinos, *The Goddess and the Warrior* (London and New York, 2000), chapter 6, pp. 110–129.

40 Ibid., pp. 117–120. See conclusions on p. 128, especially no. 3 with reference to figs. 6. 4, 6. 6, 6. 8 and 6. 15.

41 Ibid., p. 129.

42 A. Muthesius, *Studies in Byzantine and Islamic Silk Weaving* (London, 1995), study X, 'Silken diplomacy', pp. 165–172; and study XII, 'The role of Byzantine silks in the Ottoman Empire', pp. 201–216.

43 Muthesius, *Byzantine Silk Weaving*, pp. 52–53 for griffin attacking quadruped. A. Muthesius, 'The Byzantine Eagle' in A. Muthesius (forthcoming) *Studies in Silk in Byzantium*, study X, London 2000.

44 Maguire, *Earth and Ocean* p. s 47 and 51 and fig. 58, Reference to Gentiles in Anastasios, HexFmeron 6, *Migne PG*, LXXXIX, cols. 924–926.

45 Maguire, *Earth and Ocean*, p. 51. For reference to Body and Blood of Christ see St. Ambrose's commentary on Luke, Expositio Evangelii secundum Lucam, 8, 56; Ambrosii Mediolanensis Opera, part 4. (*Corpus Christianorum, Series Latina*, X1V, p. s 318–319).

46 Maguire, *Earth and Ocean*, p. 52. For John Chrysostom's interpretation see, In Epistulam I ad Corinthios Homilia, XXIV, 3, *Migne PG*, LXI col. 203.

47 Maguire *Earth and Ocean*, p. 47 and footnote 36 on p. 93, with reference to M. Guarducci, 'La piu antica catachesi figurata: Il grande mosaico della basilica di Gasr Elbia in Cirenaica: *Atti della Accademia Nazionale dei Lincei, Classe di Scienze morali storiche e filologiche Memorie*, series 8, XVIII/7, (1975), pp. 659–686.

48 The latest edition of the Romance is E. Jeffreys (ed. and transl.), *Digenis Akritis* Cambridge Medieval Classics 7 (Cambridge, 1998). For brave deeds see Grottaferrata manuscript p. 69, line 25 ff; and pp. 159 and 223.

49 Ibid., Gr. f. pp. 76–77.

50 Ibid., Gr. f. p. 119.

51 Ibid., Gr. f. p. 53.

52 Muthesius, *Studies in Byzantine and Islamic Silk Weaving*, plate 71 (here mistakenly termed bi-cephal lion motif).

Chapter 19

THE RE-APPEARANCE OF AN OLD ROMAN LOOM IN MEDIEVAL ENGLAND

Penelope Walton Rogers

Introduction

John Peter Wild's work has always been a pleasing blend of historical and archaeological research. Excavated textiles have been farmed for the secrets of their technology; the tools of production have been drawn into the discussion; and written sources have been trawled for contemporary descriptions and linguistic clues. The following text is an attempt to apply a similar approach to the later history of a loom which will be familiar to John Peter from his Roman studies. This is the two-beam vertical loom, which was in use in Gaul, Italy and the eastern provinces during the Roman Empire and which re-appeared some centuries later in England. The aim has been to draw together a variety of sources in order to pin-point when the loom re-appeared; and to outline a new theory concerning its role in Saxo-Norman England.

The two-beam vertical loom

In its simplest form, the two-beam vertical loom consists of two uprights set in a stand, with an upper and lower cross-beam. The cross-beams may be fixed permanently in position, in which case a thin rod is attached to each beam and the warp stretched between the rods. Or one of the cross-beams may have adjustable fixings at the side, which allows it to be moved as weaving progresses. In most later models of the loom, however, the cross-beams are cylindrical and rotated by means of cranks at the side of the loom (Fig. 19.1). For small pieces of weaving, the warp may be mounted directly on to the loom (in a single sheet or as a tubular warp), but for larger pieces the warp has to be prepared separately and then mounted. There does not seem to be any one standard method of doing this and the warping method used for the warp-weighted loom, in which the warp is prepared with a woven starting band, may have been transferred to this loom.

Once the loom has been warped, weaving may begin straight away, the weave being picked out by hand. Alternatively, heddle rods may be attached in front, by means of twine loops, so that different sets of warp thread may be raised for the passage of the weft, as the weave requires. It would be hard to attach any elaborate patterning device to this loom, and it is generally associated with simple weaves. Designs may, however, be worked freehand, by tapestry-weaving blocks of different colour. The main advantage of this loom for freehand work is that the weaver sits in front of the loom, and the design grows directly in front of his/her eyes (Fig. 19.1).

The hand tools associated with this loom are the single-ended pin-beater, the toothed weft-beater and the tapestry 'flute'.[1] The single-ended pin-beater, or 'pick-up', is a long pointed instrument made from bone or wood, which is used to pick out individual warp threads in pattern work and to give the weft a preliminary beating-in (Fig. 19.2). The toothed weft-beater is a comb-like tool, found in two forms: the first is made from wood or bone, with a long handle in the same plane as the teeth (modern domestic tapestry-weavers sometimes use a cut-down kitchen

Fig. 19.1 The two-beam vertical loom. The weaver is beating downwards with a toothed weft-beater; a single-ended pin-beater sits loosely in the warp, waiting to be used; three tapestry flutes are being used to weave the different colours. Drawing by Simon Chew, York Archaeological Trust.

Fig. 19.2 Bone and antler pin-beaters from 16–22 Coppergate, York. The two at the top are the double-ended form used with the warp-weighted loom (the lower of the two is an unfinished example); those in the middle are the short single-ended form held against the palm of the hand and used with the two-beam vertical loom; those at the bottom are the long single-ended form, held like a pencil, as in the Baugy sculptures. Photo by Simon I. Hill of Scirebröc, on behalf of York Archaeological Trust.

fork); and the second is a wide iron blade with teeth along the long edge, set in a wooden mount with an angled handle (Fig. 19.1).[2] Both are used to beat down the weft. Flutes are small wooden bobbins used in tapestry work, the different colours being wound on to separate flutes.[3]

The two-beam vertical loom in the Roman period

In Italy, and in several parts of the Empire, the main loom in use at the start of the first century AD was the warp-weighted loom (described below). The two-beam vertical loom seems to have begun to displace the warp-weighted during the first and second centuries in Italy and the Mediterranean provinces, but the two clearly existed side-by-side for quite some time.[4] John Peter has suggested that the warp-weighted was used for wider, especially linen, fabrics, and the two-beam loom for tapestry and for narrow wool cloths, a view supported by more recent work.[5] Illustrations of the two-beam loom can be seen in Rome, in a sculpted frieze from the forum of Nerva, in a wall-painting in the hypogeum of the Aurelii (Fig. 19.3), and also in the early fifth-century Codex Vaticanus.

In Gaul, there is a single depiction of a two-beam vertical loom on a funerary sculpture of a woman weaver, Genetiva, at Baugy, Central France (Fig. 19.4).[6] Genetiva stands with the loom on her left, a spool of yarn in her left hand and a single-ended pin-beater in her right, the pin-beater pointing diagonally downwards. A second sculpture from Baugy shows another weaver, possibly Lupula, this time without a loom, but still with a spool of yarn in one hand and a pin-beater in the other, the pin-beater held in a gesture typical of weavers working with the two-beam vertical loom (Fig. 19.4).

The main cloth loom of Iron Age Britain at the time of the Roman invasions was the warp-weighted loom and it clearly continued in use during the Roman occupation. Whether it was the only British loom at this time is debatable. There are long-handled bone 'weaving combs' from Iron Age and Romano-British sites, which resemble the toothed weft-beaters used with the two-beam vertical loom. Other authors, however, seem to associate these weaving combs with the warp-weighted loom,[7] and there are no examples of the single-ended pin-beaters which are truly diagnostic of the two-beam loom, from Iron Age or Roman sites in Britain.[8]

Fig. 19.3 Wall-painting in the hypogeum *of the Aurelii, Rome. Photo: Fototeca Unione, American Academy in Rome.*

Fig. 19.4 Roman funerary sculptures from Baugy, Central France. Centre: the weaver Genetiva holding a spool of yarn and pin-beater. 1. Drawing of the loom on Genetiva's left (not visible in photograph, due to angle of shot); 2. Drawing of the hands of the weaver ?Lupula; 3. Drawing of the hands of Genetiva. Photo: M.-E. Fonvielle; drawings: A. Ferdière.

Most textiles from Roman Britain are the same tabbies and 2/2 plain, chevron and diamond twills which were already established in the British Iron Age and which were almost certainly products of the warp-weighted loom. Alongside these are a small number of wool textile-types which are new to Britain in the Roman period. These are a tabby weave with weft-faced bands, an extended tabby known as 'half-basket weave', and 2/1 twill. The textiles with weft-faced bands are typical of the eastern provinces and by the second century AD were woven on the two-beam loom;[9] half-basket weave is also a Mediterranean weave, although it became a 'typical Gallo-Roman product';[10] and 2/1 twills are believed to have been woven on the two-beam loom.[11] In short, it seems likely that all three of these less common weaves were woven on the two-beam loom, although whether any of them was ever made in Britain is open to question.

It may be concluded that if the two-beam loom ever reached Roman Britain, it was used only in a limited way. Once the Romans had departed from Britain, the Anglo-Saxon settlers of the fifth and sixth centuries, brought with them another version of the warp-weighted loom, this time with circular clay loomweights. This was to remain the main cloth loom in England until the beginning of the tenth century.

The warp-weighted loom

The history of the warp-weighted loom is so intertwined with that of the two-beam vertical loom that an outline of its use is relevant at this point. The warp-weighted loom consists of two uprights joined together by a lower cross-beam. It has a cylindrical upper cloth beam set in crotches at the top, which is rotated in order to wind on the woven cloth.[12] The loom is generally leant against a wall, on the slant, and the warp is tensioned by attaching weights to the lower end. In contrast with the two-beam loom, the weft is beaten upwards. The artefacts recovered from archaeological excavations which are regarded as diagnostic of the warp-weighted loom are loomweights, sword-beaters and a form of pin-beater which has a working point at either end (Fig. 19.2).

There are hundreds of circular Anglo-Saxon loomweights from early and middle Anglo-Saxon sites such as West Stow[13] and Mucking[14] in Essex and Flixborough[15] in Lincolnshire; sword-beaters and double-ended pin-beaters are also well represented at this time. The weaves of the early and middle Anglo-Saxon wool and linen textiles are tabby and 2/2 plain, chevron and diamond twill, just as they were in the Iron Age. There seems, then, to be an association between these weaves and the warp-weighted loom.

The demise of the warp-weighted loom in late Anglo-Saxon England can be charted in the archaeological record. In towns such as York[16] and Winchester[17] it clearly disappeared about AD 900. In sites which were settled as 'green-field' sites after this time, there are no tools associated with the warp-weighted loom, and in sites which had been continuously occupied since before 900, a limited number of loomweights from later levels can be shown to be associated with residual ninth-century pottery and are therefore interpreted as having been churned up from lower levels of the site.[18]

In the countryside, however, the same was not the case. At Flixborough, for example, the focus of this rural settlement shifted during the tenth century, but loomweights and pin-beaters continued to be deposited in the new area well into the second half of the tenth century. At Sparkford, now in Winchester, but originally a hamlet outside the medieval town, two sets of loomweights have been found in a hut dated to the late Anglo-Saxon or early Anglo-Norman period.[19] At Rochester, Kent, an abandoned kiln containing loomweights has been dated to AD *c.* 1100.[20]

To summarise, the warp-weighted loom had disappeared from towns such as York and Winchester by about AD 900, but it continued in use in other parts until well into the eleventh century.

The arrival of the horizontal treadle loom

There is another loom which enters the picture in the eleventh century. This is the horizontal treadle-operated loom, the fore-runner of the modern craft studio loom. A horizontal loom of sorts was already in existence in the Roman period, but it was probably a form of ground loom, with multiple heddle rods, and it had only limited use in the northern provinces.[21] The treadle-operated loom did not develop out of this loom – or at any rate not in north-west Europe. Instead, it seems to have arrived as a fully developed piece of equipment, complete with treadles, some form of superstructure with pulleys to support heddle-shafts, and reed to beat in the weft. Its route(s) into Europe over the tenth to twelfth centuries can be plotted, using archaeological evidence supplemented by written sources.[22] The earliest evidence from Britain is a tentatively identified heddle cradle from Coppergate, York, dated to the late eleventh century and a heddle rod from late twelfth- or early thirteenth-century levels of the same site.[23] Grenander Nyberg has argued that this loom was regarded as a linen loom when it first reached Europe[24] and its system of pulleys/balances and treadles is certainly better suited to the tabby weaves of medieval linens, than the 2/1 twill which by the end of the eleventh century was the main weave of English wool cloth.

As far as English towns are concerned, there is an obvious gap of over a hundred years between the disappearance of the warp-weighted loom and the arrival of the horizontal treadle loom. This, it will be shown, is filled by evidence for the two-beam vertical loom.

The archaeological evidence for the two-beam loom in the medieval period

The only example of a two-beam vertical loom recovered from a European archaeological excavation is from the ninth-century royal ship burial at Oseberg, Norway.[25] This is a small loom, 1.19 m tall and 0.75 m wide at the base. It has a thin crossways rod at the top, 0.33 m long, for attachment of the warp, and drilled holes in the lower uprights where the cloth beam could be positioned and adjusted. This loom is an appropriate size to make the wall-hanging ornamented in soumak technique found at the same site, although Marta Hoffmann and Agnes Geijer both consider the warp-weighted loom a more likely tool for this.[26] There are fragments of another small loom, similar to the first, in the Oseberg burial and also a long-handled toothed weft-beater made from wood,[27] comparable with another in antler from Birka.[28]

No fragments of the two-beam vertical loom have been recognised in English excavations, but the single-ended pin-beaters, toothed weft-beaters and tapestry flutes may be regarded as evidence for the presence of the loom. The earliest single-ended pin-beaters from England are all dated to about AD 900 and appear first in towns, exactly at the point that the warp-weighted loom disappears. There are early collections of them from York, Beverley, Lincoln, Northampton, Winchester and Thetford.[29] There are also examples from Goltho, a tenth-century manor house north of Lincoln, although in most rural sites, the warp-weighted loom seems to have continued in use. They occur in two forms (Fig. 19.2), one flat in section, short and held against the palm of the hand; and the other round in section, longer, and grasped like a pencil, as shown in the Baugy sculptures (Fig. 19.4).

It is probable that single-ended pin-beaters came to England from France. As well as the Gallo-Roman evidence, there are at least four, and perhaps even eight, examples, from Brebières, a sixth- and seventh-century village, close to the royal residence at Vitry-en-Artois,[30] and there are twelve from Villiers-le-Sec, on the lands of the Abbey of Saint-Denis, of which two are as early as the eighth century.[31] If the pin-beaters are taken as a guide, it would appear that the two-beam vertical loom continued in use in France after the Romans departed, and transferred to England around AD 900.

Toothed weft-beaters of the sort found at Oseberg and Birka have not yet been identified in England, but twelfth- to fourteenth-century examples of the wider iron toothed weft-beater have been recorded at York, Winchester, Newbury (Berks) and Westbury (Bucks).[32] These wide weft-beaters had been used within the Roman Empire,[33] but they seem to be a late arrival in Britain. They were probably used for the heavier types of work such as coverlets and rugs, while the narrow long-handled weft-beater was used with the finer weaves. Two tapestry flutes are known from tenth- or eleventh-century York, but no certain examples have been recorded elsewhere.[34]

Single-ended pin-beaters dwindle in numbers in English excavations during the thirteenth and fourteenth centuries.[35] This may be because they were now being made from wood,[36] a material which does not survive as well as bone on archaeological sites; or because the two-beam loom was now only used in specialist workshops.

Pictorial sources

In the medieval period, before the advent of printing, manuscripts were copied and re-copied in religious houses across Europe. Illustrations were adjusted by each artist, so that it is often difficult to establish how much of the content of a picture is contemporary with the volume in which it appears. The two-beam vertical loom is illustrated in an English manuscript, the Eadwine Psalter (Fig. 19.5b), dated to the mid twelfth century, but the same scene appears in a ninth-century psalter from Utrecht (Fig. 19.5a) and both illustrations will almost certainly derive from some late Roman or Byzantine original. Errors have been introduced into the Eadwine Psalter version (for example, the hank of yarn looped between posts, could not in real life be removed from the posts) but the English illustrator has carefully transposed the figures into contemporary dress. The toothed weft-beater held by one of the women is also convincingly drawn and shows the line where the iron-toothed blade is mounted in the wooden frame, exactly as it is in the excavated examples.

A further illustration from an eleventh-century Italian manuscript shows a similar loom, this time with the weaver seated (Fig. 19.6). All these early illustrations show quite narrow looms, which could be managed by one person, who while seated in front could easily reach both sides of the web.

Written sources

References to spinning and weaving equipment appear in several Old English texts, especially riddles, but the terms used are often poetic, vague, or poorly understood

Fig. 19.5 a: Illustration from the Utrecht Psalter, made in the Abbey of Hautvillier near Rheims, AD 820–835. Library of the University of Utrecht, ms. 32, f. 84. b: The same scene as in Fig. 19.5a., in a mid twelfth century English manuscript, the Eadwine (or Canterbury) Psalter. Trinity College Library, Cambridge, ms R. 17.1, f. 263.

Fig. 19.6 Re-drawn copy of an illustration from De Rerum Naturis *by Hrabanus Maurus, AD c. 1022–1025 (after a tenth-century original). Redrawn from Library of Monte Casino, ms. 132, f. 364, by T. Srahan.*

at the present time. Translations into Modern English tend to depend on which loom the translator has in his/her mind's eye. There is, however, one text where it is possible to give a more exact technical translation. This is the document known as *Be gesceadwisan gerefan*, 'The wise reeve' or 'The good bailiff' (Corpus Christi College Cambridge MS 383).[37] This was probably written or compiled by Wulfstan, who was simultaneously Bishop of Worcester and Archbishop of York, AD 1002–1023.[38] The bailiff, or reeve, is advised to supply the workshops with 'many tools: flax line, spindle, reel, swift, loom uprights, heddle rods, press, comb [toothed weft-beater], temple, weft, warp, wool-comb, cross-beam, beater, crank-stick, sheath, seam-pins, shears, needle, slick-stone'.[39]

The weaving comb or toothed weft-beater, *pihten*, is distinguished from the woolcomb, *wulcamb,* in this text and the other loom parts listed are all compatible with the two-beam vertical loom. The presence of a crank stick, *crancstaef,* suggests that the loom by this time had one or more rotating beams. The term *pihten* is a French loan-word (as are *timplean,* a temple, and *presse,* a press).[40] This supports the theory that the two-beam vertical loom was introduced from France in the Anglo-Saxon period.

The evidence of the textile products

Some fragments of tapestry-work with soumak inserts, rather like the Oseberg hanging, have been found in the seventh-century ship burial at Sutton Hoo.[41] These may have been woven on the two-beam loom, but, as they come from a royal burial which includes high-status imported goods, they may not have been made locally. More significantly, there are a small number of 2/1 twills to be found in the cemeteries of East Anglia at this time.[42] 2/1 twill is not a natural product of the warp-weighted loom and several authors have already connected it with the two-beam vertical loom.[43] It is possible, then, that this loom was known in sixth/seventh-century England, but if so it can only have been used in a very limited way, perhaps attached to an East Anglian royal court.

The 2/1 twill structure seems to disappear after the seventh century, but in the tenth century it re-appears in town excavations and for over a century it overlaps with the old 2/2 twills. There are examples from York,[44] London,[45] Winchester,[46] and Durham[47] and they occur as fine diamond twills and coarser plain twills (Table 19.1). By the mid-to-late eleventh century the old 2/2 chevron and diamond twills had disappeared and 2/1 twill had triumphed in wool clothing textiles; tabby weave was now used only for linens. There is therefore a coincidence between the departure of the warp-weighted loom and the old Anglo-Saxon weave structures, and also between the arrival of single-ended pin-beaters and 2/1 twill.

Haberget, chalons and the tapiter's loom

In a paper written in 1969, Eleanora Carus-Wilson summarised the written sources concerning a twelfth- and thirteenth-century fabric known as 'haberget'.[48] This was an expensive, English-made wool textile which was of enough commercial importance to have its width set at a standard measurement, along with 'dyed cloths and russets' in Magna Carta.[49] The word seems to derive from 'hauberk', a garment of chain-mail, and it was suggested that haberget had a pattern resembling the interlocking links of mail. Drawing on the evidence she had to hand at that time, Carus-Wilson put forward 2/2 diamond twill as a candidate. Since then, many more textiles have been excavated in medieval towns and it can now be shown that the date-span of the term 'haberget' fits not 2/2, but 2/1 diamond twill. This tenth/eleventh- to thirteenth-century fabric-type displays exactly the appearance Carus-Wilson predicted, of interlocking rings.[50]

Textiles	Weave	Spin	Thread-count (per cm)	Finish	Dye or wool colour	Fleece-types
The Brooks, Winchester (1987–88 excavations), tenth century						
5824	plain 2/1	Z × S	6–7 × 5–6	none	grey	–
5869	plain 2/1	S × S	7 × 6	matted	white	HM × HM
6729	plain 2/1	Z × S	7 × 4	none	white	HM × HM
7823	plain 2/1	Z × S	6 × 6	matted	grey	–
Lower Brook Street, Winchester, mid–late tenth century						
1030	plain 2/1	S × S	4 × 5	none	?	–
1033	plain 2/1	Z × Z+S	9 × 4–5	none	weft stripes	–
Pavement, York, tenth century						
564	2/1 diamond	Z × Z	22 × 16	none	?	–
565	2/1 diamond	Z × Z	22 × 11	none	?	–
568	2/1 diamond	Z × Z	22 × 14	none	?	–
569	2/1 diamond	Z × Z	20 × 11	none	?	–
574	2/1 chevron	Z × S	20 × 14	none	?	–
575	2/1 diamond	Z × Z	27 × 16	none	?	–
588	plain 2/1	Z × S	4–5 × 5	none	?	–
593	plain 2/1	Z × Z	17 × 7	none	?	–
Milk Street, London, tenth century						
1215	plain 2/1	Z × S	11 × 9	none	no dye detected	–
1147	plain 2/1	S × S	3–4 × 3–4	none	no dye detected	–
Pavement, York, late tenth or early eleventh century						
566	2/1 diamond	Z × Z	26 × 14	none	madder	–
567	2/1 diamond	Z × Z	18 × 11	none	madder + indigotin (woad)	–
570	2/1 diamond	Z × Z	16 × 10	none	?	–
670	2/1 diamond	Z × Z	28–30 × 18	none	?	–
589	plain 2/1	S × S	4–5 × 4	none	madder	–
Saddler Street, Durham, late tenth or early eleventh century						
142	plain 2/1	Z × S	11–7–8	none	?dyed	H or HM
Lower Brook Street, Winchester, early–mid eleventh century						
1035	plain 2/1	Z × S	10 × 10	none	?	HM × GM
1036	2/1 diamond	Z × Z	32 × 2	none	?	–
Milk Street, London, eleventh century						
104	plain 2/1	S × S	4–5 × 4–5	none	?	–
Watling Court, London, eleventh century						
776	2/1 diamond	Z × S	30–32 × 20	none	no dye detected	–
1375	2/1 diamond	?	?	none	indigotin (woad) + madder	

Table 19.1 Wool 2/1 twills of late Anglo–Saxon date. Data from Hedges 1982, Pritchard 1982, Crowfoot 1979, Crowfoot 1990 and Walton Rogers unpublished (see endnotes 44–7).

One of the latest examples of 2/1 diamond twill comes from the lower leg of a man, possibly an abbot, who was buried at Tavistock Abbey, Devon, in the fourteenth century – although his vestments appear to be fifty to a hundred years older than the burial.[51] This example has a preserved starting border in which the warp threads are grouped six at a time (Fig. 19.7). This is reminiscent of the starting band of the warp-weighted loom, although for that loom the warp threads are generally arranged in pairs. It is highly unlikely that this border was made for the horizontal loom, where the warp usually begins with long knotted loops;[52] and yet the warp-weighted loom had long ago disappeared even from the most rural parts of England. All things considered, it seems likely that this textile was woven on the two-beam vertical loom.[53]

By the end of the thirteenth century, the two-beam loom had taken on the role with which we are familiar today, that of a tool for weaving coverlets, rugs and tapestries. The artisans who made such fabrics were known as 'tapiters' or 'tapeners'. When the customs of the city of Winchester[54] were written down in about 1275, the following statements were made in relation to the production of textiles: 'No citizen shall cause burels [coarse wool cloths] or chalons [coverlets] to be made outside the walls…'; '…every great loom (*grant ustil*) for making burels owes a fee to the town of five shillings per year… '; 'Of the small looms (*petiz ustilz*) for working chalons, each double (*turs*) loom owes a fee to the town of twelve pence a year, and each single (*sengle*) loom six pence…'; and 'chalons four ells long must be two yards before the tapener…' From these statements it may be concluded that the two-beam tapiter's loom, used for coverlets, was known as the 'small loom' (Woodger suggests *'des petiz ustilz'* could also be translated as 'piece looms'[55]) and this could now be wide (*turs*) or narrow (*sengle*). It was contrasted with the 'great loom' of the weavers (*telers*) of burel, which was almost certainly the large and more elaborate treadle-operated horizontal loom, and which was taxed at a much higher rate than the simple tapiter's loom.[56]

a

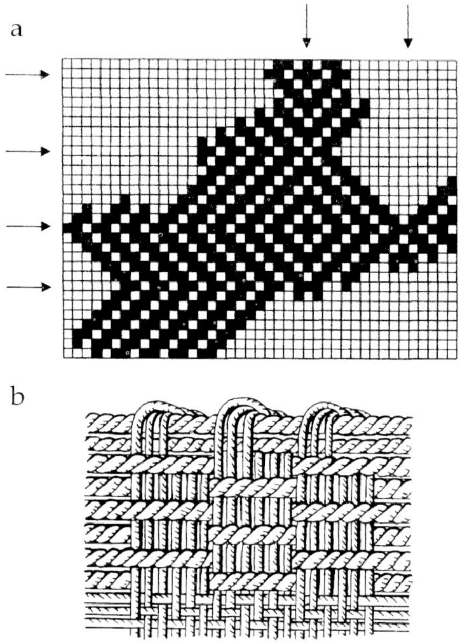

b

Fig. 19.7 Fine 2/1 diamond twill from Grave 602, Tavistock Abbey, Devon (warp 22/Z × weft 12/Z per cm). 7a: weave diagram (black squares indicate warp over weft); 7b: the starting border. Fig. 19.7a is by T. Srahan; 7b is courtesy of Exeter Archaology.

Conclusion

This study has proposed that the old Roman two-beam vertical loom continued in use in France after the departure of the Romans and transferred to England at the start of the tenth century. It has also been suggested that for a time it was a cloth loom and that the 2/1 twills of the tenth and eleventh centuries were made on it. The period of its use as a cloth loom was a time when there were many social changes in England and a loom which could be conveniently operated by one weaver may have had some advantage over the old warp-weighted loom, which functions best with two or three.

When the treadle-operated horizontal loom arrived in the eleventh century, it may have been regarded as a linen loom and for a while (how long is not known) the two looms could have existed side-by-side, the vertical two-beam loom for wool 2/1 twill and the horizontal for linen tabby-weave. This would mirror the Roman use of looms, with the two-beam for wool textiles and a second loom (in that instance the warp-weighted loom) for linens. Plain 2/1 twill probably eventually transferred to the horizontal loom, but this un-balanced weave is not a natural product of the treadle-operated loom and finally, in the fourteenth century, there was a shift back to tabby and 2/2 twill.

It has also been suggested that the fine 2/1 diamond twills which have been identified with the medieval fabric 'haberget' were made on this loom. By the end of the thirteenth century, however, production of haberget had ceased and the two-beam vertical loom had emerged as the tapiter's loom. It is in this role that it finally appears in guild records and town ordinances of the later medieval period.

Notes

1 P. Walton Rogers, *Textile Production at 16–22 Coppergate* (*The Archaeology of York* 17/11) (York: CBA, 1997), pp. 1755–62.

2 Walton Rogers 1997, *op. cit.*, pp. 1761–2.

3 Walton Rogers 1997, *op. cit.*, pp. 1761 and fig. 818.

4 J. P. Wild, *Textile Manufacture in the Northern Roman Provinces*, (Cambridge: Cambridge University Press, 1970), p. 67.

5 Wild *op. cit.*, p. 68. The change from the warp-weighted to the two-beam loom has also been detected in certain wool textiles from the Mediterranean provinces: H. Granger Taylor, 'The grouping of warp threads for areas of weft-faced decoration in textiles of the Roman period: a means of distinguishing looms?', *Vlaamse Vereniging voor Oud en Hedendaags Textiel: Bulletin,* 1992 (aan Daniël De Jonghe), pp. 18–28.

6 A. Ferdière, 'Le travail du textile en Région Centre de l'Age du Fer au Haut Moyen Age', *Revue Archéologique du Centre de la France,* XXIII/2 (1984), 209–275, pp. 218–222.

7 A. S. Henshall, 'Textiles and weaving appliances in prehistoric Britain', *Proceedings of the Prehistoric Society*, X (1950), p146–8. Wild *op. cit.*, 66–7. Other uses for these long-handled combs have been suggested, such as skin/hide preparation, the combing of wool from primitive moulting sheep, or as a hand distaff.

8 Wild 1970, *op. cit.*, p66, tentatively suggests the Iron Age bone 'gouges' may have been pin-beaters, although they are extraordinarily coarse for such a purpose.

9 Granger-Taylor *op. cit.* A. Sheffer and H. Granger-Taylor, 'Textiles from Masada, a Preliminary Selection', *Masada IV: The Yigael Yadin Excavations 1963–1965, Final Reports* (Jerusalem: Israel Exploration Society/The Hebrew University of Jerusalem, 1994), 230–1.

10 Wild in L. Bender Jørgensen and J. P. Wild, 'Clothes from the Roman Empire: barbarians and Romans', *Archaeological Textiles: NESAT II*, (Copenhagen, 1988, pp. 65–98), p. 76.

11 Wild 1970, *op. cit.*, p. 70.

12 Walton Rogers 1997, fig. 812 (p. 1751).

13 S. West, *West Stow, the Anglo-Saxon Village* (*East Anglian Archaeology* 24) (Gressenhall, 1985, 2 vols).

14 H. Hamerow, *Excavations at Mucking 2: The Anglo-Saxon Settlement* (London: English Heritage Archaeological Report, 21 (1993), pp. 66–7.

15 P. Walton Rogers in C. Loveluck in prep.

16 Walton Rogers 1997, *op. cit.*, p. 1753.

17 Derek Keene, drawing on the Winchester evidence, was the first author to suggest that the warp-weighted loom was replaced by the two-beam vertical loom, and that the new loom was for a while a cloth loom: D. Keene, 'The Textile Industry' in M. Biddle (ed), *Winchester Studies* 7 ii: *Objects and Economy in Medieval Winchester* (Oxford, 1990), I (pp. 200–214), pp. 203–8

18 Walton Rogers 1997, pp. 1799–1801.

19 J. W. Hedges, 'The loomweights' in J. Collis, *Winchester Excavations III, 1949–1960*, II (Winchester), pp. 33–9.

20 A. C. Harrison, 'Rochester East Gate 1969', *Archaeologia Cantiana* LXXXVII (1972, 121–157), pp. 123–4

21 See, for example, De Jonghe this volume. This loom may have been in Trier in the Roman period, but it is likely to have retreated to Italy, along with the weavers, when the Romans withdrew: see J. P. Wild in P. Walton, *Textiles, Cordage and Raw Fibre from 16–22 Coppergate* (*The Archaeology of York* 17/5, 1989) p. 358.

22 W. Endrei, 'Der Trittwebstuhl im frühmitelalterlichen Europa', *Acta Historica* VIII (1961) pp. 107–136; see especially the map, fig. 2, p. 122. G. Grenander Nyberg, 'Looms for linen', *Laborativ Arkeologi* VII (1994), pp. 75–7. There seems to be some confusion in the literature over the date of a loom pulley-block from Haithabu, Schleswig, but it is clearly identified as eleventh-century in Grenander Nyberg *op. cit.*, and this has been confirmed to me by the author (pers. comm.).

23 Walton Rogers 1997, 1763–66

24 Grenander Nyberg *op. cit.*

25 S. Grieg, 'Kvindearbeidet', in A. W. Brøgger and H. Schetelig (eds), *Osebergfundet* II (Oslo, 1928, pp. 173–198), pp. 176–9.

26 M. Hoffmann, *The Warp-Weighted Loom* (Oslo: Universitetsforlaget, 1974), p. 185.

27 Grieg *op. cit.*, p. 194 .

28 J. Graham-Campbell, *Viking Artefacts: a Select Catalogue*, (London, 1980), pp. 21, 207.

29 Walton Rogers 1997, pp. 1755–7, 1760–1.

30 P. Demelon, *Le Village Merovingien de Brebière (VIe–VIIe Siècle)*, (Arras 1972), passim.

31 Anon., *Un Village au Temps de Charlemagne: Moines et Paysans de l'Abbaye de Saint-Denis du VIIe Siècle à l'An Mil* 1988, p. 280ff.

32 Walton Rogers 1997, pp. 1761–2.

33 R. Patterson, 'Spinning and Weaving', in C. Singer, E. J. Holmyard, A. R. Hall, T. I. Williams (eds), *A History of Technology* II (1957), fig. 180, p. 212.

34 Walton Rogers 1997, *op. cit.*, p. 1761.

35 P. Walton Rogers, 'Textile making equipment', in A. MacGregor, A. J. Mainman and N. S. H. Rogers, *Bone, Antler, Ivory and Horn from Anglo-Scandinavian and Medieval York* (*The Archaeology of York* 17/12, 1999), p. 1967–8.

36 Modern pin-beaters are made of wood. The rise of professional butchers in towns of the post-Norman period meant that animals were no longer slaughtered in the back yard and bone was not so immediately available as a raw material for hand-tools. Bone spindle whorls also decline at about the same time.

37 F. Liebermann, *Die Gesetze der Angelsachsen* (Halle, 1903), Vol 1, 453–5

[38] D. Whitelock, *Sermo Lupis ad Anglos*, (London, 1963), p. 12

[39] Author's translation, modified since publication in Walton Rogers 1997, p. 1823

[40] R. G. Poole, 'The textile inventory in the Old English *Gerefa*', *RES* New Series, XL, No. 160 (1989, pp. 469–478), p. 473

[41] E. Crowfoot, E., 'The textiles' in R. Bruce-Mitford *The Sutton Hoo Ship Burial* 3/1 (London, 1983, pp. 409–479), p. 428–42.

[42] E. Crowfoot 1983, *op. cit.*, pp. 440–2. E. Crowfoot, 'The textiles', in B. Green and A. Rogerson, *The Anglo-Saxon Cemetery at Bergh Apton, Norfolk* (Gressenhall: Norfolk Archaeological Unit, 1978), pp. 98–112.

[43] Wild 1970, *op. cit.*, p. 70; Hoffmann *op. cit.*, p. 253; E. Crowfoot 1983, *op. cit.*, pp. 440–2.

[44] J. W. Hedges, 'Textiles', in A. MacGregor, *Anglo-Scandinavian Finds from Lloyds Bank, Pavement, and Other Site* (*The Archaeology of York* 17/3, 1982), p. 103

[45] P. Walton Rogers unpublished data. E. Crowfoot, 'Personal possessions: textiles' in M. Biddle (ed), *Winchester Studies* 7 ii: *Objects and Economy in Medieval Winchester* (Oxford, 1990), I, pp. 467–494.

[46] F. Pritchard, 'Textiles from recent excavations in the City of London' in L. Bender Jørgensen and K. Tidow (eds) *Textilsymposium Neumünster: Archäologische Textilfunde* (*NESAT* I, 1982, pp. 193–208), p. 204.

[47] E. Crowfoot, 'Textiles' in M. O. H. Carver, 'Three Saxo-Norman tenements in Durham City', *Medieval Archaeology* XXIII, pp36–39.

[48] E. Carus-Wilson, 'Haberget: a medieval textile conundrum', *Medieval Archaeology* XIII (1969), pp. 148–66.

[49] '...*una latitudo pannorum tinctorum et russetorum et halbergettorum scilicet due ulne infra listas*': AD 1215, Magna Carta article 35. Re-issued in 1216, 1217 and 1225, and confirmed 1297 and 1300.

[50] Hedges 1982, *op. cit.*, Plate IVc.

[51] P. Walton Rogers in prep.

[52] Luther Hooper, *Hand-Loom Weaving* (London: Pitman Publishing, 1979, 1st edn 1910), pp. 101–4. Edward F. Worst, *Foot-Power Loom Weaving* (Milwaukee, Wis: The Bruce Publishing Co., 1924), p. 33.

[53] Starting borders with paired warp threads sometimes occur in late medieval 2/1 twills from Norway and Sweden. As the warp-weighted loom continued in these countries long after it had disappeared elsewhere, it is possible that this loom was eventually adapted for 2/1 twill. M. Lindström, 'Textilier', in A. W. Mårtenson (ed), *Uppgrävt förflutet för PKbanken I Lund* (*Archaeologica Lundensia* VII, 1976), pp. 279–292. The broken remains of a border which may be similar to the Tavistock example has been recorded on a fifteenth-century coarse 2/1 twill from Oslo: A. Kjellberg, 'Medieval textiles from the excavations in the old town of Oslo', in L. Bender Jørgensen and K. Tidow (eds) *Textilsymposium Neumünster: Archäologische Textilfunde* (*NESAT* I, 1982, pp. 135–149), pp. 142 and 148.

[54] E. Smirke, 'Ancient consuetudinary of the city of Winchester', *Archaeological Journal*, IX (1852), pp. 69–89.

[55] A. Woodger, 'The eclipse of the burel weaver: some technological developments in the thirteenth century', *Textile History* XII (1981, pp. 59–76), p. 68.

[56] Woodger (*op. cit.*), writing in 1981, believed that the great loom (*grant ustil*) on which burels were made was the warp-weighted, but, this loom is now known to have disappeared from England long before the Winchester customs were written down.

Chapter 20

WHERE ARE THE ROMANS? CLASSICAL INFLUENCES ON WOMEN'S FASHIONABLE DRESS FROM THE LATE EIGHTEENTH TO THE TWENTIETH CENTURY

Naomi Tarrant

In 1812 Henry Moses engraved a series of scenes for Thomas Hope of Deepdene in which contemporary men and women are seen in various neo-classical settings suitable for Le Beau Monde of the period (Fig. 20.1).[1] The purpose of this small book of 1812 is not clear. Only one copy is known to exist and it may have been a private publication Hope gave to friends.[2] There is no text, but it was possibly intended to show how people could copy details of dress from the admired classical period and incorporate it into their everyday wear. The men wear the typical clothes of the time but the women are clad in a curious mixture. The main shaping of their dresses is contemporary but certain details of design, cut and hairstyle have a classical touch. The rooms all have furniture and decorations in the neo-classical style.

Fig. 20.1 Plate from Thomas Hope's 1812 book.

Fig. 20.2 Plate from Thomas Hope's Costume of the Ancients, *showing a Grecian figure wearing what may be the prototype for Fig. 20.1.*

This set of plates of 1812 raises an interesting question for a costume historian. The classical elements are all Greek, the Romans being conspicuous by their absence. Looking through various books produced about dress of this period there is nothing which relates to Roman dress and virtually no item of clothing is given a Roman name. However, Greek names abound and it is Greek examples that are copied particularly in women's dress, throughout most of the nineteenth century.[3]

Most writers on costume mention classical influences on dress in the late eighteenth and early nineteenth century during the period when neo-classicism in art was at its height. However, the term 'classical' is not defined further, yet there are at least two major artistic and literary traditions that are covered by the term, those of Greece and Rome. Greece was of course a major influence on Rome so that the almost exclusive use of the term classical in costume history terms to mean Greek may perhaps be excused. However, some parts of Roman tradition were much admired by writers and artists in Europe over the period of the mid eighteenth and early nineteenth centuries. Certain themes from early Roman history were illustrated in paintings by Jacques Louis David and other artists, for instance the Oath of the Horatii, Corialanus, Brutus and the Rape of the Sabine Women.[4]

Roman dress had been used in portraits in an earlier period. Statues of Roman emperors in military uniform were well known to seventeenth-century artists and many portraits of the period showed men in Roman military uniform of various degrees of accuracy. But this was a period where most portraits showed their sitters in some sort of fancy or antique clothing. Roman military dress gave the idea that the sitter was a skilled soldier whilst portraits of women as mythological subjects fitted the rather easy-going atmosphere of the Restoration court in London. However, these women were not painted in a recognisable style of dress, unlike the men, so that it would be difficult to say which civilisation provided the inspiration.[5]

In the mid eighteenth century classical drapery was again used by Reynolds, Coates and other portrait painters for their portraits of women.[6] Although artists and men with a classical education might see the draperies of Greece and Rome as less capricious than that of contemporary dress, there was a revulsion against its supposed indecency when anyone tried to copy it, such as the outcry that greeted Elizabeth Chudleigh in 1749 when she went to a masquerade as Iphigenia. Reynolds in particular developed a theory on the virtues of a timeless dress based on that of the classical world. Like their earlier counterparts women were painted as mythological figures in drapery, which bear no relationship to either Greek or Roman dress. In some instances it is very difficult to believe the artist actually had any in front of him, so contrived are the folds. Whilst most of these eighteenth century portraits show women wearing silk and satin the original Greek and Roman garments were more likely to be in wool, a point that may not have been appreciated by the artist and certainly this would have affected the way the fabric draped and fell.

How did fashionable dress of the eighteenth century with its wide skirts and large patterned silk fabrics change into the 'classical' line of the early years of the nineteenth century? All fashion in clothing takes a well-known progression from the merest hint of a new style to the fully developed idea, followed by its rapid collapse as some other element is then exploited. Change in shape in the dresses could only follow if the fabrics became less stiff and more diaphanous, able to take tight gathers rather than pleats. The correct weight of fabric is needed for any style of clothing, regardless of period, as each type can only be manipulated by the tailor or dressmaker in certain ways. The very lightest fabric available at this period was the hand spun and hand woven cotton from India, but this was expensive. By the early nineteenth century various mechanical processes needed to produce large quantities of machine spun and woven cotton cloth were at last achieved. But before this, silk fabrics had become lighter in weight with smaller patterns. Very lightweight satins and plain silks replaced the heavier varieties that had been needed for the voluminous skirts of the earlier period to sit well.[7]

Dress reflects the general decorative style of its period and its shaping must also follow the requirements of any code of manners; people have to be able to move correctly in the clothes. The formality of most European Courts in the early part of the eighteenth century meant that lightweight silk dresses would have met with disapproval. The lightness and asymmetrical style of Rococo decoration that followed suggested frivolity and was frowned on by the more serious minds of the period. The reaction against Rococo excesses led to a wish to see a 'correct' or 'true' style being developed by those engaged in the intellectual excitement and enquiry of the Age of Enlightenment. The importance of philosophy in this process helped to fuel the interest in the 'antique' and the art of ancients, because of the major role this had played in Antiquity. For artists this was a return to first principles and various models were revered, not all of them antique. By the end of the eighteenth century a return to Nature, an idea which we would see as somewhat artificial today, was the desire of most artists. These saw Nature as an essence rather than the reality of what they saw around them and it is this that lies at the heart of the so-called Neo-classical movement. Whilst this movement can most clearly be seen in the work of artists, architects and sculptors, more peripheral subjects, such as interior decoration, furniture and dress were influenced by it to some extent. In the case of clothing for the very fashionable the style had to fit in with the new interiors or look out of place. It is within this general movement that attempts to dress contemporaries, particularly women, in the antique style should be seen.

A change in dress had already begun in the 1770s in Britain, where lightweight fabrics and more informal styles were being worn. This was exported to France where, during the 1780s, even Marie Antoinette was painted in an informal white 'chemise' dress, thus giving royal approval to the fashion. A further impetus to classical styles was the French Revolution starting in 1789. One of the bases for this had been the philosophy of the Enlightenment, so that 'antique'styles were very popular, being seen as a return to uncorrupted ways after the excesses of the Ancien Regime. The high moral tone and puritanism of the Jacobins in 1793–4, which led on to the Terror, found the excesses of citizens of the new republic in matters of dress shocking. The ruling Convention was determined to reform dress in order to do away with the anarchy and looseness in clothing that had been unleashed. They admired the old Roman virtues and wanted to reform society along the lines of a moral secular state. The artist David was asked in May 1794 by the Comité de Salut Public to present his views on the means of improving the present costume, and providing ideas to give it an appropriate republican slant which would reflect the character of the Revolution. Unsurprisingly the clothing reforms were not adopted – another instance of a government's attempted interference in personal appearance miscarrying.[8]

The apparent nakedness which Greek statues revealed perhaps attracted the somewhat raffish society that the uncertainties of the Revolution in France produced. They used clothing as a way of flaunting their disdain for authority now that the dead hand of the old life had been lifted. As dress had been rigidly codified under the monarchy a certain freedom and licence was adopted in matters of dress by both men and women. Classical dress therefore afforded many opportunities for women who wished to attract male attention to show off their figures. Classical dress was used extensively by David as inspiration in the number of pageants he was asked to design, particularly those staged during 1794.

For various reasons, fashion news from Paris was limited during the 1790s and, even if it got through, was not always taken up by the fashionable ladies of Britain. Contrary to popular belief, most women of the late eighteenth and early nineteenth century did not damp their muslin dresses to reveal un-corseted figures clad in flesh-coloured tights. The majority of women continued to wear a corset, different in shape from that worn with hooped skirts, but still a substantial garment. Underwear was generally white linen the fineness depending on the wearer's income, the layer nearest the skin being known as a smock or chemise, and at least one petticoat was worn. All these layers were worn under the much less full skirts of the years between 1790 and 1820. The amount of fabric in a dress did not reduce dramatically from the 1780s to the 1800s but the type of fabric changed which had more of an effect. The closely woven lightweight silks of the 1780s were tightly pleated or gathered to the bodice so as to throw out the fabric from the low waist and create a rounded shape away from the legs. The 1800s dresses were of fine cottons, the waist under the bust and the front panel of the skirt with no gathering, all the fullness being concentrated into about three inches at the centre back (Fig. 20.4).[9] This brought the dress against the legs when the wearer walked. What women wore therefore did not really resemble any Greek or Roman statue and most would not have wanted to do so.

However, colour in dress at this period also played a part in attempting to produce classical dress. The purity of white marble was much admired and the way the fabrics draped and clung to unfettered figures; no stiff corsets were discernible on a classical statue. The most admired sculptor in marble of the late eighteenth and early nineteenth centuries was Antonio Canova. His perfect, stylised naked statues, such as the Three Graces are an example of what he and many others admired most about classical sculpture. White cotton and linen were available to be the equivalent of marble, as it was impractical for contemporary women to go around nude. These fabrics could be pleated and gathered into straight, tight skirts and made to cling to the figure in a way which was aesthetically more pleasing than the original. That we today find them less than convincing is perhaps due to our better understanding of Greek and Roman dress and our concern for accuracy. Possibly it was not realised that Greek women in antiquity often wore wool garments and that the gathers and pleats seen on the statues were not made with such a fine fabric as muslin. How far the folds of drapery on a Greek statue were stylised may not have been appreciated or even thought about by the majority.

It was perhaps hairstyles that came nearest to reflecting accurately the antique mode. In 1791 the great French actor Talman played the role of Titus in Voltaire's play *Brutus* and the fashion for the short cropped hairstyle he wore for this part was copied by both men and women. Women copied the more elaborate plaited and curled hairstyles, often with a bandeau or metal circlet found on both Greek and Roman statues. These rather tight-to-the-head styles went well with the narrower skirts helping to complete the vertical effect that the slim line dresses gave to women. Apart from the 'Titus' hairstyle most others are described as 'à la grecque'. However, the red cap of Liberty of the French Revolution was based on the caps Roman slaves wore when they obtained their freedom

The success of neo-classicism in dress is difficult to evaluate because there are not many comments on it by contemporary women and little survives in the way of unaltered garments (Fig. 20.4). We are left with the fashion plates and portraits with which to assess it. Fashion plates are the hand coloured engravings published in women's magazines from the late 1790s and throughout the nineteenth century, which showed the most recent fashions in Paris, London and other major cities. These plates attempted to give some idea of what was new and fashionable at that moment, rather than showing what fashionable people were wearing, as had earlier plates in pocket books published in the eighteenth century. It is not possible to tell if the garments existed or whether they were drawings from one or other of the main dressmakers, from which a customer could select an outfit. The providers of information for these plates are the dressmakers and they knew what outfits their clients would wear. The garments shown are therefore unlikely to be too outré, so that fashion progressed at fairly slow steps over the year.

The costume historian C. W. Cunnington described the period from 1800–1821 as the Vertical Epoch, with the years 1800–07 as the period of Pure Classicism, marked by extreme exhibitionism.[10] Classicism was marked by an exaggerated emphasis on vertical lines with a high waist and a long narrow skirt, although as the latter was often trailing on the ground the vertical line was spoilt by the need to lift it up when walking (Figs. 20.3–20.4). By the 1820s the nakedness of antique sculpture as a model for contemporary dress was seen as indelicate, and the main influences on fashionable dress were historical, fuelled by the Romantic poets, novels such as 'Waverley' and figures such as Mary, Queen of Scots. Throughout the rest of the nineteenth century classical allusions are few. The very large crinoline skirts of the 1860s were perfect for bold patterns such as the Greek key, which appeared on a dress in 1863,[11] and the peplum returned in a vaguely Greek style in an evening dress of 1866.[12] The dress reform movement mostly looked to medieval models but the department store Peter Robinson's produced a Greek costume for an evening dress in 1888,[13] whilst Liberty's made an Empire line dress in 1890 which looked back to 1810 styles copying antique modes.[14]

Throughout the nineteenth century and the early years of the twentieth, references back to earlier styles of dress were constantly being made. There was more than one period – the 1840s and 1880s in particular – when dress of the years before 1780 was the model. The Empire, that is, the French Empire, was popular in the 1890s whilst around 1910 it was the French Directoire of the 1790s which provided the

Fig. 20.3 An 1803 French fashion plate showing a fine muslin dress with trained skirt. (National Museums of Scotland, Adam Dickson Collection, H.RHI.21(ix)).

Fig. 20.4 White cotton dress with trained skirt, trimmed with pleats and small acorn-shaped buttons at the back, about 1800–05 (National Museums of Scotland, A.1975.5).

inspiration for the slim line garments with high waists. However, these returns to past eras of dress never saw an exact copying of the former styles of clothes, because women were not necessarily prepared to return to some of the disadvantages of the clothing. For example, by 1910 women's shoes had become much more practical and suited their way of life, which a return to 1790s shoes would not have done. Nomenclature for the styles of these revivals nearly always related to the historical period, so that little dress of 1910–14 had an antique name, whatever the source of the original inspiration.

Perhaps the most interesting attempt to produce clothes after the antique style were the gowns of Mariano Fortuny, a Spanish artist who lived in Venice.[15] He invented a way of pleating very fine silk satin inspired by the Ionic *chiton* of preclassical *korai*. The dress he used this fabric on was originally based on the Delphic Charioteer, an idea he patented in 1909. These pleated dresses were a success with many women who lived in the artistic and musical worlds of Paris, Vienna and London. Their sale was controlled by Fortuny who sold them through friends and shops that were accustomed to less conventional lifestyles. These dresses were produced with virtually no change over the years in several different styles until Fortuny's death in 1949. With him died the recipe for pleating the fabric. The pleated 'delphos' dress, as it was called, enjoyed a comeback in the 1970s when the first major books on his fabric and clothing designs were published (Fig. 20.5). Examples were bought at auction by women to wear and several modern designers have attempted to discover the secret of the pleating and revive it.

Fig. 20.5 A Fortuny 'delphos' dress in eau de nil satin trimmed with Venetian beads (National Museums of Scotland, A.1975.261).

Another icon of the twentieth century was the Kestos brassiere, the first one being worn by many young girls because of its gentle shape and the way it fastened at the front. Invented in about 1926–7 by Mrs Rosalind Klin in the USA, the prototype was based on two small handkerchiefs folded to form two triangles which crossed over at the front. The bra was fastened by two long elastic straps, which went from one side to the other across the back and buttoned under each bust. Mrs Klin took the name for her invention from the *kestos* of Aphrodite.[16]

But where does this leave the Romans? So far nearly all the examples quoted are to Greek dress and most of the inspiration appears to be from Greek sources. Did the Romans contribute nothing to neo-classical dress (Fig. 20.6)? If not why not? Perhaps one answer to this may be found in Thomas Hope's earlier work, a series of engravings called *Costume of the Ancients*, published in two volumes in 1809.[17] Filled with line drawings in the style of John Flaxman, it reproduces figures from Greek and Roman vases and statues, either in Hope's own collection or seen and drawn by him in other collections. This obviously inspired his interest in producing his engravings of 1812, ironically just as the fashions were starting to develop along less classical lines (Fig. 20.1–20.2). Had he published them ten or fifteen years earlier they might have had more resonance with the public and perhaps it was this recognition that the drawings were now out of step with contemporary styles that made the issue of the book so limited.

In contrast with the Roman, the Greek figures in Hope's book show several very attractive garments that could be adapted for wear, as he himself showed in his 1812 plates. The twists of heavy fabric shown on the Roman figures must have been impractical in ancient times and were certainly so by the 1790s. The soft cashmere wool shawls from India, or their European equivalents in wool and silk, were worn by women for warmth and were manipulated with ease to wrap the body when the weather required it. It was one thing to drape yards of fabric elegantly round the body for a portrait and quite another to be faced with the same amount to be manipulated whilst carrying out even fairly mundane tasks at home.

Fig. 20.6 English fashion plate from The Lady's Magazine *for November 1809. The left figure wears a muslin dress and purple velvet Roman cloak, one of the few instances of a garment with a Roman attribution (Private Collection).*

Fashion as worn by people is never quite as ludicrous as some commentators would have us believe. A sense of reality and practicality surfaces when necessary and each age requires their clothes to fit contemporary aesthetics. The adaptations of classical dress, whether from Greek or Roman models, was therefore made with contemporary dress in mind. However much the dressmakers thought they were adhering to correct classical modes there was always something which betrayed their own time in the adaptations.

Notes

1 Reprinted as *Designs of Modern Costume 1812* (London: Costume Society Extra Series No. 4, 1973), from a copy in a private collection. The original cannot now be traced.

2 Thomas Hope (1769–1831) was the son of John Hope, a banker in Amsterdam, who studied architecture whilst on an unusually long and varied Grand Tour, which included countries in Asia and Africa as well as Europe. After he settled in Britain in the late 1790s he acquired, amongst other things, a large collection of antique sculpture and vases. He was a patron of several contemporary sculptors and artists and was a champion of the Greek Revival. Hope's publications were varied, including furniture and interior decoration as well as a novel. See David Watkin, *Thomas Hope and the Neo-Classical Idea* (1968).

3 For example see the index to C. W. Cunnington, *English Women's Clothing in the Nineteenth Century* (London: Faber and Faber, 1937), pp 447–460, the standard work on the period. Names given to various articles of dress can be very confusing. Throughout the nineteenth century it was the custom to name a garment after a famous figure, someone in a play of the moment or a beautiful princess. For example virtually the same style of cap can be a called an Alexandra one year, an Eugenie the next and an Elisabeth the third, all named after the most beautiful royal women of the mid century. When naming styles after particular countries the resemblance to any genuine garment of that country might be very tenuous.

4 Hugh Honour, *Neo-Classicism* (London: Penguin Books, 1968).
Arts Council of Great Britain, *The Age of Neo-Classicism* (London: Arts Council of Great Britain, 1972), catalogue of an exhibition held at the Royal Academy and the Victoria and Albert Museum, London.

5 There is a splendid full length of the Marquis of Atholl, *c.* 1680 by Jacob de Wet in Roman armour illustrated in Andrew Wilton, *The Swagger Portrait* (London, 1992), cat. No. 19. See also cat. No. 13 for a portrait of the Duchess of Norfolk, *c.* 1677, by Sir Peter Lely in drapery.

6 Wilton, *op. cit.*, cat. No. 35, Three Ladies Adorning a Term of Hymen, 1773–5, by Sir Joshua Reynolds, and Aileen Ribeiro, 'Muses and mythology: classical dress in British eighteenth-century female portraiture', in A. de la Haye & E. Wilson (eds) *Defining Dress: dress as object, meaning & identity* (Manchester: MUP, 1999), pp. 104–113.

7 For a general discussion of eighteenth century dress see Anne Buck, *Dress in Eighteenth-Century England*, London, 1979, C W & P Cunnington, *Handbook of English Costume in the Eighteenth Century*, London, rev. ed 1972 and Aileen Ribeiro, *Dress in Eighteenth-Century Europe* (London, 1984).

8 See Aileen Ribeiro, *Fashion in the French Revolution* and K le Bourhis (ed), *Costume in the Age of Napoleon. Costume from Revolution to Empire: 1789–1815*, New York, 1989.

9 For the patterns of dresses in this period see Janet Arnold, *Patterns of Fashion I: Englishwomen's dresses and their construction, c. 1600–1860* (London, 1964).

10 Cunnington, *op. cit.*, p. 25

11 Cunnington, *op. cit.*, p. 217

12 Cunnington, *op. cit.*, p. 226

13 Cunnington, *op. cit.*, p. 345

14 Cunnington, *op. cit.*, p. 371

15 Guillermo de Osma, *Mariano Fortuny, his Life and Work* (London, 1980).

16 Maureen Alden, 'The Beguilement of Zeus – In All the Better Shops', in *Costume*, 33, 1999, pp. 68–73.

17 Reprinted in one volume as Thomas Hope, *Costume of the Greeks and Romans* (New York: Dover, 1962).

Chapter 21

THE CONTRIBUTION OF EXPERIMENTAL ARCHAEOLOGY TO THE RESEARCH OF ANCIENT TEXTILES

Elizabeth E. Peacock

Introduction

A contribution on the theme of experimental archaeology may seem out of place in this volume dedicated to John Peter Wild. After all, it is not an aspect of archaeology one most readily associates with John Peter. This is even more so the case if it is the flint-knapping and boat-building experimental archaeology that first comes to one's mind. Quite the contrary! John Peter has been involved in many aspects of the practical experimental process, perhaps more than he himself is aware. This has been either through his own work or through his enthusiastic support of the diverse research topics his students have pursued over the years, this author included.

In fact, in his classic *Archaeology by Experiment*, John Coles[1] singles out John Peter's *Textile Manufacture in the Northern Roman Provinces*,[2] along with Audrey Henshall's 'Textiles and weaving appliances in prehistoric Britain'[3] as two works which lay foundations for experimental work. Their 'specialised observations of ancient textiles ... go a long way towards deducing the precise type of weaving procedures used.'[4] Another element in John Peter's contribution to the experimental approach in ancient textile studies has been as a driving force behind both the North European Symposium for Archaeological Textiles (NESAT) and the *Archaeological Textiles Newsletter* (ATN), forums which disseminate current studies in archaeological textiles, including those of an experimental nature.

Experimental archaeology has become an important part of modern archaeology. It stands at the interface between processual archaeology and archaeological science. There is much debate about what does and does not constitute experimental archaeology.[5] Even experimental archaeologists cannot agree upon what it is. In essence, experimental archaeology is practical attempts by trial and experiment to reconstruct past conditions and circumstances. It deals with the basic sources of archaeological data – the surviving material remains of a culture, both artefacts and sites. Pictorial and descriptive sources and ethnological parallels greatly enhance this archaeological record.

Experimental archaeology permeates many textile projects which venture beyond cataloguing the attributes of structure and scale, patterning and design, yarn and fibres, and coloration. It also forms part of the current moves to take the traditional technical, historical and aesthetic studies of ancient textiles further and relate the material to site formation, past cultures and human behaviour. Coles[6] groups experiments into three levels: simulation, production methods and function testing. We are all familiar with simulation of ancient costumes for display purposes, where attention is concentrated on the visual three-dimensional effect. Original materials, appropriate technology and functionability are not the issue. An example of production experiments would be research directed to producing fabrics which replicate Bronze Age finds using the technology of the two-beam vertical loom and wool from descendants of Bronze Age sheep. Pressing into service sails produced for sea-going replicas of Viking ships aptly illustrates function testing.[7]

The survey presented here is not comprehensive, nor is it intended to be. Some aspects, time periods or geographical regions have been over- or under-represented. No attempt is made to judge the merit or contribution of single pieces of research or long-term projects. Rather, it is the aim to bring together and draw attention to the wide range of seemingly disparate pursuits to provide an overview of the diversity and impact of experimentation's contribution to ancient textile studies. Perhaps John Peter, on reflection, will feel on familiar territory after all.

The textiles and their raw materials

The tangibles of textile studies are the textiles, their raw materials and the tools used in their production. Traditional studies of textile remains begin with the quantifiable attributes of structure and scale, patterning and design, yarn and fibres, and coloration. Experimental archaeology is one means of building on these purely technical studies.

Perhaps the earliest applications of experimental archaeology in ancient textile research were attempts to interpret the technique of manufacture by analysis of the textile's structure. There is a long tradition of taking the deciphered structure of fragments and proposing a hypothesis about how the fabric was constructed. Today, we are so familiar with this step, that we take it for granted, but the actual unravelling of how a textile was produced was a big step forward in the experimental process. Here we have the classic work of Margrethe Hald.[8] She worked out careful reconstructions not only of woven fabrics, but also ones produced by tablet weaving, *nålebinding*, braiding and sprang. Furthermore, she devised methods of graphically illustrating her reconstructions so that these crafts could be brought to life.

The next logical step was producing the experimental version of the careful diagram reconstructions. The corpus of experimental work carried out in the reconstruction of ancient fabrics is too numerous to detail. Both the textile workshop at the Historical-Archaeological Research Centre at Lejre in Denmark and the Weaving School at the University College of Borås, Sweden have long-term research programmes reconstructing ancient fabrics. Each generation of experiments resolves some questions and raises new ones. Of recent interest has been the 'time trial'. How many working hours are involved in production, and what is the cost and value of the product? Sundström[9] calculated that a complete set of horsehair tablet-woven bands for a Migration Period costume takes 1740 hours' work. This would make these a veritable treasure. On the other hand, Nørgaard[10] clocked up 402 hours reconstructing the Vejen (Denmark) blanket, also dating to the Migration Period.

Researchers and practitioners have come a long way in mastering the production of the fabrics, the braids and the bands, as well as sorting out the colours. The natural next step in the experimental process is the reconstruction of the ancient costumes and functional textiles. With regard to garments, this too has a long tradition, but is currently an area of intensive experimental research, as well as the subject of heated discussions regarding what does and does not constitute a useful contribution. Serious problem-orientated researchers often condemn the 'weekend' novice or the 'dumbing down' of sophisticated ancient skills for education purposes. Nonetheless, exciting, research-based creations are being produced, such as the costume of King Canute (National Museum of Denmark),[11] the Viborg (Denmark) linen shirt,[12] the 'Iceman's' clothing[13] and the sails for the replica Viking ships.[14]

In addition to its technique, the excavated textile, through its physical condition, can provide insight into both its function and use prior to burial and its microbiological degradation during burial. Evidence of creasing, wear and fibre damage, which occurred during use, is often preserved. Characterising fibre damage and creasing using fibre fracture morphology provides insight into degree and type of wear. Cooke and co-workers have studied surface damage in numerous Roman wool fabrics from Vindolanda.[15] They subjected a common fabric-type, produced on the warp-weighted loom, to experimental abrasion to simulate the type of wear registered in the archaeological fragment and calibrate its severity.[16] Initial results showed that the wear in the replica was similar in nature but much more extensive than in the original. Wear and damage simulation is an area of experimental research with many possibilities.

The raw materials of textiles, the fibres, are the subject of many studies. Long-range programmes at Lejre,[17] Butser Ancient Farm in the UK,[18] Düppel Open Air Museum in Berlin[19] and the Tømmervik Textile Trust in Central Norway[20] continue to address the production and processing of fibres that approach the characteristics of fibres employed in the construction of ancient textiles. Much of this work has involved sheep and wool.[21] One recent project in Israel researched harvesting, fibre preparation and weaving of milkweed fibres.[22] Another carried out at Lejre by Mannering[23] undertook the entire process of growing and transforming stinging nettle (*Urtica dioica*) from plant, to fibre, to fabric. Because flax (*Linum usitatissimum* L), another fibre of antiquity, continues to be used, its characteristics and methods of preparation are known; whereas, those of stinging nettle have been lost. The study found, among other things, that the prepared fibres made up only 4%–5% of the dry weight of the plants following retting, that they are of a very high quality, and that they can be distinguished from flax by microscopy of their cross section.

In the study of ancient textiles, the identification of fibres is of primary importance. Here both optical and scanning electron microscopy are invaluable tools. For many fibres, especially those of animal origin, fibre morphology is specific enough to assist in characterisation. Meanwhile, the morphologies of other fibres, in particular those deriving from plant stems, such as nettle and hemp, are less distinct. Here is one way in which Mannering's experimental work with nettles will feed back to assist in the analysis of ancient fragments. In North America, a plant fibre collection has been established, consisting of material that has been processed from the stems of plants employed by prehistoric Native Americans, for comparison with fibres in ancient textiles.[24] Processing methods have attempted to simulate those used in prehistoric times in order to produce fibres with 'ancient' fibre characteristics.

Other textile evidence

Natural textile fibres are highly perishable. Their long-term survival in archaeological deposits is the result of special circumstances of extreme dryness, cold or anoxic conditions. The actual artefact database from which textile specialists draw is more extensive than just the 'organic' textile remains. Additional forms of textile evidence include mineral-preserved fragments and impressions in previously plastic liquid surfaces.

Textile fragments in intimate contact with metal artefacts in archaeological contexts can be preserved by the metal corrosion products that develop as the result of the corroding metal. This type of survival is common in burials in which grave goods such as coins, buckles, swords and brooches accompany the corpse. Mineralization can be a continuum from partial to total replacement of the organic matrix of the textile with an inorganic one. In the proximity of copper alloy objects, the biocidal properties of copper ions in solution can prevent biological degradation of natural fibres, leaving them still flexible and recognisably textile. Higher levels of impregnation can lead to a hard, obviously inorganic facsimile of the textile. Mineralized textile remains survive in two forms: positive and negative casts. Positive casts occur when minerals form within the fibre, whereas, negative casts result from the deposition of minerals on the fibre surface after which the organic original disappears. Mineralized fibres have been documented associated with alloys of copper, silver, iron and lead, and have encompassed both protein- and cellulose-based fibres. Although mineralization is most commonly associated with metals, it has been reported for other materials such as the calcified cast of a silk-moth cocoon and part of the enclosed pupa.[25]

For the most part, mineral-preserved textiles are of interest for what light they can shed on the technical nature of the fabric. The actual mechanisms of and interrelationships between fibre decay and mineralization are poorly understood. Using analytical techniques such as x-ray diffraction (XRD), scanning electron microscopy (SEM) and energy dispersive x-ray spectrometry (EDS), both Janaway[26] and Jakes and Sibley[27] proposed models for the formation of mineral-preserved fibres. Gillard *et al.*[28] and Jakes and Howard[29] took these models further and simulated the mineralization of fibres in the laboratory. Both studies found that fibre morphology, but not chemistry, was preserved by the replacement minerals, and Jakes and Howard reported that the resulting 'fibre' was larger than the original fibre. This is in agreement with measurements carried out on a group of wool and plant-fibre textiles recovered from a Late Germanic Iron Age cemetery on Bornholm (Denmark) in which several fabrics were present in both organic and mineral-preserved state.[30]

Not only have the mechanisms of mineral preservation been of interest but also the time-scales over which mineralization takes place. The common 'hunch' seemed to be that mineralization takes place relatively quickly following burial. Actualistic field studies of the early stages of the *in situ* mineralization process are reported by several researchers. Both Barford[31] and Janaway[32] examined the degradation of modern textiles in association with metal artefacts in experimental refuse pits. Janaway found a rapid onset of corrosion for both copper-alloy and iron samples, with iron being the more aggressive, and that corrosion was more extensive on linen than on the protein-based fabrics. Closer investigation of iron-corroded wool and linen revealed fibre longitudinal surface morphology typical of that seen in archaeological fragments, that is, negative casts of well-preserved wool fibres and unidentifiable negative casts of fibres that could no longer be characterized as linen. In an earlier study, Janaway[33] replicated Anglo-Saxon inhumation graves. Differences were seen in the textile and metal samples between the coffin and non-coffin burials with general trends following those seen in the refuse-pit trial, but the rate of mineralization was slower in the coffins. In hindsight, the refuse pit was not typical of archaeological deposits in which mineral-preserved fragments are found. In addition, recent investigation of mineral-preserved saprophytic invertebrates and textiles in Anglo-Saxon graves indicates that the onset of mineralization in coffin-protected graves may be as long as several years after burial.[34]

The long-term experimental earthwork project near Wareham in the UK, which consists of a full-scale bank and ditch constructed on sand in 1963, included textile material in association with metals among the buried materials. Reported results of the deterioration of the fabrics highlight that preservation was better where they were in contact with the metals, but further study to provide insight into the mineralization process is lacking.[35]

Some of the oldest indications of fibre-based technology are in the form of carbonised fragments and impressions in fired clay or plaster. Many finds of prehistoric North American textiles are in a carbonised state. As the result of carbonising, the fibres sometimes have an altered morphology that defies identification even with the greater depth of focus and resolution of the SEM. Srinivasan[36] carried out a series of high-temperature carbonising experiments of modern plant fibres to produce similarly altered carbonised fibres that could assist in the identification of such fibres found in prehistoric textiles.

In most instances carbonised fibres prove to be of plant origin. As a rule, cellulose-based fibres are not well preserved in wet burial environments. When they are, severely degraded fragments often metamorphose into inflexible, collapsed, corrugated, black fragments upon excavation and exposure to the air. These can be mistaken for carbonised fibres. Experimental soil burial studies carried out by Peacock[37] have addressed this transformation and further work is addressing the causative mechanisms.

Textile impressions are most commonly found in fired clay,[38] plaster[39] and metal artefacts. In many regions of the world, such as eastern North America, the scarcity of organic textile remains emphasizes the importance of these forms of evidence. These materials have not to date been a major focus of experimental investigation. Because thread density is frequently used as an indicator of fabric quality, the extent to which impressions represent the true density should be of interest. The 'impression' process has been studied in experiments that have focused on the production of copper-alloy brooches from Late Iron Age Sweden. Woven fabrics were traditionally employed in the casting process, and are evidenced by impressions on the convex, that is, the interior face, of excavated brooches. Malmius[40] investigated the function of the textile in the casting process, and the relationship in thread density between the resulting impression and the original fabric.

Tools and equipment used in the production of textiles

Loom weights, shuttles, heddles, spindle whorls, bone and metal needles, weaving tablets, scissors, thimbles, smoothing stones, sword beaters, comb beaters and teasels are all part of the panoply of finds in the archaeological record that contribute to our understanding of the production of textiles. As is the case for the textiles, technical studies of the tools provide the foundation for experiments.[41] With the textile fragments as the point of departure, these tools have been the subject of extensive testing both of their function, and of their suitability in producing replica textiles. One of the most investigated aspects of function and production continues to be the operation of the warp-weighted loom. Some of the earliest experiments were attempts to weave replicas of ancient fabrics on the warp-weighted loom. Schlabow's extensive experiments began prior to World War II,[42] and those at the Norwegian Folk Museum followed soon thereafter.[43] As was the case for the reconstruction of fabrics and garments, experiments focusing on the tools and equipment have also evolved through several generations. Many of the research programmes being carried out today, such as those at Lejre or at Düppel Open Air Museum build upon the earlier investigations of others.

Environments

There is a scattered but growing corpus of studies that investigate the effect of soil burial on textile materials. Some of this work aims to synthesize archaeological textiles from modern material for use as experimental samples in conservation research.[44] The importance of the role of conservation in stabilising textile fragments with minimal intervention and alteration cannot be stressed enough. It is the most crucial stage in the post-excavation process. Experimental research in archaeological textile conservation is handicapped by the nature of the subject material. Archaeological textiles are quite often fragmentary and do not exist in the numbers necessary for experimental research where variables must be controlled, measurements must be accurate, statistics must be used to analyze the data, and the experiment must be replicated a number of times. These textiles are rarely released for destructive research; and, since they are characterized by a high degree of variability, they are rarely suitable for experimental research, where variations in results could be attributed to the nature of the specimen. Simulated samples bridge the gap, between precious artefacts and unsuitable modern materials.

The archaeological textile, the 'artefact', is the end product of a cumulative process. It will have been subjected to several chemical and physical processes to bring it from the fibre stage to the yarn stage, and through to the finished product. This in turn would go through a lifetime of 'wear and tear' before becoming part of an archaeological deposit. Once in the archaeological context, factors such as soil chemistry, subsidence and microbiology contribute further to its transformation. Recovered textiles 'look and feel' different – different beyond that of simply being worn out. Often experimental archaeology is the research approach undertaken to address these differences. Unlike textiles recovered from dry sites or arctic sites, textiles from excavations in Northern Europe are characterized by their thematic brown colour. Great advances in putting colour to these 'brown rags' have been made through techniques developed to analyse for dyestuffs in archaeological textiles where not only the chemical compound is identified but also possible candidates for its source, such as woad or lichen purple.[45] Meanwhile the workshop at Lejre has investigated plant dyes, both growing suitable plants, extracting dyestuffs, and dyeing and fixing the colours.

Soil burial has also been used to investigate the impact of burial on dyed textiles. When dye analysis does not detect colorants, a negative result does not necessarily indicate that the textile was never dyed, only that any dye present is no longer detectable. Speculations about the dyestuff decaying beyond recognition or being removed by interaction with the soil solution have been postulated. Needles and his colleagues[46] investigated metal-ion exchange, and carried out laboratory burial studies to determine the effect of mordanting and burial on the shade and depth-of-shade of dyed modern cotton and wool. The fabrics underwent underwent extensive colour change, but the significant net absorption of a range of elements from the soil precluded metal-ion exchange as the cause. Another study carried out by Peacock[47] in which unmordanted, undyed natural fibre fabrics were buried in two soil types, showed that colour changes following burial can result from absorption of elements from the burial environment.

The textile workshop at Lejre has carried out several long-term experiments on the effects of burial in a bog on natural-dyed wool fabrics.[48] As early as 1970, dyed wool samples were buried in a bucket of peat. At that time techniques for the analysis of dyestuffs in archaeological textiles had not been developed. It was known that dyeing was practised in the Iron Age, yet it was difficult to find evidence for this in the spectacularly preserved Danish textile finds. The workshop sought to replicate the famous oak coffin bog burials and see what effect there would be on the coloured fabrics. The bucket experiment was followed in 1972 with several undyed and plant-dyed wool fabrics being packed into three miniature oak coffins, which were submerged into the Centre's bog for up to 11 years. A similar series was begun in 1976 and those samples removed after two years. Visual comparisons were made with the unburied controls, with the 11-year samples looking like convincing archaeological 'brown rags'.

Several programmes of experimental research have addressed the interactions of textiles within entire systems. The refuse pits and inhumation graves described earlier are examples of this. The completely preserved costumes found in well-preserved oak coffins in burial mounds form some of the most remarkable textile discoveries from prehistoric Denmark. The central parts of these mounds, which include the coffins, are surrounded by a strongly cemented iron pan that completely encapsulates the wet core, providing the preservative environment for the coffins and their contents. Different theories have been proposed to explain the development of these pans. An experimental mound was constructed at Lejre, scale 1:5, of the famous Egtved mound to investigate iron pan formation.[49] Included in the mound was a miniature oak coffin containing a rib roast, a copper-alloy badge and a piece of undyed wool fabric that was a replica of the original textile[50] Within a week the installed monitoring system indicated the chemical conditions required for the formation of an iron pan had developed. Excavation three years later revealed an established iron pan, and the contents of the coffin were quite 'fresh'. Analysis of the changes in the textile, which are being carried out at NTNU in Trondheim, are not yet complete.

Large-scale experiments in the formation and transformation of archaeological environments that are relevant to ancient textiles are the two experimental earthworks constructed in the UK in the 1960s. A full-scale bank and ditch were constructed on chalk subsoil at Overton Down and a similar structure was built on sand near Wareham. A wide range of objects and materials were buried including modern wool and linen fabrics, and cotton fabric (Overton Down) and flax and hemp rope (Wareham). Recovery on a progressive scale from one to 132 years provides the possibility to study the deterioration progress of these textile materials. In hindsight, there is much discussion about the suitability of the selected textiles, such as chrome-mordanted wool, and about the inclusion of this material in a structure that would not have contained textiles originally. However, the spirit and scale of the enterprise are to be commended.

Another aspect of ancient textiles being investigated by burial experiments concerns degradation pathways operating in different burial environments. This area of research is currently of utmost relevance for all types of archaeological materials and sites. For ethico-political and financial reasons it is increasingly necessary to preserve the archaeological heritage for future generations through *in situ* preservation. If re-burial of excavated materials or *in situ* preservation is to be a policy method of managing the archaeological heritage, its efficacy has to be established. We need to know whether textiles left buried in archaeological deposits are at risk. A newly established comparative burial programme at NTNU, in co-operation with Lejre, has buried a series of organic materials similar to those found in the archaeological record in several climatic zones in Scandinavia for a period of up to eight years.[51] The textiles include unbleached linen and dyed and undyed wool fabrics. The Maritime Research Centre in Roskilde, Denmark has been studying re-burial preservation of boat timbers found in maritime environments. Programmes have been established in which samples of modern wood and cotton fabrics have been submerged in both sea-water and the sea-bed.[52] The cotton did not survive sea-water burial but was better preserved in sediments on the sea-bed. The next phase of experiments will include the same textile materials as those in the NTNU study described above.

Conclusion

Experimental archaeology is a recognised and well–worn research method that continues to make valuable contributions to ancient textile studies. These include producing appropriate raw materials, reconstructing ancient fabrics and garments, physically modelling the function and efficiency of tools and equipment, and studying decay processes. Today's understanding of the role and contribution of textiles in past societies would be much poorer without this input.

Notes

1 J. Coles, *Archaeology by Experiment* (London: Hutchinson University Library, 1973).

2 J. P. Wild, *Textile Manufacture in the Northern Roman Provinces* (Cambridge: Cambridge University Press, 1970).

3 A. S. Henshall, 'Textiles and weaving appliances in prehistoric Britain', *Proceedings of the Prehistoric Society*, XVI (1950), pp. 130–162.

4 J. Coles, (note 1) *op. cit.* p. 143.

5 See J. Coles, *Experimental Archaeology* (London: Academic Press, 1979). J. Coles, ibid. D. Ingersoll, J. E. Yellen and W. Macdonald, *Experimental Archaeology* (NewYork: Columbia University Press, 1977). J. Malina, 'Archaeology and experiment', *Norwegian Archaeological Review*, XVI, no. 2 (1983), pp. 69–85. D. Olausson, 'Experimental archaeology in Sweden', *Bulletin of Experimental Archaeology*, no. 8 (1987), pp. 13–14. M. B. Schiffer, J. M. Skibo, T. C. Boelke, M. A. Neupert and M. Aronson,' New perspectives on experimental archaeology: surface treatments and thermal response of the clay cooking pot', *American Antiquity* LIX, no. 2 (1994), pp. 197–217.

6 J. Coles, (note 5), ibid.

7 E. Andersen, J. Milland and E. Myre, *Uldsejl i 1000 år* (Roskilde: Vikingskipshallen, 1989).

8 M. Hald, *Ancient Danish Textiles from Bogs and Burials* (Copenhagen: The National Museum of Denmark, 1980). H. C. Broholm and M. Hald, 'Skrydstrupfundet' *Nordiske Fortidsminder*, III (Copenhagen: Det Kongelige Nordiske Oldskriftselskasb, 1939). H. C. Broholm and M. Hald, 'Danske Bronzealders Dragter', *Nordiske Fortidsminder*, II (Copenhagen: H. H. Thieles Bogtrykkeri, 1935).

9 A. Sundström, 'Reproduction of horsehair tablet braids from Scandinavia's Migration Period', *Archaeological Textiles Newsletter*, no. 21 (Autumn 1995), pp. 24–26.

10 A. Nørgaard and E. Østergaard, 'The reconstruction of a blanket from the Migration Period', *Archaeological Textiles Newsletter*, nos. 18–19 (November 1994), pp. 17–19.

11 E. Munksgaard, 'Kopien af dragten fra mammengraven' in M. Iversen (ed), *Mammen. Grav, kunst og samfund I vikingetid*, Jysk ArkFologisk Selskabs Skrifter XXVIII (Højberg: Jysk Arkæologisk Selskab, 1991), pp. 151–4. L. Bender Jørgensen, 'I Knud den Stores Klær' *Nationalmuseets Arbejdsmark* 1992 (Copenhagen: Nationalmuseet, 1992), pp. 32–42.

12 M. Fentz, 'Viborgskjorten. En hørskjorte fra 1000-årene', *Viborg Stiftsmuseums* række, bind 2 (Viborg: Jysk Arkæologisk Selskab, 1994). M. Fentz, 'An 11th-century linen shirt from Viborg Søndersø, Denmark', in L. Bender Jørgensen and E. Munksgaard (eds), *Archaeological Textiles in Northern Europe*, Tidens Tand Nr. 5 (Copenhagen: Konservatorskolen, 1992), pp. 83–92.

13 M. Fansa, *Experimentelle Archäologie in Deutschland*, (Oldenburg: Staatliches Museum für Naturkunde und Vorgeschichte, 1998).

14 L. Bender Jørgensen and T. Damgaard-Sørensen, 'Textiles of seafaring' *Archaeological Textiles Newsletter*, no. 27 (Autumn 1998), pp. 6–9

15 Cooke and B. Lomas, 'The evidence of wear and damage in ancient textiles', in P. Walton and J.-P. Wild (eds), *Textiles in Northern Archaeology* (London: Archetype Publications, 1990), pp. 215–226. W. D. Cooke, *'Creasing in ancient textiles'*, Conservation News, no. 35 (1988), pp. 27–30.

16 J. P. Wild, W. D. Cooke, C. R. Cork and L. Fang Lu, 'Vindolanda: some results of the Leverhulme Trust Programme', in L. Bender Jørgensen and C. Rinaldo (eds), *Textiles in European Archaeology* (Göteborg: Göteborg University,1998) pp. 85–95.

17 T. Hatting, *Fåret i Oldtid & Nutid*, Forsøg Med Fortiden 4 (Lejre: Historisk Arkæologisk Forsøgscenter, 1993).

18 P. Reynolds, 'Butser Ancient Farm, Hampshire, UK', in P. G. Stone and P. G. Planel (eds), *The Constructed Past: Experimental Archaeology, Education and the Public* (London: Routledge, 1999), pp. 124–135.

19 A. Goldmann, 'Die Skudde: Ein alte mittel- und osteuropäische Landschafrasse', in L. Bender Jørgensen and C. Rinaldo (eds), *Textiles in European Archaeology*, GOTARC Series A, Vol. 1 (Götenborg: Göteborg University, 1998), pp. 233–242.

20 A. Lightfoot, 'Ullseil i tusen Dr, *SPOR*, XII, no. 2 (1997), pp. 10–15.

21 See M. Fansa, *Experimentelle Archäologie*, (Oldenburg: Staatliches Museum für Naturkunde und Vorgeschichte, 1999 and 1991). M. Fansa, *Experimentelle Archäologie in Deutschland*, (Oldenburg: Staatliches Museum für Naturkunde und Vorgeschichte, 1998, 1997 and 1990).

22 T. Friedman and Z. Amar, 'Milkweed: fibres to fabric', *Archaeological Textiles Newsletter*, no. 24 (Spring 1997), pp. 4–7.

23 U. Mannering, 'Oldtidens bræendenældklæde', in M. Meldgaar and M. Rasmussen, *Arkæologiske experimenter i Lejre* (Copenhagen: Rhodos, 1986), pp. 73–80.

24 K. A. Jakes, 'Clues to the past: further development of the comparative plant fiber collection', in M. V. Orna (ed), *Archaeological Chemistry*: Organic, Inorganic and Biochemical Analysis, ACS Symposium Series, DCXXV (Washington DC: American Chemical Society, 1996), pp. 202–222.

25 E. Panagiotakopulu, P. C. Buckland, P. M. Day, C. Doumas, A. Sarpaki and P. Skidmore, 'A lepidopterous cocoon from Thera and evidence for silk in the Aegean Bronze Age', *Antiquity*, LXXI (1997), pp. 420–429.

26 R. C. Janaway, 'The preservation of organic materials in association with metal artifacts deposited in inhumation graves, in A. Boddington, A. N. Garland and R. C. Janaway (eds), *Death, Decay and Reconstruction* (Manchester: University of Manchester Press, 1987), pp. 127–148.

27 K. A. Jakes and L. R. Sibley, 'An examination of the phenomenon of textile fabric pseudomorphism', in J. B. Lambert (ed.), *Archaeological Chemistry* – III, Advances in Chemistry Series, CCV (Washington DC: American Chemical Society, 1994), pp. 403–424.

28 R. D. Gillard, S. M. Hardman, R. G. Thomas and D. E. Watkinson, 'The mineralization of fibres in burial environments', *Studies in Conservation*, XLIX, no. 2 (1994), pp. 132–140.

29 K. A. Jakes and K. H. Howard III, 'Formation of textile pseudomorphs', in J. S. Olin and H. J Blackman (eds.), *Proceedings of the 24th International Archaeometry Symposium* (Washington DC: Smithsonian Institution Press, 1986), pp. 165–177.

30 U. Mannering and E. Peacock, 'A note on mineral-preserved textiles from the Late Germanic Iron Age cemetery at Nørre Sandgård Vest, Bornholm, Denmark', *Archaeological Textiles Newsletter*, no. 26 (1998), pp. 8–13.

31 P. M. Barford, *Mineral Pseudomorphs of Organic Materials:A Study in Burial Experiments*, unpublished (London: University of London, 1979).

32 R. C. Janaway, 'Corrosion preserved textile evidence: mechanism, bias and interpretation', in R. C. Janaway and B. Scott (eds), *Evidence Preserved in Corrosion Products: New Fields in Artifact Studies* (London: United Kingdom for Conservation, 1989), pp. 21–29.

33 R. C. Janaway, (note 22) *op. cit.*

34 G. Turner-Walker and C. J. Scull, 'Microfauna in Anglo-Saxon graves: entomological evidence at Boss Hall and the Butter Market, Ipswich', in A. Sinclair, E. Slater and J. Gowlett (eds), *Archaeological Sciences 1995*, Oxbow Monograph 64 (Oxford: Oxbow Books, 1997), pp. 320–327.

35 J. G. Evans and S. Limbrey, 'The experimental earthwork on Morden Bog, Wareham, Dorset, England: 1963–1972. Report of the Experimental Earthworks Committee of the British Association for the Advancement of Science', Proceedings of the Prehistoric Society, XL (1974), pp. 170–202.

36 R. Srinivasan, *Exploration of the Effects of Carbonisation on Apocynum Cannabinum Fibers*, MSc Thesis (Columbus: Ohio State University, 1993) cited in K. A. Jakes, 'Clues to the past: further development of the comparative plant fiber collection', in M. V. Orna (ed), *Archaeological Chemistry: Organic, Inorganic and Biochemical Analysis*, ACS Symposium Series, DCXXV (Washington DC: American Chemical Society, 1996), pp. 202–222.

37 E. E. Peacock, 'Biodegradation and characterization of water-degraded archaeological textiles created for conservation research', *International Biodeterioration & Biodegradation*, XXXVIII, no. 1 (1996), pp. 49–59. E. E. Peacock, *The Drying of Simulated Water-degraded Archaeological Textiles*, PhD thesis (Manchester: University of Manchester, 1993).

38 J. M. Adovasio, O. Soffer and B. Klíma, 'Upper Palaeolithic fibre technology: interlaced woven finds from Pavlov I, Czech Republic, *c.* 26,000 years ago', *Antiquity* LXX (1996), pp. 526–534. C. A. Giner, 'Traces of cloth, rope and wickerwork on oil amphoras in Monte Testaccio (Rome)', *Archaeological Textiles Newsletter*, nos. 18–19 (1994), pp. 6–8.

39 A. Betts, K. van der Borg, A. de Jong, C. McClintock and M. van Strydonck, 'Early cotton in North Arabia', *Journal of Archaeological Science XXI*, no. 4 (1994), pp. 489–499.

40 A. Malmius, 'Textile impressions on tortoise brooches from Birka and Vendel, Sweden', *Archaeological Textiles Newsletter*, no. 23 (1996), pp. 10–13.

41 See for example I. Øye, 'Textile equipment and its working environment, Bryggen in Bergen c 1150–1500', *The Bryggen Papers, Main Series*, II (Bergen: Norwegian University Press, 1988). E. Andersson, Textilproduktion i arkeologisk kontext', *Institute of Archaeology Report Series* nr. 58, (Lund: University of Lund, 1996). M. Hald (note 8) *op. cit.* J. P. Wild (note 2) *op. cit.* A. S. Henshall (note 3) *op. cit.*

42 K. Schlabow, *Der Thorsberger Prachtmantel, der Sclüssel zum altergermanischen Webstuhl* (Neumünster: 1952).

43 M. Hoffmann, *The Warp-Weighted Loom* (Oregon: Robin and Russ Handweavers, 1974).

44 E. E. Peacock, (note 33) *op. cit.* K. S. Tarleton and M. T. Ordoñez, 'Stabilization methods for textiles from wet sites', *Journal of Field Archaeology*, XXII, no. 1 (1995), pp. 81–95.

45 See for example P. Walton and G. W. Taylor, 'The characterisation of dyes in archaeological excavations', *Chromatography and Analysis*, XVII (June 1991), pp. 5–7; and other papers in the journal *Dyes in History and Archaeology*

46 H. L. Needles, 'Burial-induced color changes in unmordanted and mordanted alizarin-dyed cotton and wool fabrics', in K. Grimstad (ed) *ICOM Committee for Conservation 8th Triennial Meeting Sydney, Australia 6–11 September,* 1987 (Marina del Rey: Getty Conservation Institute, 1987), pp. 403–406. H. L. Needles, V. Cassman and M. J. Collins, 'Mordanted natural-dyed wool and silk fabrics: light- and burial-induced changes in color and *Historic Textile and Paper Materials,* tensile properties', in H. L. Needles and S. H. Zeronian (eds) ACS Symposium Series, CCXII (Washington DC: American Chemical Society, 1986), pp. 199–210. H. L. Needles and M. E. Regazzi, 'Burial-induced color changes in unmordanted and mordanted madder-dyed cotton and wool fabrics', Preprints (Washington DC: The American Institute for Conservation of Historic and Artistic Works,1987), pp. 78–84.

47 E. E. Peacock, 'X-ray fluorescence analysis of burial-degraded textiles', in V. Mejdahl and P. Siemen (eds), Proceedings from the *6th Nordic Conference on the Application of Scientific Methods in Archaeology, Esbjerg 1993*, Arkæologiske Rapporter nr. 1 (Esbjerg: Esbjerg Museum, 1996), pp. 13–22.

48 A. Norgaard, L. Dokkedal and E. Jensen, *Moseforsøg: natur- og plantefarvede stofprøver,* 10/72 (Lejre: Historiske-Arkæologisk Forsøgscenter, 1983). E. E. Peacock, 'Moselik på kunstig vis', *SPOR*, XIII, no. 2 (1998), pp. 49–51.

49 H. Breuning-Madsen and M. K. Holst, 'Recent studies on the formation of iron pans around the oaken coffins of the Bronze Age burial mounds of Denmark', *Journal of Archaeological Science,* XXV (1998), pp. 1103–1110.

50 H. Breuning-Madsen, M. K. Holst and M. Rasmussen, 'Jernkapper i bronzealderens gravhøj – forsøg ved en minimodel af Egtved-pigens gravhøj', in M. Meldgaard and M. Rasmussen (eds.) *Arkeologiske eksperimenter i Lejre* (Copenhagen: Rhodes, 1996), pp. 113–120.

51 E. E. Peacock, 'Moselik på kunstig vis', *SPOR*, XIII, no. 2 (1998), pp. 49–51.

52 D. Gregory, 'Opbevaring af tømmer i havet', *Marinarkeologisk Nyhedsbrev fra Roskilde,* no. 12 (1999), pp. 25–29. D. Gregory, 'Re-burial of ship timbers in the marine environment as a method of in-situ preservation', Proceedings of the 7th ICOM-CC *Working Group on Wet Organic Archaeological Materials Conference* (Grenoble: ARC-Nucléart, 1999), pp. 78–84.

Chapter 22

JOHN PETER WILD: A BIBLIOGRAPHY

1963

'Die Ausgrabungen unter dem Universitätsgebäude Bonn im März 1962' *Bonner Jahrbücher* 163, pp. 342–67 (joint authorship)

'The *Byrrus Britannicus*', *Antiquity* XXXVII, pp. 193–202

1964

'The *Caracallus*', *Latomus* XXIII, pp. 532–36

'The textile term *scutulatus*', *Classical Quarterly* NS XIV, pp. 263–66

1965

'How were provincial Roman brooches worn?', *Latomus* XXIV, pp. 610–13

'Zwei Textilproben aus Xanten', *Bonner Jahrbücher* 165, pp. 275–77

'A Roman silk damask from Kent', *Archaeologia Cantiana* LXXX, pp. 246–50

1966

'Papyrus in Pre-Roman Britain?' *Antiquity* XL, pp. 139–42 and 308ff.

'Mantus', *Zeitschrift f. vergl. Sprachforschung* LXXX, 247f.

'Manchester University Excavations at Brough-on-Noe (Navio) 1966', *Derbyshire Archaeological Journal* LXXXVI, pp. 99–101, (joint authorship)

1967

'Soft-finished textiles in Roman Britain', *Classical Quarterly* NS XVII, pp. 133–5

'Two technical terms used by Roman tapestry-weavers', *Philologus* CXI, pp. 151–55

'The *gynaeceum* at Venta and its context', *Latomus* XXVI, pp. 648–76

'Römische Textilreste im Saalburgmuseum', *Saalburg-Jahrbuch* XXIV, pp. 77–8

'Manchester University excavations 1967: 3. The Grey Ditch, Bradwell', *Derbyshire Archaeological Journal* LXXXVII, p. 160

1968

'Die Waffen des Burgus in Froitzheim, Kr. Düren', *Beiträge zur Archäologie des römischen Rheinlandes* I, pp. 111–4

'The Roman flax-hackle (AENA)', *Museum Helveticum* XXV, pp. 139–42

'Die Frauentracht der Ubier', *Germania* XLVI, pp. 67–73

'Excavations at Brough-on-Noe (Navio) 1968', *Derbyshire Archaeological Journal* LXXXVII, pp. 89–96 (joint authorship)

'Clothing in the North-West Provinces of the Roman Empire; *Bonner Jahrbücher* 168, pp. 166–240

Note on textile from Lombard St., London, in: *Transactions of the London and Middlesex Archaeological Society* XX, p. 42

Note on textiles in: I. E. Anthony, 'Excavations in Verulam Hill Fields, St. Albans, 1963–4', *Hertfordshire Archaeologist* I, pp. 9–50

Note on textile in: E. J. Mason, 'Ogof-yr-esgyrn, Dan-yr-ogof caves, Brecknock, excavations 1938–50', *Archaeologia Cambrensis* CXVII, p. 52

1969

'Manchester University Excavations at Brough-on-Noe (Navio) 1969' *Derbyshire Archaeological Journal* LXXXIX, pp. 99–106 (joint authorship)

'The *tarsikarios*, a Roman linen weaver in Egypt', *Hommages à Marcel Renard* (Brussels), pp. 810–19

'A note on TITULUM', *Archaeologia Cambrensis* CXVIII, pp. 133–4

Note on a *genius cucullatus* from Springhead in: *Antiquaries Journal* XLIX, p. 382

Note on textile in: P. R. Franke, 'Pachten: Der älteste Baumwollfund nördlich der Alpen (300 n. Chr.)', *16. Bericht der Staatlichen Denkmalpflege im Saarland*, pp. 161–3

1970

Textile Manufacture in the Northern Roman Provinces (Cambridge University Press)

'Gewebeabdrücke auf dem ziegel Nr sl/XIII 3c', *Saalburg-Jahrbuch* XXVII, pp. 49–50

'Borrowed names for borrowed things?', *Antiquity* XLIV, pp. 125–30

Notes on fragments of Diocletian's Price Edict from Aphrodisias in: *Journal of Roman Studies* LX, 126ff

'Die Textilfunde aus der Memoria IIk in Xanten', *Bonner Jahrbücher* 170, pp. 267–70

'Button-and-loop fasteners in the Roman provinces', *Britannia* I, pp. 137–155

1971

'The South Shields heddle' *Archaeologia Aeliana* 4th Series, XLIX, 230f.

'Castor, Normangate Field, 1969', *Bulletin of the Northamptonshire Federation of Archaeological Societies* V, pp. 7–12

'Castor, Normangate Field, 1970', *ibid.* pp. 12–15

'Longthorpe, 1970', *ibid.* pp. 20–22

1972

'Prehistoric and Roman Textiles' in J. G. Jenkins (ed.), *The Wool Textile Industry in Great Britain* (London), pp. 3–18

'Castor, *praetorium*, 1971', *Bulletin of the Northamptonshire Federation of Archaeological Societies* VII, pp. 13–19

'Longthorpe, 1971', *ibid.* pp. 22–26

The Romans in the Nene Valley (Peterborough)

1973

'A fourth-century potter's workshop and kilns at Stibbington, Peterborough' in: A. P. Detsicas (ed.), *Current Research in Romano-British Coarse Pottery (CBA Research Report* 10), pp. 135–8

'Zwei Textilreste aus Brunnen 49 der Saalburg', *Saalburg-Jahrbuch* XXX, p. 140

'Longthorpe, 1972', *Northamptonshire Archaeology* VIII, pp. 7–8

'Lynch Farm, Site 2, 1972', *ibid.* pp. 9–12
'The Year's Work 1972', *Durobrivae* I, pp. 4–6
'Longthorpe, an essay in continuity', *ibid.* pp. 7–11
'The Roman fishpond at Lynch Farm', *ibid.* pp. 20–1

1974

Note on textile in J. Rhodes, 'The Oldcroft (1971–2) hoard of bronze coins and silver objects', *Numismatic Chronicle* Series 7, XIV, pp. 73–4
'Castor, Normangate Field, 1973', *Northamptonshire Archaeology* IX, 1974, 86–8
'Lynch Farm, Site 2, 1973', *ibid.* pp. 92–5
'Roman Settlement in the Lower Nene Valley', *Archaeological Journal* CXXXI, pp. 140–170
'Wooden tent-pegs from the Roman Fort at Melandra Castle, Glossop, Derbys.', *Antiquaries Journal* LIV, pp. 302–5
'The Year's Work: 1973', *Durobrivae* II, pp. 4–6

1975

'Roman Textiles from the Walbrook (London)', *Germania* LIII, pp. 138–43
The Year's Work: 1974', *Durobrivae* II, pp. 4–6
'Longthorpe, 1974', *Northamptonshire Archaeology* X, pp. 155–6
'Castor, 1974', *ibid.* pp. 153–4
'Lynch Farm, Site 2, 1974', *ibid.* pp. 158–61
'Textiles' in H. Osborne (ed.), *The Oxford Companion to the Decorative Arts* (Oxford), pp. 769–71

1976

'The Year's Work: 1975', *Durobrivae* IV, 4ff
'A Roman Farm at Castor, 1975', *Durobrivae* IV, p. 26
'Textiles' in: D. E. Strong, P. D. C. Brown (eds), *Roman Crafts* (London), pp. 167–177
'Durobrivae' in: R. Stillwell (ed.), *The Princeton Encyclopedia of Classical Sites* (Princeton) p. 288
'Loanwords and Roman Expansion in North-West Europe', *World Archaeology* VIII, pp. 57–64
'The *gynaecea*' in R. Goodburn, P. Bartholomew (eds.), *Aspects of the Notitia Dignitatum,* (*BAR* S15), pp. 51–8
'Castor, Normangate Field, 1975', *Northamptonshire Archaeology* XI, pp. 186–191 (joint authorship)

1977

'The Year's Work: 1976', *Durobrivae* V, p. 4
'Eine militärische Töpferei beim Legionslager in Longthorpe, Peterborough', *Studien zu den Militärgrenzen Roms* II, *Beihefte der Bonner Jahrbücher* XXXVIII, pp. 75–80
'Classical Greek Textiles from Nymphaeum', *The Textile Museum Journal* IV, 4, pp. 33–4
'The Aezani copy of the Prices Edict', *Zeitschrift für Papyrologie und Epigraphik* XXVI, pp. 125–51 (joint authorship)
The Textiles, Vindolanda III (Haltwhistle, Northumberland)

1978

'The Warp-Weighted Loom', *Antiquity* LII, p. 59
'Cross-Channel trade and the textile industry' in J. du Plat Taylor, H. Cleere (eds), *Roman Shipping and Trade: Britain and the Rhine Provinces* (*CBA Research Report* XXIV), pp. 79–81

'The textiles' in G. Dennis, 'Southwark Excavations 1972–1974: 1–7 St. Thomas Street', *London and Middlesex and Surrey Archaeological Societies Joint Publication* I, pp. 405–7

'Villas in the Lower Nene Valley' in M. Todd (ed.), *Studies in the Romano-British Villa* (Leicester), pp. 59–69

'The Year's Work: 1977', *Durobrivae* VI, p. 4

'Le bouton-agrafe', *Revue Archéologique de Narbonnaise* XI, p. 194

1979

'Fourth-century underwear with special reference to the *thoracomachus*' in M. W. C. Hassall (ed.), *De Rebus Bellicis,* (*BAR* S63), pp. 105–10

'Roman and Native in Textile Technology' in B. C. Burnham, H. B. Johnson (eds), *Invasion and Response: the Case of Roman Britain* (*BAR* 73), pp. 123–131

'The textiles from the Mummy 1770' in A. R. David (ed.), *The Manchester Museum Mummy Project* (Manchester), pp. 133–6

'Roman Textiles from Vindolanda, Hexham, England', *The Textile Museum Journal* XVIII, pp. 19–24

Note on textile impression on Roman sherd from Mucking in: *Antiquaries Journal* LIX, p. 413

'Textile' (from Red House Corbridge), *Archaeologia Aeliana* Series 5, VII, 74f.

'The Dunstable Textile', *The Manshead Magazine* XXV (Jan. 1979), p. 13

'The Aezani Copy of the Prices Edict', *Zeitschrift für Papyrologie und Epigraphik* XXXIV, pp. 163–210 (joint authorship)

'The Year's Work: 1978', *Durobrivae* VII, p. 4

1980

'The four mother goddesses from the Roman riverside wall: comments on the dress', *London & Middlesex Archaeological Society Special Paper* III, 193f. 'Textile from the Kirk Michael Hoard', *Journal of the Manx Museum* VIII, p. 8

'Textiles from Rough Castle', *Proceedings of the Society of Antiquaries of Scotland* CX (1978–80), pp. 273

1981

'A find of Roman scale armour from Carpow', *Britannia* XII, 305f.

'Some ancient silk from the Crimea in the British Museum', *Antiquaries Journal* LXI, pp. 302–6 (joint authorship)

1982

'Wool production in Roman Britain' in D. Miles (ed.), *The Romano-British Countryside* (*BAR* CIII), pp. 109–22

'Some new light on Roman textiles' in L. Bender Jørgensen, K. Tidow (eds), *Textilsymposium Neumünster: Archäologische Textilfunde: 6.5–8.5.1981* (Neumünster), pp. 10–24

1983

'Textile fragments from the later Butt Road Cemetery' in N. Crummy (ed.), *The Roman Small Finds from Excavations in Colchester 1971–9* (*Colchester Archaeological Report* II), 147f.

'Early finds of Chinese Silk in NW Europe', *Association pour l'Etude des Textiles d'Asie (Acta)* II, pp. 32–6

1984

'The Textiles' in: P. Crummy (ed.), *Excavations at Lion Walk, Balkerne Lane and Middleborough, Colchester, Essex* (*Colchester Archaeological Society Report* III), pp. 44–7.

'A group of early pottery' in: F. M. M. Pryor, *Excavations at Fengate, Peterborough, England: the Fourth Report, Northants Archaeological Society Monograph* II, (Toronto) pp. 177–9.
'The triangular loom weights from the Cat's Water and Storey's Bar Road subsites', *ibid.* p. 168
'Early silk finds in North-West Europe', *The Textile Museum Journal* XXIII, pp. 17–23
'The Year's Work: 1980–83', *Durobrivae* IX, 4f.
'The Textiles from Building 32' in: O. Brogan, D. J. Smith, *Ghirza: A Libyan Settlement in the Roman Period, Libyan Antiquities Series* 1 (Tripoli), pp. 291–308
'Camulodunum and the Silk Road', *Current Archaeology* XCIII, pp. 44–7

1985

'A socketed toothed terminal from the Saalburg vicus', *Saalburg Jahrbuch* XL–XLI, 28f.
'Excavations on the western defences and the interior, 1970' in B. J. N. Edwards and P. V. Webster, *Ribchester Excavations I: Excavations within the Roman Fort* (Cardiff), pp. 19–40 (with G. D. B. Jones)
'Economy: the arrival of money' in: C. Haigh (ed.), *The Cambridge Historical Encyclopaedia of Great Britain and Ireland* (Cambridge), pp. 32–36.
'The Clothing of Britannia, Gallia Belgica and Germania Inferior' in H. Temporini, W. Haase (eds), *Aufstieg und Niedergang der römischen Welt* II, 12, 3 (Berlin) pp. 362–422
'The Germanies/Raetia/Noricum' and 'The Rhine-Danube Limes' in R. J. A. Talbert, *Atlas of Classical History* (London).

1986

'Wool production in Roman Britain', *Ark* XIII, 8 (June 1986), pp. 205–9.
'Four bone weaving tablets' in: A. D. McWhirr, *Houses in Roman Cirencester* (*Cirencester Excavations*) III, p. 114
'Bath and the identification of the *Caracalla*', *Britannia* XVII, pp. 352–3
'Textile impression on the tile from Hockwold-cum-Wilton', *East Anglian Archaeology* XXXI, p. 84, pl. XV
(with C. Green, C. Dallas, I. Green) Excavations at Castor, Cambridgeshire in 1957–8 and 1973', *Northamptonshire Archaeology* XXI (1986–7), pp. 109–148

1987

'Ein römischer Seidenstoff aus dem Wallis: Vallis Poenina auf der Seidenstrasse?', *Helvetia Archaelogica* LXX, pp. 59–73
'The dress of the figures' in G. W. Meates, *The Roman Villa at Lullingstone, Kent* II: *The Wallpaintings and Finds* (Maidstone), pp. 40–1
'*titulus/titulum*' reply to Henderson and Keppie, *Britannia* XVIII, p. 284
'The Roman horizontal loom', *American Journal of Archaeology* XCI, pp. 459–71
'Textile impressions' in C. Going, *The Mansio and Other Sites in the SE Sector of Caesaromagus: The Roman Pottery* (*CBA Research Report* LXII), p. 90
Longthorpe II: The Military Works Depot, an Episode in Landscape History (*Britannia Monograph*) VIII

1988

'Textiles' (map spread), *Past Worlds: The Times Atlas of Archaeology* (London), pp. 40–1
'Clothes from the Roman Empire: Barbarians and Romans' in: L. Bender Jørgensen, B. Magnus, E. Munksgsaard (eds), *Archaeological Textiles: Report from the 2nd NESAT Symposium 1.–4. V. 1984* (*Arkaeologiske Skrifter* 2) (Copenhagen), pp. 65–98

'Textiles' in: L. Allason-Jones, M. C. Bishop, *Excavations at Roman Corbridge: The Hoard*, (London: HBMC), pp. 86–93, 107–8

'Textile impressions 1599, 3366 on tile from Beauport Park', *Britannia* XIX, pp. 169–70

Textiles in Archaeology (Shire Books)

1989

'Tile impression' in: D. Wilson, *Excavation of a Romano-British Villa at Worley, Gloucestershire: Fourth Interim Report 1988* (Keele), p. 32

(with H. G. Taylor, I. Jenkins) 'From Rags to Riches: Two Textile Fragments from Cyprus' in V. Tatton-Brown (ed.), *Cyprus and the Eastern Mediterranean in the Iron Age: Proceedings of the Seventh British Museum Classical Colloquium, April 1988*, pp. 146–152

'Roman silk and the horizontal loom in the Maas-Rhine region' *Middeleeuws Textiel in het Bijzonder in het Euregiogebied Maas-Rijn', Handelingen van het congres Alden Biesen 13.2.–16.2.1989* (Provinciaal Museum voor Religieuze Kunst, Sint-Truiden), pp. 209–221

1990

'An Introduction to Archaeological Textiles Studies' in S. A. O'Connor, M. M. Brooks (eds), *Archaeological Textiles (Occasional Papers of the UKIC)*, X, pp. 3–4

'Tile fragment with a textile impression' in R. J. Ling *et al.* 'Excavations at Carsington 1983–84', *Derbyshire Archaeological Journal, CX*, p. 48

Textiles in Northern Archaeology, NESAT III: Textile Symposium in York 6–9 May 1987, (London: NESAT/Archetype) (edited by P. Walton and J. P. Wild)

1991

'Grewelthorpe Moor: the textiles', *Britannia*, XXII, pp. 197–201

1992

'The Roman loom in Western Europe: the evidence of art and archaeology', *Vlaamse Vereniging voor oud en hedendaags Textiel Bulletin* (Festschrift for Daniël De Jonghe), pp. 12–17.

'Vindolanda 1985–1989: first thoughts on new finds' in L. Bender Jørgensen and E. Munksgaard (eds), *Archaeological Textiles in Northern Europe: Report from the 4th NESAT Symposium, 1–5 May 1990 in Copenhagen (Tidens Tand* 5), pp. 66–74.

'Colorator', *Glotta* LXX, pp. 96–99

1993

(with G. B. Dannell, B. R. Hartley, J. R. Perrin), 'Excavations on a Romano-British pottery production site at Park Farm, Stanground, Peterborough, 1965–67', *Journal of Roman Pottery Studies*, VI, pp. 51–93

'Vindolanda 1985–1988: The Textiles' in R. E. Birley (ed.), *Vindolanda III: Preliminary Reports on the Leather, Textiles Environmental Evidence and Dendrochronology*, (Bardon Mill, Northumberland), pp. 76–90

'The textiles' in D. E. Farwell, T. I. Molleson, *Poundbury: Volume 2: The Cemeteries* (London), pp. 111–113

'Central and Northern Europe' in J. Harris (ed.), *5000 Years of Textiles* (London British Museum Press), pp. 66–67

'Textile' in M. Rule, J. Monaghan, *A Gallo-Roman Trading Vessel from Guernsey: The Excavation and Recovery of a Third-Century Shipwreck (Guernsey Museum Monograph* V), p. 99

1994

'Tunic no. 4219: An Archaeological and Historical Perspective', *Riggisberger Berichte* II, pp. 9–36

'A hairmoss cap from Vindolanda' in G. Jaacks, K. Tidow (eds), *Archäologische Textilfunde – Archaeological Textiles: Textilsymposium Neumünster 4.–7.5.1993* (NESAT V), (Neumünster), pp. 61–68

'Textile' in M. G. Fulford, J. R. C. Allen, S. J. Rippon, 'The Settlement and Drainage of the Wentlooge Level, Gwent: Excavations and Survey at Rumney Great Wharf 1992' *Britannia* XXV, p. 196

1995

(with C. R. Cork, W. D. Cooke) 'The characterisation of archaeological textile fibres using Advanced Image Analysis software', *Archaeological Textiles Newsletter* XVIII/XXIX, pp. 16–17

'Berenike 1995', *Archaeological Textiles Newsletter* XX, p. 8

1996

(with C. R. Cork, W. D. Cooke) 'The use of image analysis to determine twist level in archaeological textiles', *Archaeometry* XXVII, Pt 2, pp. 337–345

(with F. C. Wild) 'The Textiles' in S. E. Sidebotham, W. Z. Wendrich (eds), *Berenike 1995: Preliminary Report of the 1995 Excavations at Berenike (Egyptian Red Sea Coast) and the Survey of the Easter Desert*, Research School CNWS (Leiden) pp. 245–256

'Wool', 'Linen', 'Byssus', 'Silk', 'Textile Production', 'Dyeing' in S. Hornblower, A. Spawforth (eds), *The Oxford Classical Dictionary* (third edition, OUP 1996), pp. 266, 499, 1407, 1489–90, 1626

(with F. C. Wild) 'Berenike 1996', *Archaeological Textiles Newsletter* XXII, pp. 20–21

Translator of : C. B. Rüger, 'Germany' in *Cambridge Ancient History* X (2nd edition, Cambridge), pp. 517–534

1997

(with C. R. Cork, W. D. Cooke, L. Fang Lu) 'Analysis and Evaluation of a Group of Early Roman Textiles from Vindolanda'' *Journal of Archaeological Science* XXIV, pp. 19–32

'Cotton in Roman Egypt: Some Problems of Origin', *Al-Rāfidān* XVIII (special volume: Festschrift for Professor Hideo Fujii, Kokushikan University), pp. 287–298

'The Textiles' in C. Johns, *The Snettisham Roman Jeweller's Hoard* (London), pp. 47–49

1998

'...and clothing to match', *The Colchester Archaeologist* XI, p. 5

'A Sling from Melandra', in J. Bird (ed.), *Form and Fabric: Studies in Rome's Material Past in Honour of B. R. Hartley* (Oxford: Oxbow Books), pp. 297–300

'The Textiles', in H. E. M. Cool, C. Philo (eds), *Roman Castleford: Excavations 1974–85 I: The Small Finds (Yorkshire Archaeology* 4), pp. 346–347

(with F. C. Wild) 'The Textiles', S. E. Sidebotham, W. Z. Wendrich (eds), *Berenike 96: Report of the Excavations at Berenike (Egyptian Red Sea Coast) and the Survey of the Eastern Desert* (Research School CNWS, Leiden), pp. 221–236

(with W. D. Cooke, C. R. Cork, L. Fang Lu) 'Vindolanda: some results of the Leverhulme Trust Programme', in: L. Bender Jørgensen, C. Rinaldo (eds), *Textile in European Archaeology: Report from the 6th NESAT Symposium 7–11th May 1996 in Borås* (Gothenburg: University of Gothenburg), pp. 85–95

1999

'Clothing and textiles', in M. J. Aldhouse Green, *Pilgrims in Stone: Stone Images from the Gallo-Roman Sanctuary of Fontes Sequanae* (*BAR* S754), pp. 64–66.

'Textile manufacture: a rural craft?', in M. Polfer, *Artisanat et productions artisanales en milieu rural dans les provinces du nord-ouest de l'Empire romain*, Monographies *instrumentum* IX (Montagnac), pp. 29–37.

Plate I. Fragment of tunic from Didymoi, in damask weave with purple clavus *(see Chapter 2). Photo: D. Cardon*

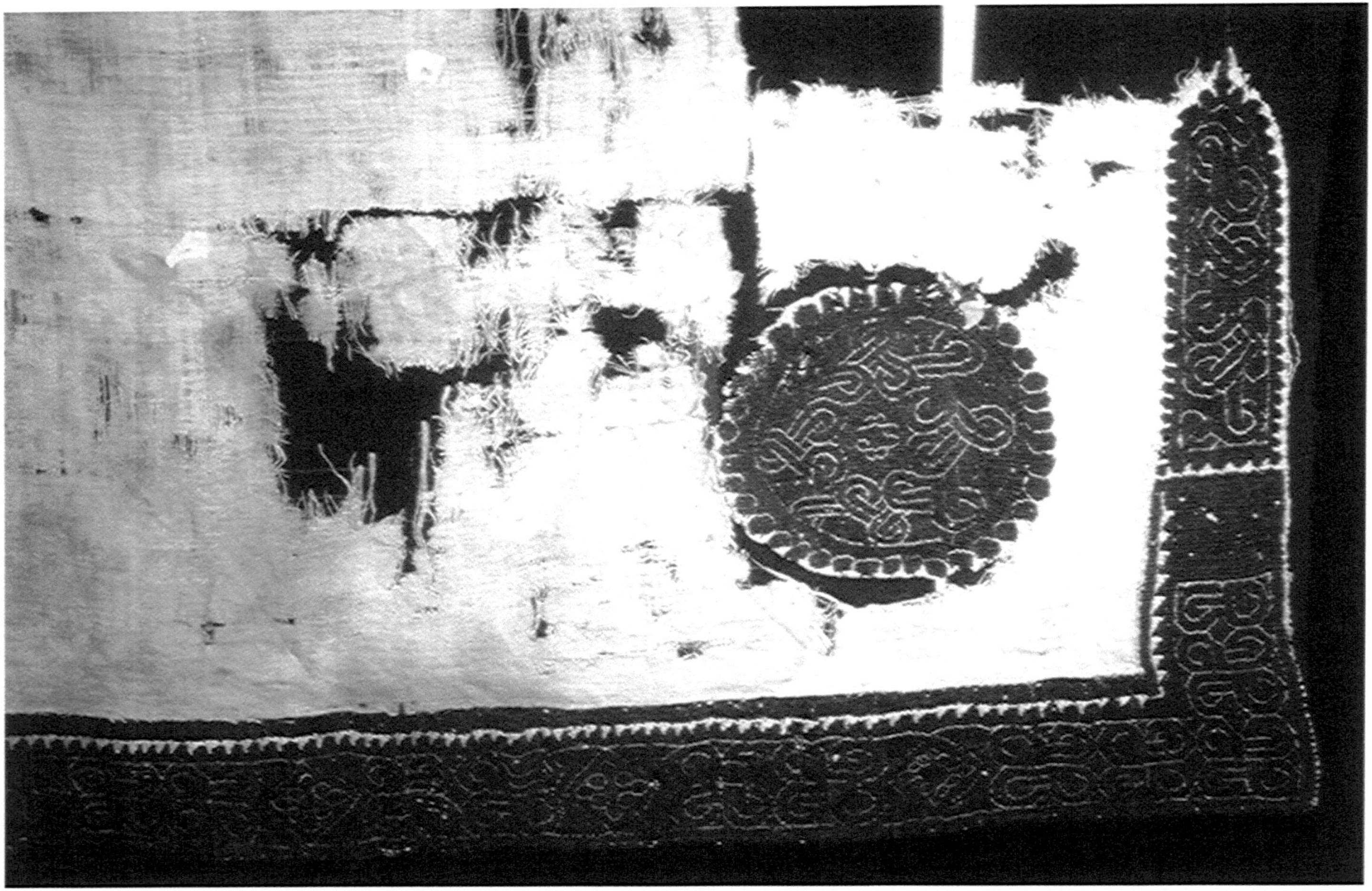

Plate II. Detail of Tunic B from Roman Egypt, showing hem band (see Chapter 3), during conservation. Photo: A. Tullo, Whitworth Art Gallery

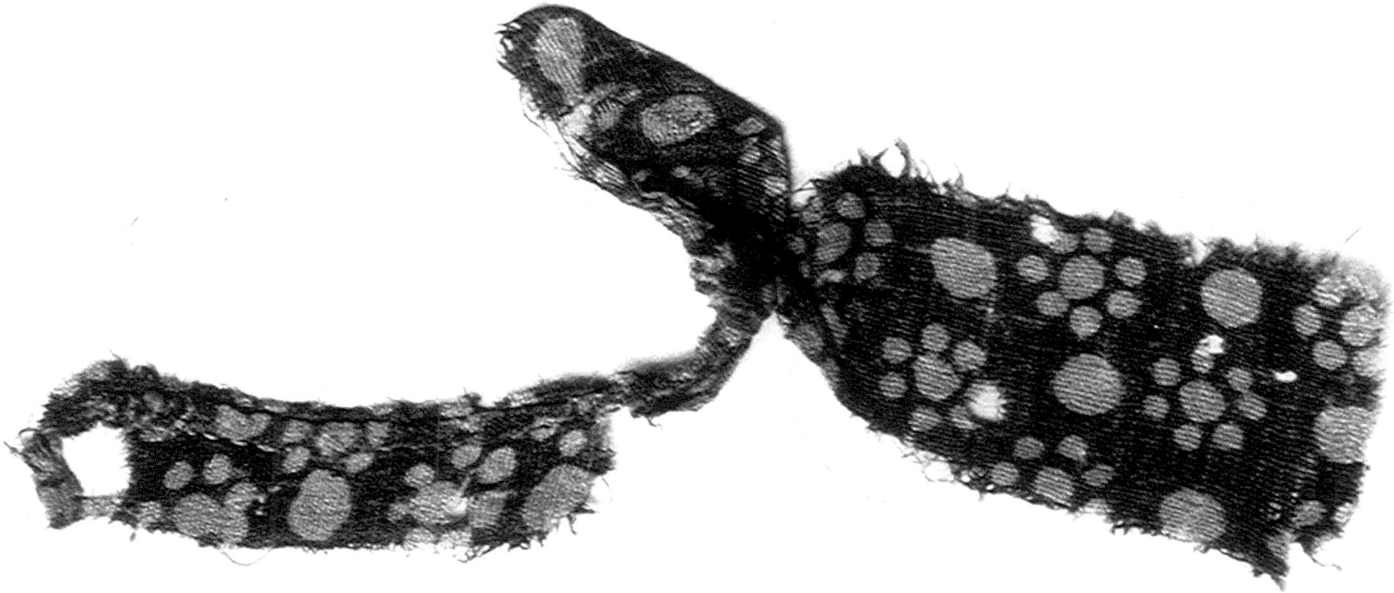

Plate III. Resist-dyed cotton from Karadong (see Chapter 6). Photo: Sino-French archaeological mission in Xinjiang.

Plate IV. Late Roman tapestry-woven emblem from the at-Tar caves, Iraq, depicting Dionysus as a female (see Chapter 7). Photo: ICSAI, Kokushikan University.

Plate V. Late Roman tapestry-woven emblem from the at-Tar caves, Iraq, showing a woman with a decorated cap (see Chapter 7). Photo: ICSAI, Kokushikan University.

Plate VI. Lion silk from Canterbury, front view (see Chapter 18). Photo: A. Muthesius, with permission from Canterbury Cathedral Authorities.

Plate VII. Lion silk from Canterbury, reverse (see Chapter 18). Photo: A. Muthesius, with permission from Canterbury Cathedral Authorities.